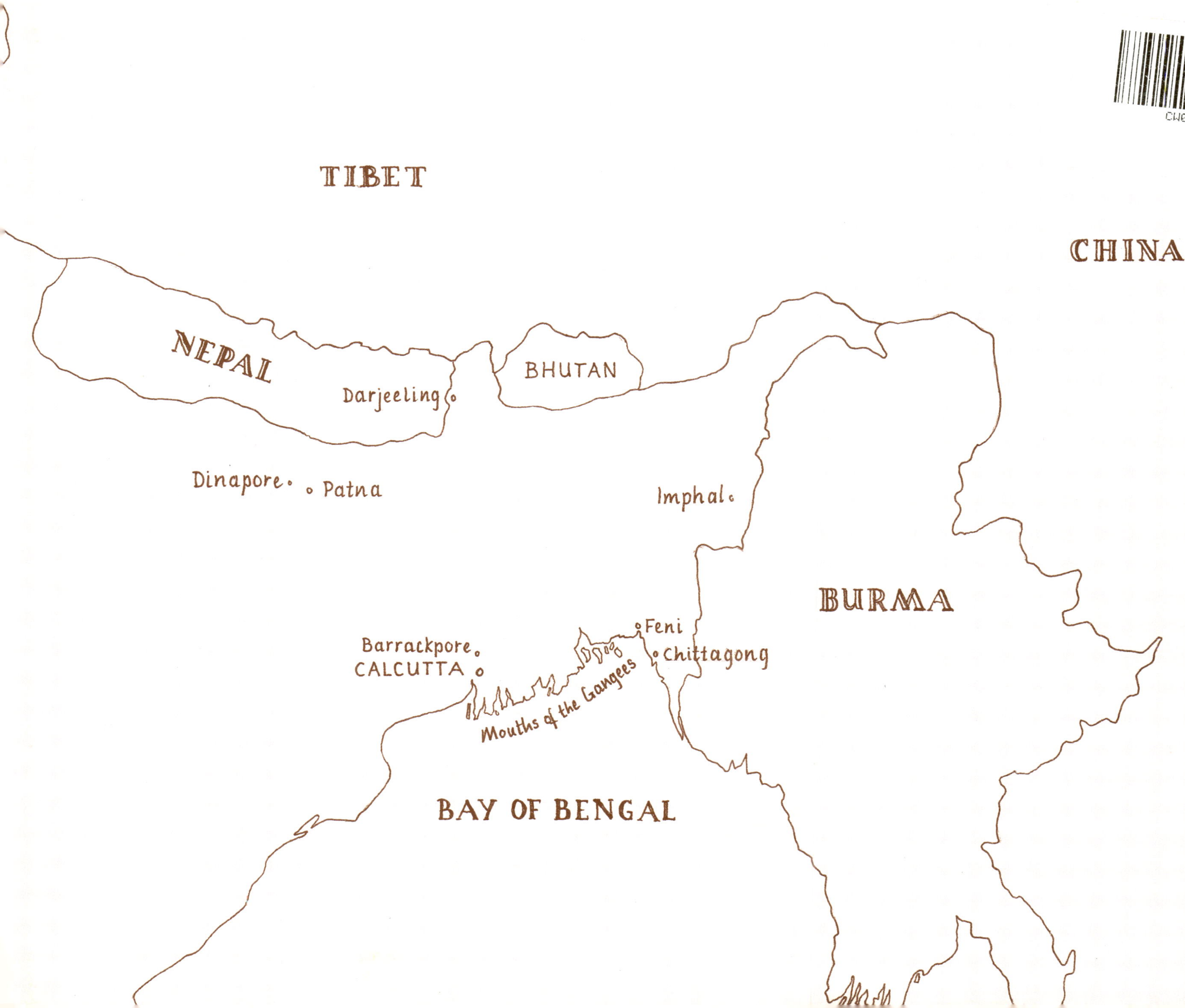
TIBET
CHINA
NEPAL
BHUTAN
Darjeeling
Dinapore
Patna
Imphal
BURMA
Feni
Barrackpore
CALCUTTA
Chittagong
Mouths of the Gangees
BAY OF BENGAL

Soldier Artist in Wartime

INDIA

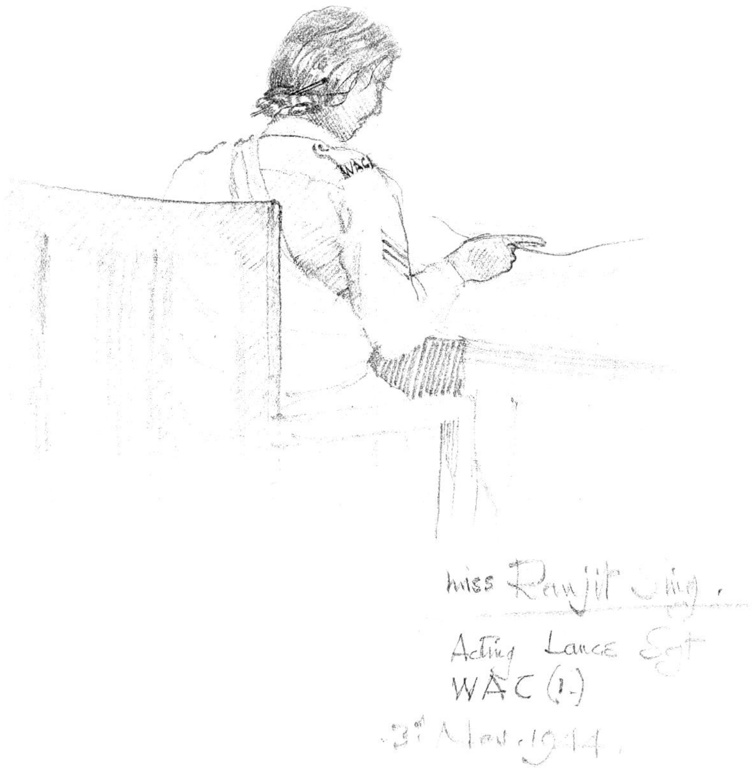

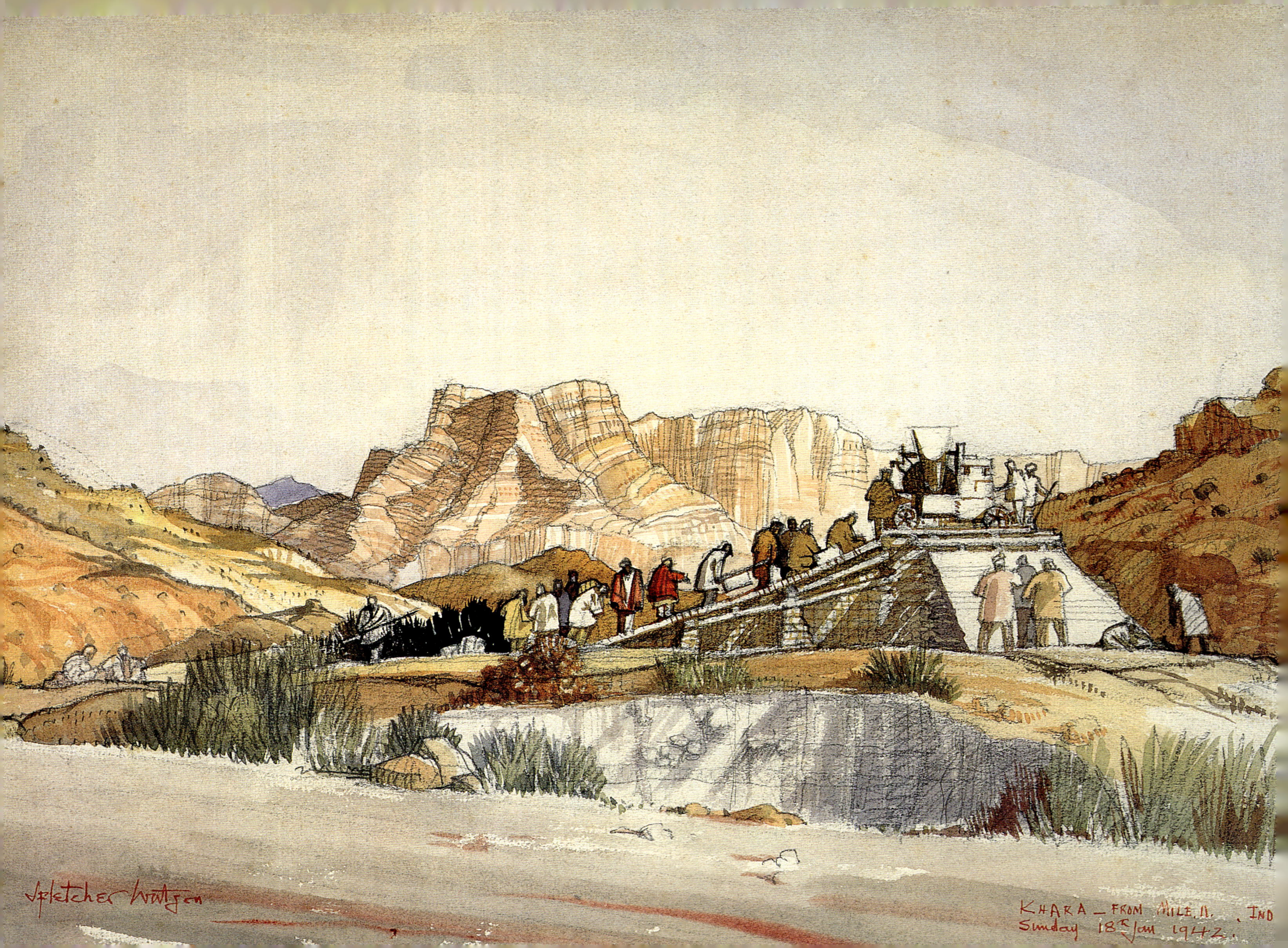
JFletcher Watson
KHARA – FROM MILE 11. IND
Sunday 18th Jan 1942.

Soldier Artist in Wartime
INDIA

1941-1945

James Fletcher-Watson

COUNTRY HERITAGE

ACKNOWLEDGEMENTS

Special thanks to my daughter Josephine Neil who has been responsible for the editing and publication of this book. I am so very grateful for her professional help and all the skill she has given to this book's production.

My thanks to General Sir John Stibbon, himself a watercolour painter, for so kindly writing the up-to-date Foreword. Also thanks to my daughter Vanessa Whinney, my nephew Matthew Parker, Tim Clarke, Andrew Hucklesby and Winston Oh for their help.

First published in 2000 by Country Heritage

Designed by Nigel Partridge

ISBN 0-9538491-0-4

Colour Reproduction by Colourpath Ltd, London
Printed in Singapore by Kyodo Printing Co Pte Ltd

CONTENTS

DEDICATED TO THE
SAPPERS IN INDIA

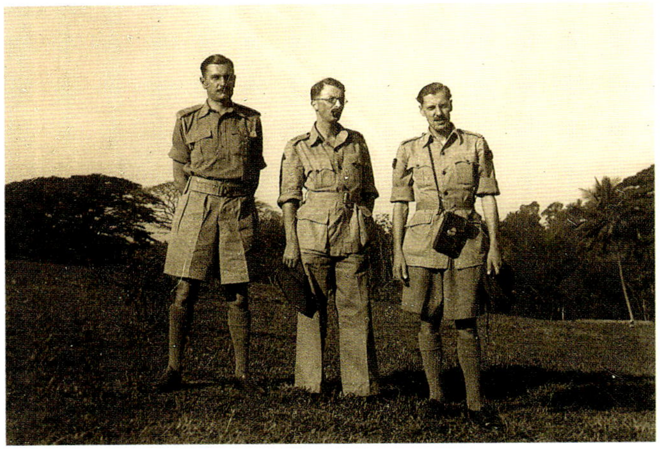

Major Fletcher-Watson (right) with fellow sappers

LIST OF COLOUR ILLUSTRATIONS

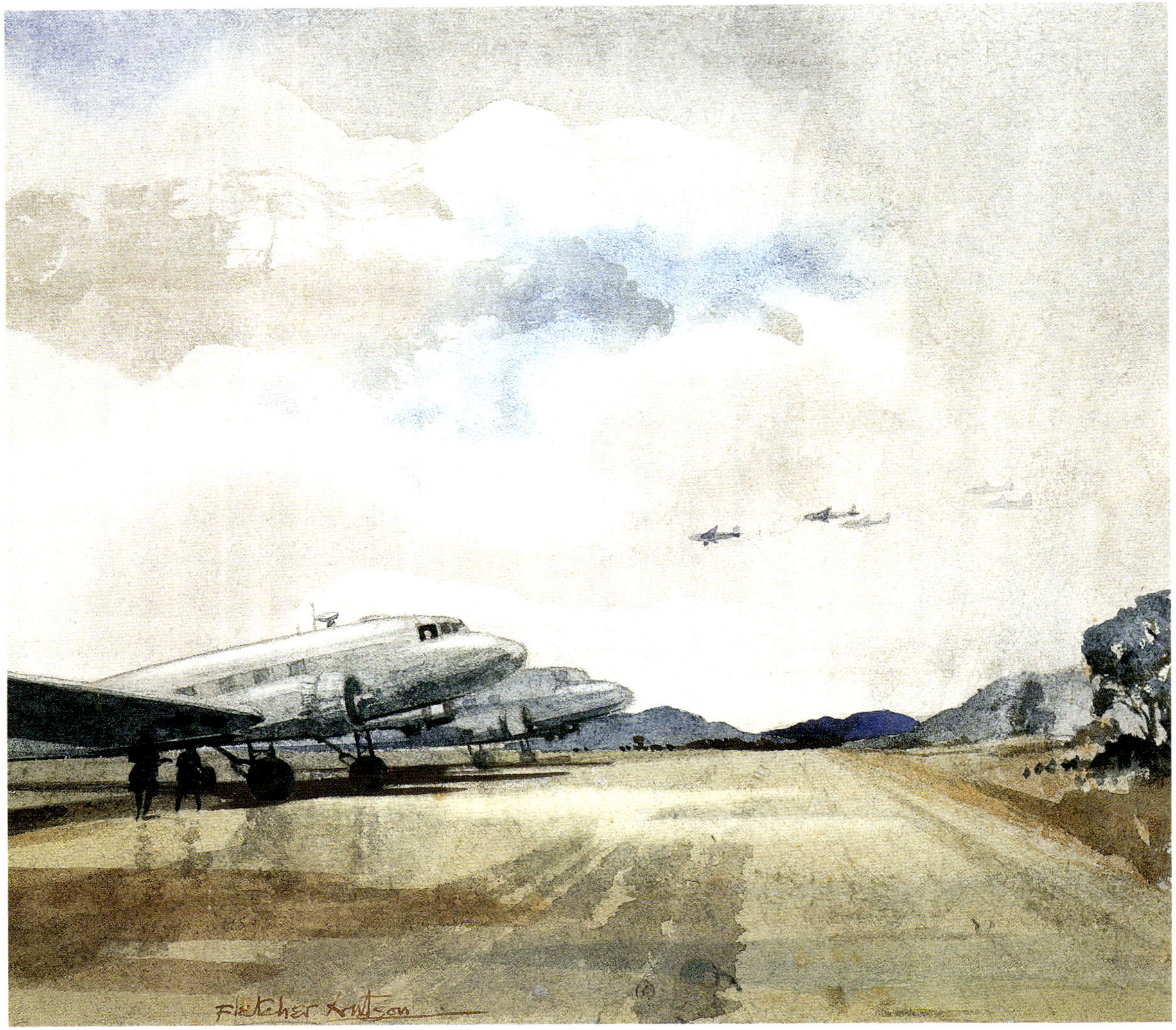

Imphal Aerodrome

FOREWORD

I am delighted to have been invited to write the Foreword to this wonderfully entertaining book which James Fletcher-Watson has generously dedicated to the Sappers who served with him in India. *Soldier Artist in Wartime India* is an account of a short but highly significant period in the life of a young, recently qualified architect whose professional career was almost immediately disrupted by four years of war service in India and Burma.

It is full of beautiful sketches crafted by the hand of an extremely gifted artist, but there is much of the trained eye of the architect in them also. One must remember that the text, apart from a few updating editorial notes, remains unchanged from when it was first drafted fifty-six years ago. There has been no recourse to rely on memory, which makes the telling authentic and of the time and occasion – and in a sense makes the appreciation more poignant.

This book is much more than a diary. James has used his talented mix of watercolour and prose to bring home to the reader the balance between the rich beauty and the poverty that was India in the 1940s – be it his description of the blue-black colour of the mid-Atlantic, the changing greens of the Kurram Valley, the rose-pink hues of the hills or the rugged beauty of the North West Frontier; not to mention the turgid brown of the Indus and the squalor and poverty of Calcutta. It is all there and makes for a wonderfully entertaining read.

I have also been fascinated by the tales of his military exploits as a young Garrison Engineer, his 'graduation' into the camouflage arena and his involvement in the development of Prefabricated Bituminous Surfacing. P.B.S. was a key to the provision of rapidly laid runways – so vital for the replenishment and later advance of General Slim's 14th Army. With little military training, James's exploits demonstrate for me his adaptability and resourcefulness, aspects of Sapper character which remain as relevant to the young officer today as they were then.

I commend this book strongly, not only to my fellow Sappers, but to anyone with an interest in the Indian sub-continent, a fondness for James Fletcher-Watson's marvellous watercolours – or just as a very enjoyable and rewarding read.

General Sir John Stibbon KCB, OBE
Chief Royal Engineer (1993-99)

PREFACE

During the last three years I have been fortunate in seeing, in the course of many military postings, a varied selection of the Indian landscape. I have been impelled by the sheer beauty of the scene to make sketches as opportunities occurred and sometimes when they did not occur. Some of these sketches I sent home to England but the majority of them are still with me here in India.

When I recently spent my first war leave in this country at Darjeeling, I had a chance of going through the collection in a quiet, detached atmosphere, away from the restless push and rush of military organisms. The idea then came to me of putting together these sketches with a few memoirs easily recalled when looking at the pictures, and compiling them into book form before sending any more home or distributing them amongst friends over here.

I should like to emphasise that no attempt has been made to give the stranger to India a 'typical' collection illustrating the people, the beauty spots, architectural masterpieces or customs of the country. The pictures have been arranged more or less in the order in which they were painted and the selection of subject has been largely, if sub-consciously, dictated by the Army who has been considerate enough to place me in some of the most remote corners of this vast Peninsula. I did not always think that they were very considerate at the time.

The somewhat random account of my haphazard wanderings, leads me with all diffidence to present this record, and I sincerely trust that it will be of interest to civilians and servicemen alike and especially my friends and temporary colleagues, the Sappers.

NOVEMBER 1944

FOREWORD

Early in 1941 the first Emergency Commissioned Officers of the Royal Engineers arrived in India. Major Fletcher-Watson was one of them. Their arrival was opportune as the programme of engineer work was beginning to assume serious proportions.

This programme opened with the Defence Works on the North West Frontier, and with large camps to house thousands of Italian prisoners of war. The programme grew month by month and year by year to very large dimensions embracing airfields, roads, ports and many other activities.

To assist in the undertaking of these works, further batches of R. E. officers continued to arrive at regular intervals from the United Kingdom. Engineer officers were also directly recruited in India, and the services of others were loaned by the Dominions. Together they have been responsible for a vast amount of construction, the execution of which has taken them to every corner of India, and beyond India into Burma.

Most officers, in the course of their service, have been transferred from one station to another, but few can have seen as much of India as Major Fletcher-Watson. He has taken full advantage of the opportunities afforded to record in a most pleasing manner so much of what he saw and experienced. The beauties of India, its attractions and its waywardness, have been sympathetically treated by his pen and brush. This record of engineer activity will appeal to all his brother Sappers in India and to a much wider circle beyond.

Major General M. Roome
Engineer-in-Chief, India
New Delhi, 1 February 1945

CHAPTER ONE

'GOING OUT'

Glasgow to Bombay via the Cape; ten thousand miles of hostile waters safely traversed, and one more British convoy gets through with its precious cargo of troops and war materials. We took eight weeks going out to India, and eight weeks is a long time to be couped up in a crowded troop ship, especially when four of you share a third class cabin built for two! The convoy consisted of fifty passenger liners and cargo vessels of all shapes and sizes with at least ten escorting naval craft.

All things considered, we were a very quick convoy compared with others and averaged 12 or 13 knots throughout the whole voyage. We stopped nearly a week at Freetown and three days at Cape Town. Fifty ships is an enormous flock for the Navy to shepherd such a tremendous distance and they certainly did their job well. Fortunately it was a completely uneventful voyage as far as enemy action was concerned, but there were quite a number of other sorts of diversion of a very much pleasanter nature which helped to break the monotony of the long voyage.

In spite of our cramped sleeping quarters we managed to get a lot of enjoyment out of life on board ship. There was deck quoits when one was clever enough to book the deck,

Right: 1 Convoy

Below: Our sister ship

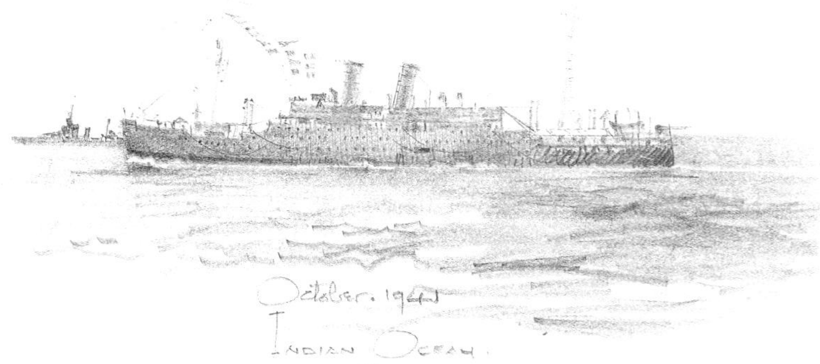

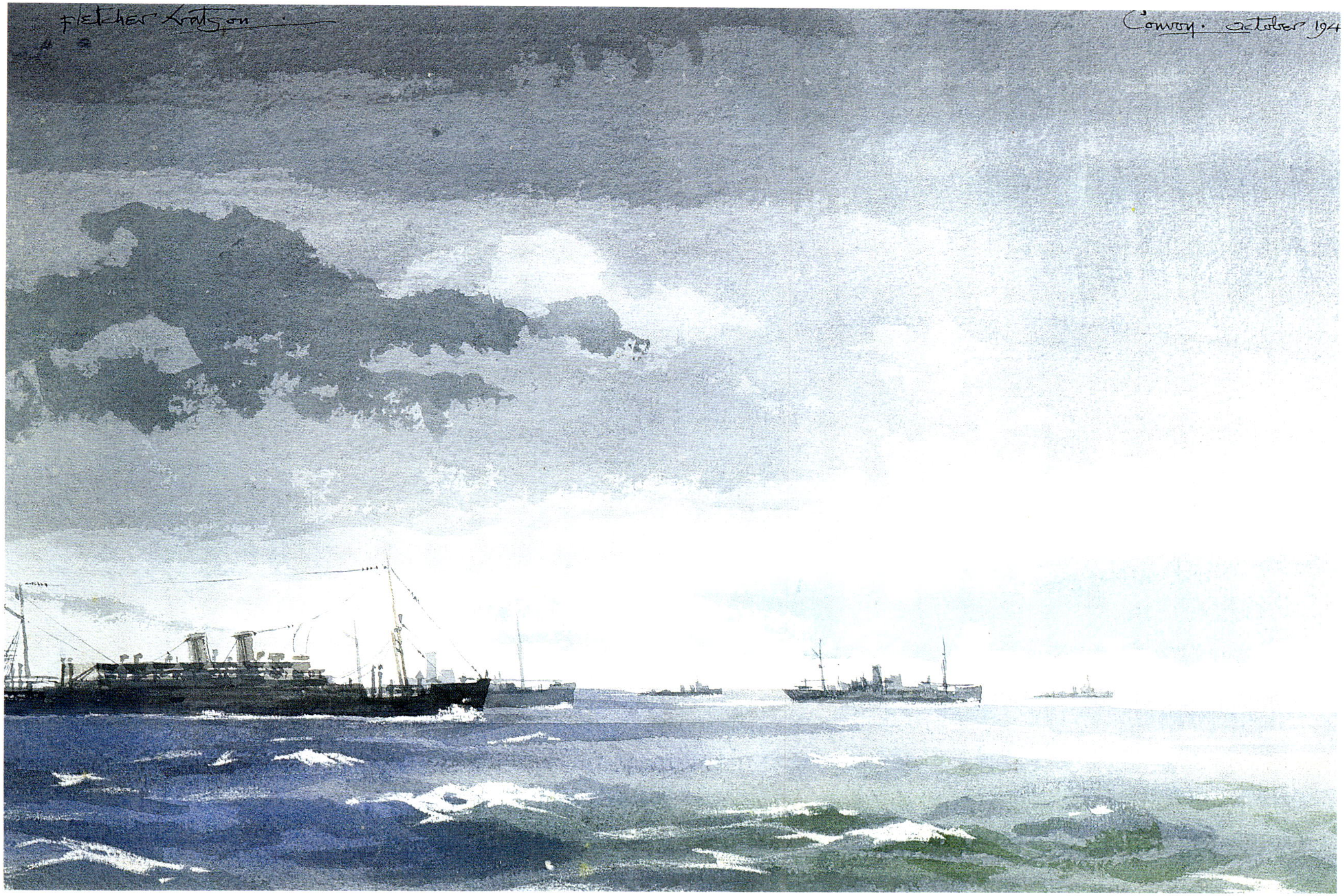
Fletcher Watson
Convoy. October 194

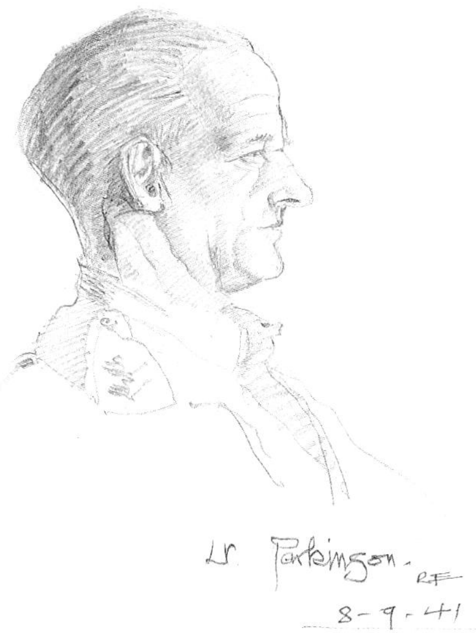
Lt. Parkinson. RE
8-9-41

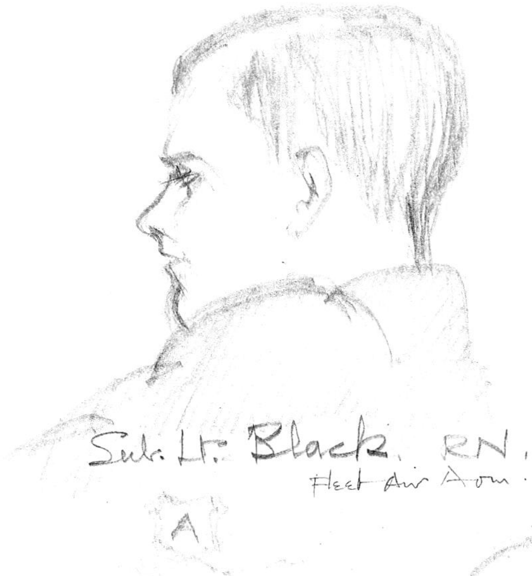
Sub. Lt. Black. RN.
Fleet Air Arm.

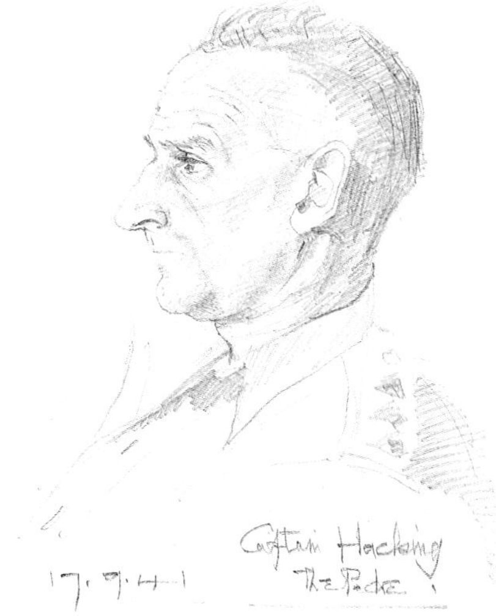
17.9.41
Captain Hacking
The Padre!

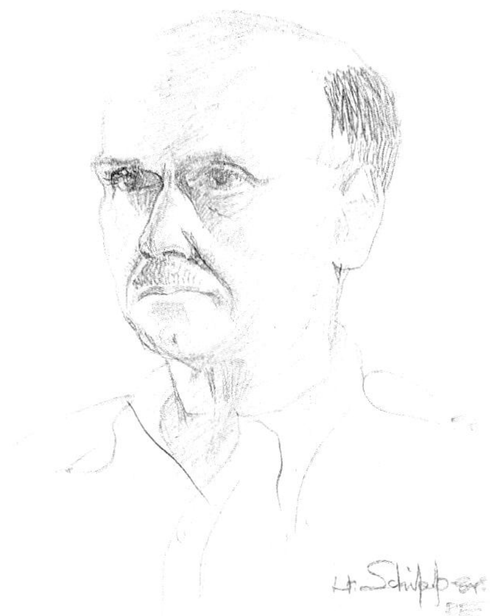

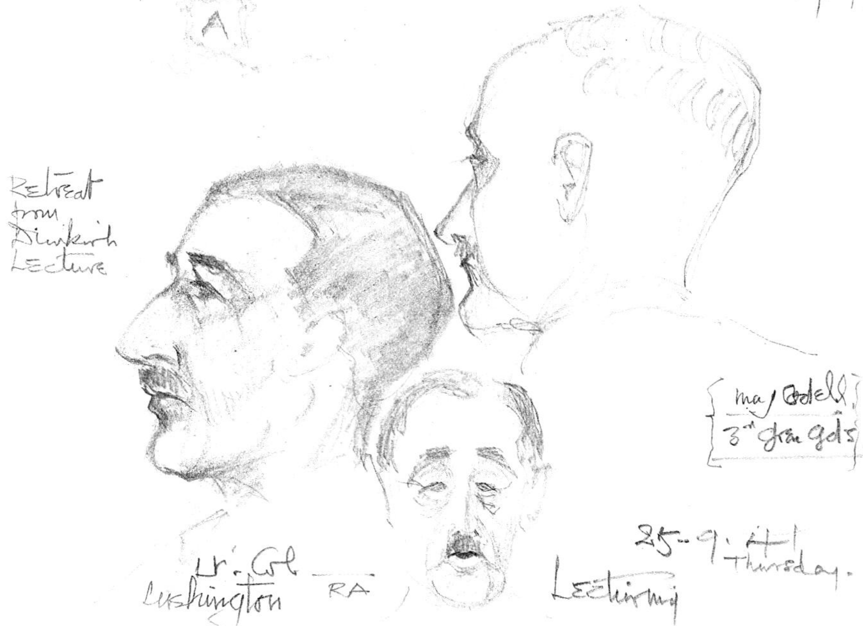
Retreat from Dunkirk Lecture
Lt. Col. Lushington RA
Lecturing
25-9-41
Thursday.

deck tennis when one felt energetic enough, and deck chairs when one didn't feel clever or energetic. I spent quite a lot of my time in the latter occupation, armed with pencil and sketch block, making studies of the men in our draft or of the ships in the convoy. There was a certain amount of restlessness about my brother officers which I deplored when I was trying to draw them. Either they had a quoits engagement or an Urdu lesson or the bar was just opening, but for one reason or another they 'Could not stop long' for me to draw portraits. I am not suggesting that I didn't visit the bar myself but my best sitter was George the deck hand who was always delighted to sit and gaze out to sea like a statue for as long as I wanted. I managed to get quite a good likeness of the old boy; he had a fine, typical seaman's face with those squashed-up eyes and a wrinkled, weather-beaten skin.

We were the Commodore's ship which meant that all the other ships in the convoy took orders from us as regards, speed, lighting, formation etc. Consequently, our ship was situated in a forward and central position which enabled one to have an excellent view of all the other ships. The watercolour entitled 'Convoy' (No.1) is just a typical everyday scene, but an impressive one nevertheless, especially towards evening when the ships would close in and become not much more

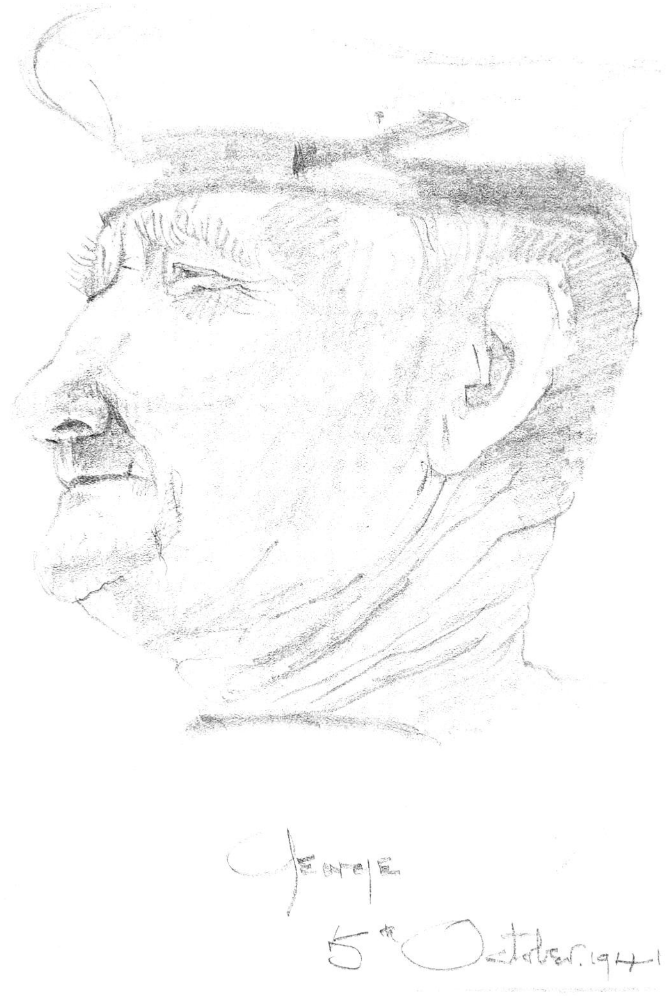

ABOVE: George

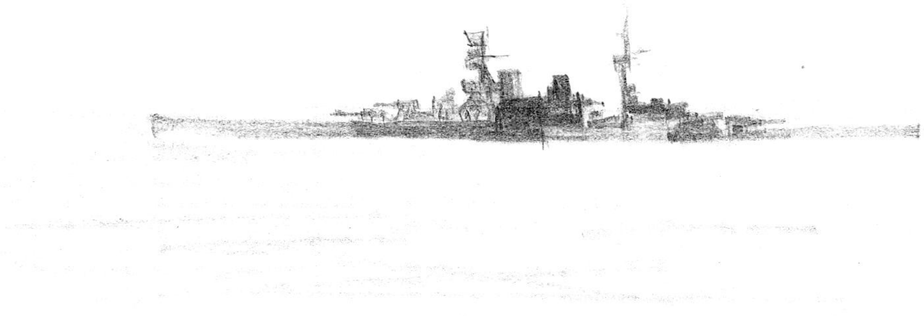

than silhouettes in the fading light. Day after day, week after week, we had this identical view, the same ships to port and the same ships to starboard. No further in front and no further behind but always in the same position, breasting the waves together in perfect unison.

The naval craft did move about, of course, especially our battleship the *Repulse*, who was constantly shifting her position in the convoy. It was very interesting to watch her through glasses shooting off her reconnaissance plane, a Walrus, and then picking it up again with extraordinary skill. She was a grand battleship, having a very graceful outline and distinctive camouflage. I did a very small sketch of her which I feel will be no breach of security in reproducing here, as she is now, alas, sunk.

Looking back on the whole voyage, I think the most impressive scene of all was the foregathering of the convoy before we left England, or rather I should say Scotland. Ships arriving one by one at the rendezvous in the Firth of Clyde on the evening of Saturday 30th August 1941. The last time I had been on the Clyde was in precisely the same month of 1937 when on a sailing holiday. We had been a light-hearted young party then with few cares as we sailed happily about the Firth. Little did I think that four years hence I should be there again in uniform, grimly leaning over the rail of a troop ship looking at those same purple hills of the beautiful Clyde Valley, about to proceed to an unknown destination overseas.

Above: HMS Repulse

We soon adjusted ourselves to life on board ship. Perhaps one of the most striking features at first was the food. Oranges were thrust on us, things one had not seen for months, and eggs and bacon in plenty for breakfast. It seemed a little unfair to be wolfing such luxuries almost within sight of our homes and families who were so strictly rationed.

We reached Freetown after exactly fifteen days' sailing. Nothing of great interest happened on the way apart from destroyers firing at an occasional unexploded surface mine. Boat drill and sleeping in a bunk became a habit and we got used to queuing up for baths and doing certain items of washing and ironing ourselves. Fifteen days was a long time to take in covering a distance of 3,000 odd miles, but we travelled many extra miles out of our way in order to delude the lurking U boats. This included quite a big detour into mid Atlantic and I had my first view of the deep blue-black colour of that ocean. It is certainly a most lovely colour and not to be compared with any other waters through which we passed. Further south, near Cape Town, the sea lost its blueness and turned duller and greener and the Indian Ocean from Madagascar onwards had a brownish tinge.

Below: Mr Blackout

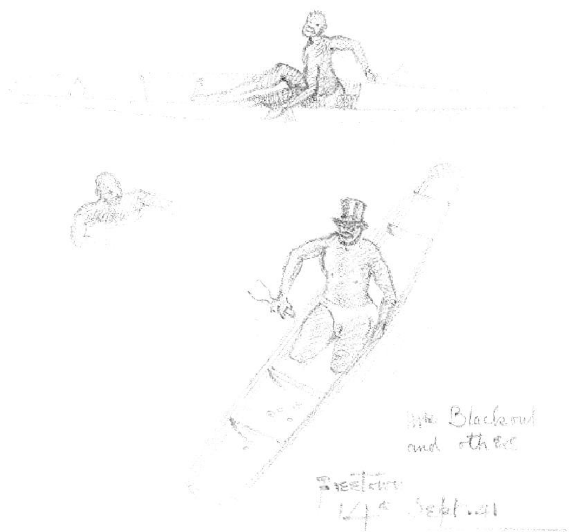

Freetown was not a pleasant experience; it was very hot and sticky with absolutely no breeze. The only man allowed ashore was the O.C. troops and we noticed he took his golf clubs in the motor launch which did not help to lessen our impatience with the place. The only form of amusement was the locals who paddled out to the waiting ships in their canoes and dived for pennies. They called out for 'Glasgow sixpence' but not many were lavish enough to give them that. The most amusing of these visitors that came to our ship had 'Mr Blackout' painted on the side of his canoe and he wore an old top hat. He imitated a drill sergeant, giving words of command like 'Forms, Fours', 'Form two deep, halt' and sang 'Kiss me goodnight, Sergeant Major' so well that it brought him plenty of applause and a great many pennies.

The small harbour was absolutely crammed with shipping

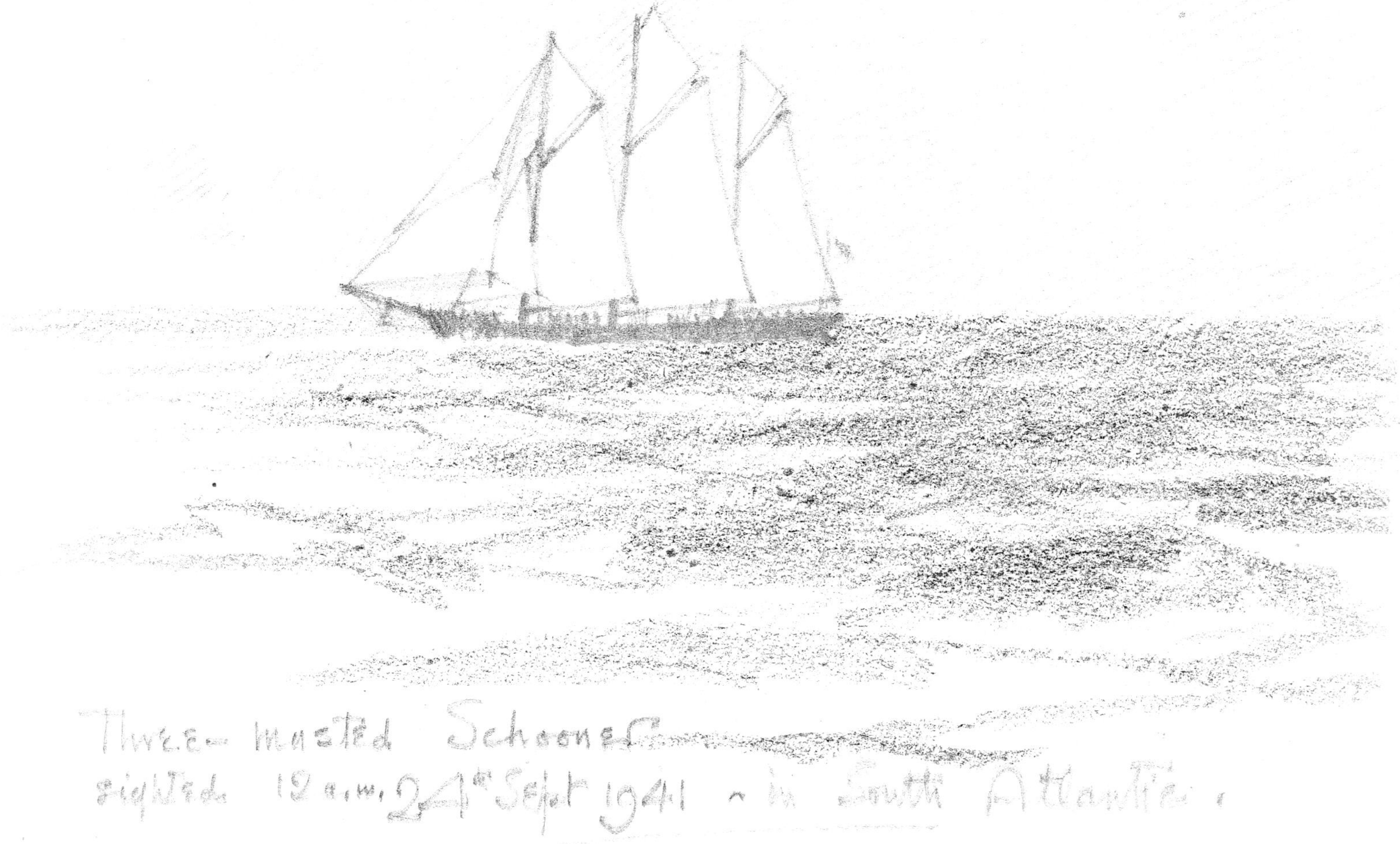
Three-masted Schooner
sighted 12 a.m. 24th Sept 1941 - in South Atlantic.

and we had to wait our turn to be refuelled with oil and water. But at last we got off and everybody was thankful for the cool breeze again.

We now had the long hop to Cape Town in front of us. Some people said that they saw the Ascension Islands in the distance as we passed. I was not one of them but I did see a very much lovelier sight one morning: a three-masted schooner about fifteen miles to starboard. We soon left her behind but she was a pleasing picture, her big white sails shining in the sun. She was too far away to do more than a thumb-nail sketch, but even that was worthwhile as it is a rare occasion these days to see a large sailing vessel on the high seas.

The day before we reached Cape Town we were given a lecture by our O.C. troops on how to behave on shore. It appeared that a previous convoy, carrying certain troops of our noble Empire, had behaved in a manner far from noble. Consequently, the Cape Towners had grown a trifle anxious about convoys, and every strict regulation was imposed to ensure that troops always returned to their ships by 1.00 a.m.

We were not always good boys but we did behave decently. And how could we behave otherwise in the face of such tremendous hospitality? The way in which the South Africans welcomed convoys during those years of 1940 to 1943 will remain a lasting memorial of their goodwill and generosity. They literally threw open their doors and said help yourself. They freely lent their cars and fed you in their houses and clubs, they gave you golf clubs or tennis rackets and even took you shopping to buy presents for your family at home. No wonder there were a lot of long faces on board the morning we sailed. After three days of hilarity and dancing, a lot of close friendships were made which had to be rudely severed at short notice. No warning could be vouchsafed to us about when we would sail; it was simply announced in the morning that no one would go ashore that day as we were leaving, and that was that. All the appointments of the previous night had to remain unkept. My diary entry for that day is short and reads: 'No shore leave. Blast. Sail 2.15 p.m. Nasty cross swell. Teddy leant me his cabin 169C.' I am a rotten sailor and a cabin on C deck for a day or two was a great luxury compared with mine way down on E deck.

I was unlucky enough to be orderly officer on one of these shore leave days, but even in two days I made pretty good headway. Two dances, a visit to Groot Constantia to see the delightful old Dutch buildings, and other tea, lunch and dinner

LEFT: A Three-master in the South Atlantic

parties. Few cities in the world can have a finer setting with the big natural harbour basin and Table Mountain towering up in the background.

As the convoy slowly pulled out to sea and the shores of South Africa receded towards the horizon, the unanimous opinion of everybody on board was that Cape Town must receive a further visit as soon as the happier days of peace would allow.

We were joined by the other half of our convoy who had put in to Durban and had, as I heard afterwards, received an equally warm welcome.

The O.C. Troops received a wireless message from the Mayor of Cape Town saying that everybody had behaved themselves extremely well. This news he passed on to us in the lounge with a proud smile on his face. But he never heard the muttered comments of some of my friends: 'That's what you think!'

The remainder of the journey was punctuated with a series of cocktail parties. Infantry units gave them, the Gunners gave one, the Engineers, the Navy and the Captain all gave them. One party was given by the aforementioned Teddy, a mysterious civilian gentleman on board who kept his secret mission very dark. He had been a sailor and was on naval work of some

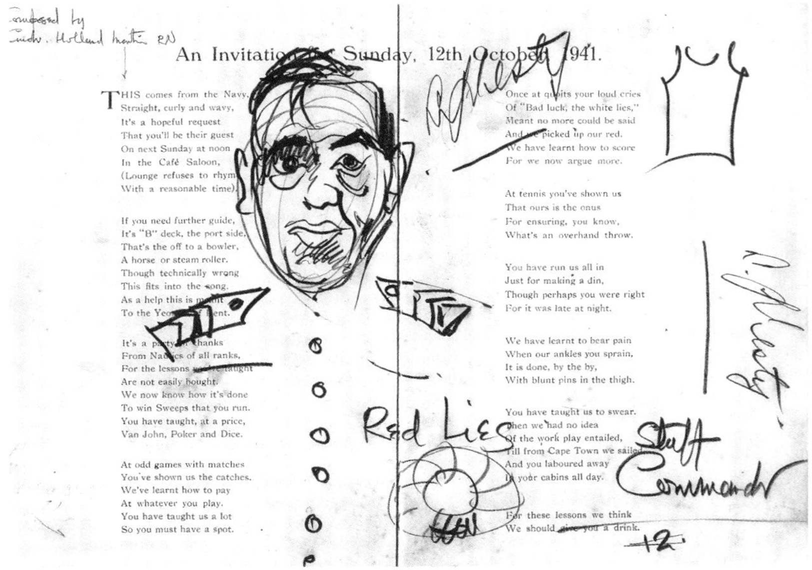

An Invitatio[illegible] Sunday, 12th Octob[illegible] 1941.

THIS comes from the Navy,
Straight, curly and wavy,
It's a hopeful request
That you'll be their guest
On next Sunday at noon
In the Café Saloon,
(Lounge refuses to rhym
With a reasonable time).

If you need further guide,
It's "B" deck, the port side,
That's the off to a bowler,
A horse or steam roller.
Though technically wrong
This fits into the song.
As a help this is [illegible]
To the Yeo[illegible]ent.

It's a pa[illegible]ty [illegible] thanks
From Nau[illegible]ics of all ranks,
For the lessons [illegible] taught
Are not easily bought.
We now know how it's done
To win Sweeps that you run.
You have taught, at a price,
Van John, Poker and Dice.

At odd games with matches
You've shown us the catches.
We've learnt how to pay
At whatever you play.
You have taught us a lot
So you must have a spot.

Once at qu[illegible]its your loud cries
Of "Bad luck, the white lies,"
Meant no more could be said
And [illegible] picked up our red.
[illegible]e have learnt how to score
For we now argue more.

At tennis you've shown us
That ours is the onus
For ensuring, you know,
What's an overhand throw.

You have run us all in
Just for making a din,
Though perhaps you were right
For it was late at night.

We have learnt to bear pain
When our ankles you sprain,
It is done, by the by,
With blunt pins in the thigh.

You have taught us to swear.
[illegible]hen we had no idea
[illegible]f the work play entailed,
[illegible]ill from Cape Town we sail[illegible]
And you laboured away
[illegible] your cabins all day.

F[illegible]r these lessons we think
We should [illegible]

Above: Naval invitation

sort but beyond that we got no further information out of him. He gave a very good party anyway.

The one I enjoyed the most was given by the naval passengers on board. The senior officer, a certain red-headed commander, wrote a poetic invitation to start with. I reproduce it here although it is somewhat mutilated by my drawing over it during the course of the evening. Incidentally the drawing on it is a very good likeness of the Staff Commander. When one draws in a slightly inebriated state (only slightly, of course) and sees the subject dimly, one puts down the salient features, the smaller ones being lost to eye and hand. This produces precisely the bold and striking results which art masters are so often at pains to teach their students. I am not suggesting for one moment that art students should follow this practice; it might lead to a certain lack of discipline in the drawing class. But it is a useful theory to have up one's sleeve, and I hold it responsible for the good likeness I achieved in this case!

Coinciding with the navy party was a farewell display by the *Repulse*. Her ratings lined the decks and straddled the big gun barrels as she paraded up and down the lines of ships at close quarters, with her marine band playing at full blast. She was a magnificent sight close to, and one realised what a colossal ship she was, having only viewed her at a distance previously. Cheer upon cheer was sent up from the troop ships as she passed. It was the only way we could show our appreciation of the safe conduct she had given us through these many miles of ocean, and we gave it lustily.

The rumours were fairly strong after leaving Cape Town that we were heading for Bombay, although some thought our destination could be Singapore or the Persian Gulf. Until then, our ultimate destination had been entirely unknown. In fact, our topis and our tropical kit were the only tangible clues and as topis are worn in a great many parts of the world, this had not helped very much.

The guardianship of the convoy was taken over by a cruiser which arrived the same day that the *Repulse* left. On the following day half the convoy parted from us and headed off in a northerly direction for the Gulf. The day after that we crossed the line for the second time and in eight more days we reached our journey's end safely. Bombay it was.

CHAPTER TWO

TRIBESMEN AND CONCRETE

After landing at Bombay all officers and men were despatched to different destinations all over India. I felt myself fortunate in being posted to the North West Frontier where army fortifications were being reinforced against possible invasion. It turned out to be the most dramatic and spectacular part of the world, particularly for someone with the eye of an artist. Four of us new arrivals were sent to Manduri hill village and I was given the job of supervising the construction of some eight concrete gun emplacements.

The tribesmen of the North West Frontier of India, that renowned body of cut-throats whose hostile activities drive the peaceful inhabitants of the province to forms of life comparable with Feudal England, introduced themselves to me with typical audacity in the following way.

By a skilfully pre-arranged plan they brought off a large scale night theft of our complete stock of thick steel concrete-reinforcing bars, sixty in all, which we were about to use in our defence construction work. In order to do this successfully they first had to bribe our night guards, if they were not already collaborators. They then had to arrange means of removing these heavy fifteen-foot rods which were over an inch thick and about as much as one man could carry. Lastly, a place had to be found where rods could be well hidden without fear of discovery. The guards, I should mention, were not regular troops but consisted of local men enlisted into a semi-official guard force under the political Testildar who is about the equivalent of a chief constable at home. These men were supplied with a rifle of not very modern manufacture and with even less up-to-date ammunition. The principle was that if the British were decent enough to employ local men and pay them well, then it was in the interests of the tribesmen – who were virtually the same people as the guards – not to give offence to the British.

A total of no less than sixty bars were removed on this fateful night from four different sites where work was going on.

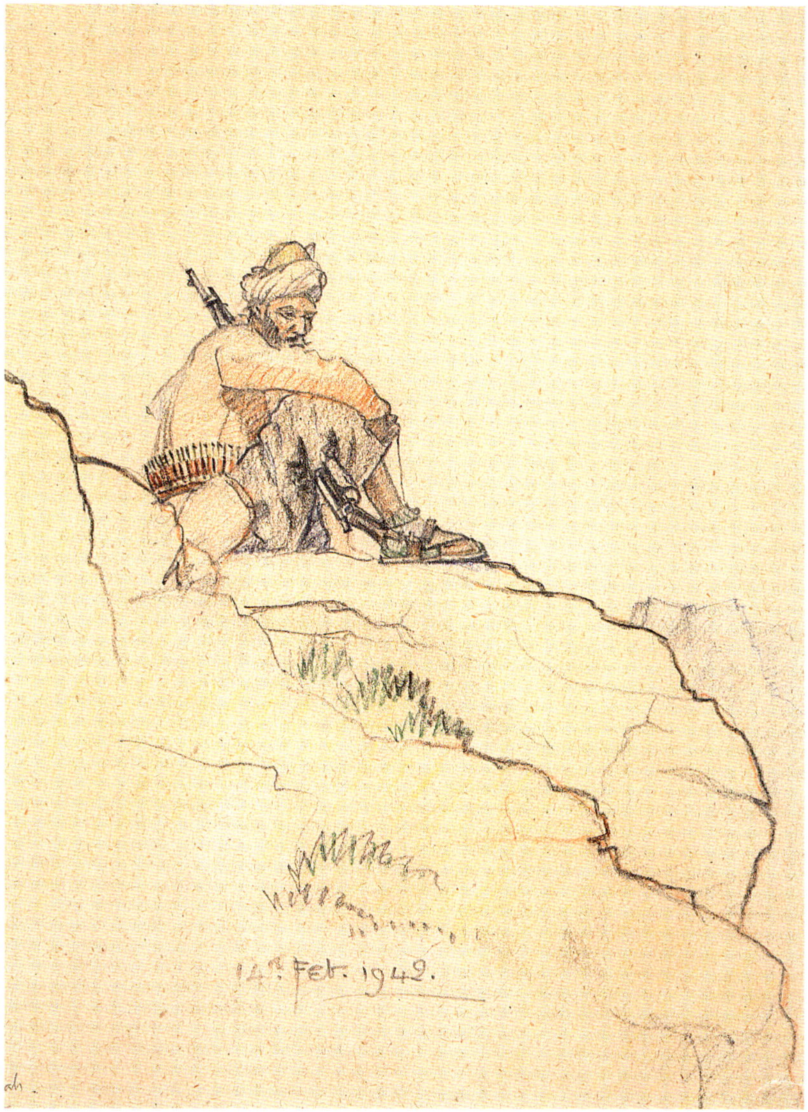

The Budraggar guards professed ignorance, of course, saying that they had not heard a sound all night. Imagine removing twenty odd steel bars from behind barbed wire in the middle of the night with no light and making no noise! Our problem was how to prove the guards had been involved. We had to turn detective and the first question was 'motive'. That we soon answered: these bars were an almost perfect size for making rifle barrels and once they could be got to the arms factory that the tribesmen worked in near Peshawar, they would have enough steel to make around 200 rifle barrels. But where had they hidden them?

The whole matter was put into the hands of the Testildar. He told the guards they would not get their pay until the steel was returned, and threatened to take away the village people's grain supply, and adopted his own tactics. One day, when our car swung into the little courtyard of military huts, in the village where we were stationed, we were presented with an astonishing sight. Three men were stuck up at the top of three tall poles, fifteen feet high, their arms hung over cross bars of wood. The Testildar was reclining back in a big chair smoking a cigar and cross-questioning the victims. He was telling them that

Left: 2 My badruggah

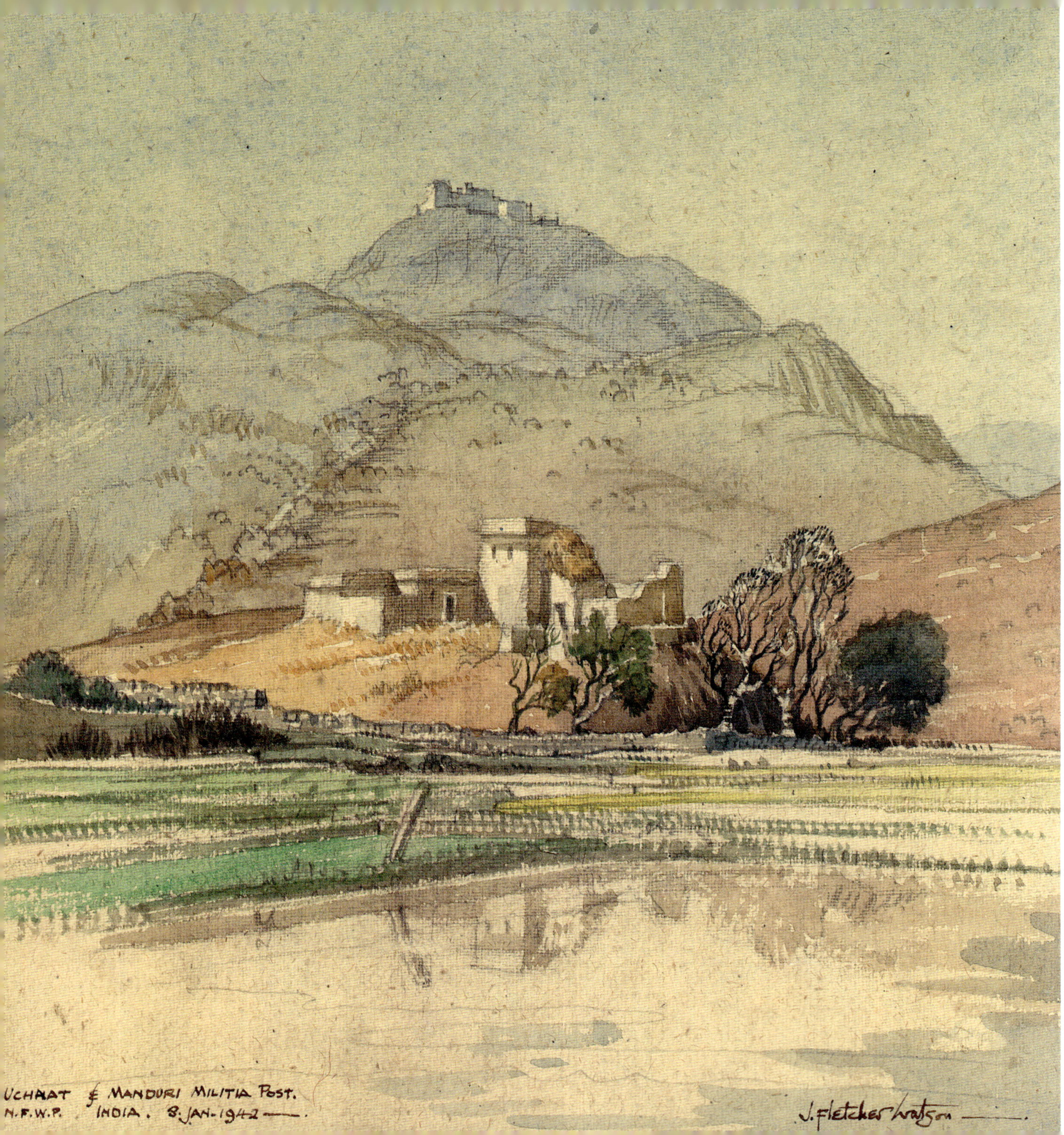

LEFT: 3 North West Frontier Province fort

they would stay there until they gave some satisfactory answers. I asked him if these third degree methods were wise and he assured me it was the only thing that impressed certain types of frontier men. Before too long he got the lot back for us.

I eventually heard the whole story of exactly how the steel bars had been stolen. The tribesmen had arranged for camels to carry the bars across country to villages four or five miles away where they had squared the Malikhs (the head man of a village) to take charge of the booty. By dawn it was all safely buried below ground. The tribesmen were quite content to wait six months or a year before removing them to the rifle factory. We were learning that these people can be cunning and daring as well as ruthless.

This, then, was the world in which I and three other young Second Lieutenants found ourselves two or three weeks after our arrival in India. It was a world that existed in habit and custom as it had for five centuries or more, and in which modern machinery seemed strangely out of place.

Large modern army lorries carrying troops armed with service rifles would speed through small villages where the women carried water pots on their heads, and past land where the men laboured as their forefathers had done for centuries behind the clumsy wooden plough drawn by two slowly plodding bullocks.

The urgent job we had in hand immediately on arrival did not unfortunately allow much time for admiring the scenery and certainly none for sketching it. It was four solid months before I had a moment to do a single sketch apart from the briefest of pencil jottings. In those days of November 1941 to the following March, the big defensive construction programme on the North West Frontier was considered India's Number One priority war job. Our C.R.E. (Commander Royal Engineers) directing the work was one of those Colonels who believed in working officers until they drop, then chucking them out and getting in some fresh ones! We had no Sundays off, no half days, working from eight in the morning until eight at night, and we certainly achieved a great deal. I did not drop until Christmas when I had to go into hospital for a couple of weeks with a touch of malaria. By March the back of the work was broken and the slave-driving Colonel was sent to the Burma front where other urgent tasks had arisen and awaited his push and drive methods.

There were sighs of relief after he had gone, but there was an awful falling off of progress on the jobs. And the clerical staff lost a lot of their former alertness which did not make our work easier. On the whole I would rather have a slave-driving but efficient Colonel.

Manduri is a tiny village fourteen miles up the Kurram valley from Thal, deep into tribal territory. At Thal there was a big fort and garrison. People lived in comparative comfort there and some senior officers even had their wives with them, about ten in all. I never met any of the wives while I was there but I did meet one a year later and she told me that after living for several months in the confines of Thal fort, there was not much that those ten women did not know about each other. This particular wife, having rather sporting tendencies and not much regard for discipline, used to venture beyond the barbed wire compound unescorted, a thing which was strictly prohibited, and make long rides on her horse into the unknown. On several occasions she was brought back by a Gurkah guard who proudly marched his European Mem Sahib prize to the Guard Room from where she had to be rescued by an embarrassed husband.

On one occasion this same restless wife dressed herself as a man and went on a long trip by car up the valley with a reconnaissance party where she got a change of atmosphere and view. She was safely back in the Fort again that night, a female once more, and a much refreshed one at that. It must have been a very trying life being couped up in the fort with no where to go but the two funny little shops, like village shops at home, selling everything from hair pins to tin trunks.

When we were sent to Manduri, people pitied us for having to go to such a lonely spot, miles from anywhere, with no fresh water arrangements, only mud huts to live in and a bad malarial district. Situated in tribal territory rather than British India, some feared it was sufficiently unprotected and isolated to be good game for the tribesmen. These reports were mostly false or exaggerated, though, and it was not long before we had settled down in our mud huts very comfortably. One advantage was that we were not bound in any way by the officialdom that existed at Brigade Headquarters in the Thal Fort.

When we arrived two officers were already established at Manduri. One was a tea planter in civilian life and he did tremendous good work in showing us the ropes. The work in which we were involved was no small task considering our work force: Kashmeries, Baluchis, men from Afghanistan, and the local Pathans themselves. The locals were usually the worst workers as they were not far from home and were apt to pop off to their village when they felt like it to do a bit of farming. The Afghans were probably the best, although the Kashmeries ran them pretty close for hard work. Most of these people were Muslims, but we imported a few Hindu gangs from southern

Right: 4 Manduri Militia post

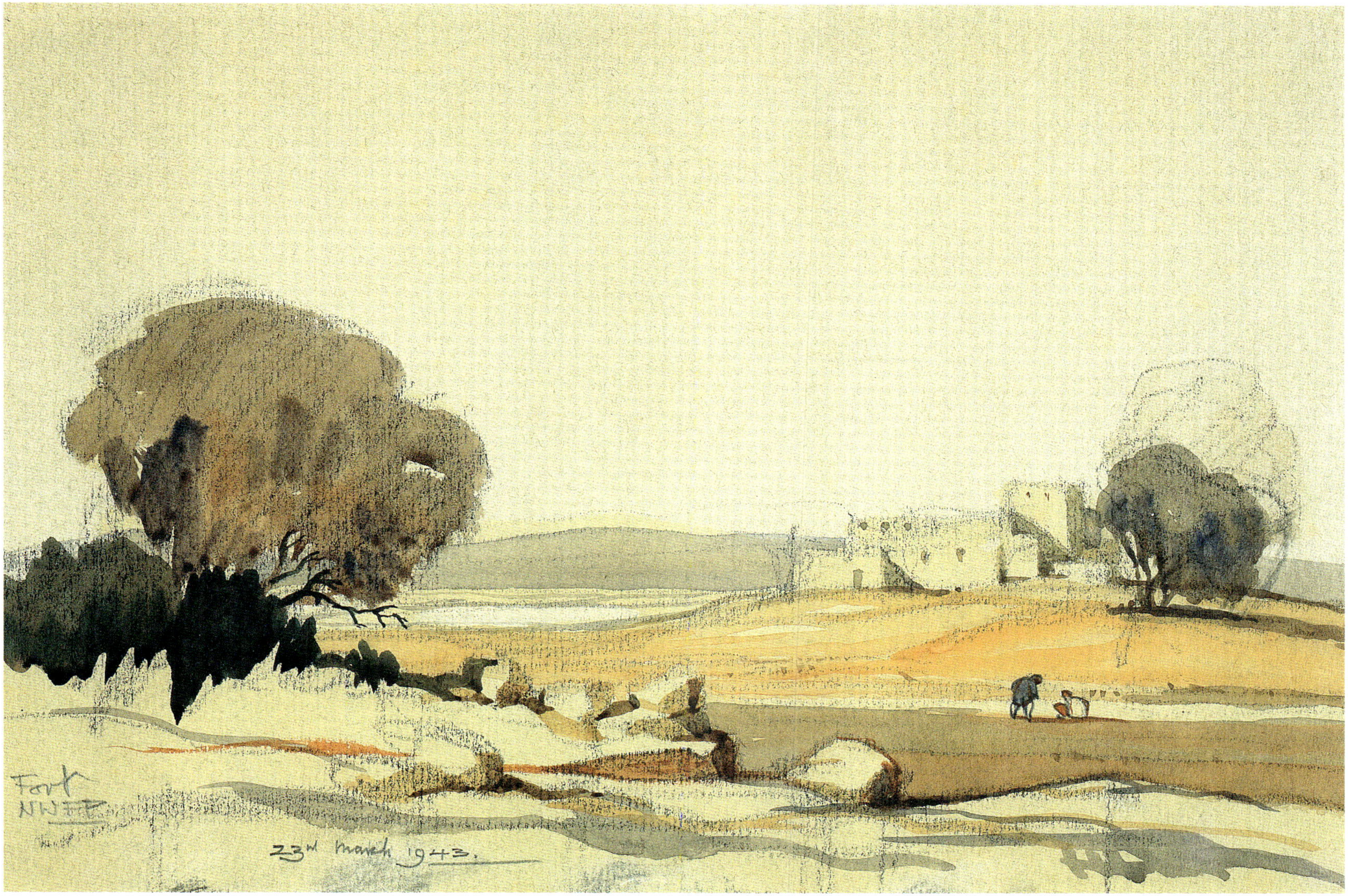
Fort
NWFP
23rd March 1943.

regions. All these various assortments of peoples lived apart from each other in their separate camps and it was wise to arrange for them to work apart, otherwise arguments on the job soon led to fights and even murders. Each group was divided into a number of gangs according to its size and each gang was led by a mate. There was, therefore, some modicum of control and discipline. If one wanted forty men for a certain job, one ordered two mates with a gang of twenty each, and the job was arranged.

It was not always as simply done as that, however, and one learnt to assess the quality of each gang and allotted heavy or light work accordingly.

I do not think I shall be giving away any military secrets when I say that one of the biggest jobs of all was on concreting days when the roofs of the projects we were building had to be completed as quickly as possible. The designs and arrangements of the steel reinforcing in these roofs had to be completed in one operation to produce the strongest possible shell-proof roof. (If the concrete was made in stages a large construction joint would have to be used, so weakening the whole structure.) So 2,500 cubic feet of concrete had to be mixed in one day, which was a major task for unskilled labourers who had never seen or heard of concrete before.

My first two or three roofs took us working well into the night, finishing only by the use of car headlights and petrol lamps. This was strictly against regulations as the political authorities would not hold themselves responsible for our safetly after 4.30 p.m., when all the pickets went off duty and only local Badruggah guards remained on the site of works. Another problem was that the coolies tended to slip away under cover of darkness and reduce the total workforce quite considerably. This threw extra work on the remainder and strained already tired men to the point of mutiny. Several times it was touch and go whether we would get the job finished; murmerings could be heard criticizing 'the boss' and only by threats and promises did we scrape through.

However, a grand idea came to me when talking to my overseer one day. He was a capital fellow, a Muslim from Kashmir and he told me these people loved a band. There was a good three-man band in our village of Manduri, and he could get them if I could arrange to pay them well. An A.G.E. (Assistant Garrison Engineer) is not much good if he cannot work out how to pay three extra men on a labour roll of some 600 odd coolies. So we decided to try music while you work.

I was out early the first day of our band trial. The band walked to work with the coolies from their camp some three miles away. They consisted of tom-tom drums, pipe and symbol, and they were playing enthusiastically as I passed them on the road in the car. There seemed to be a smile on the faces of the coolies already and they evidently took a good view of this band although they did not appreciate its purpose.

Right: The band

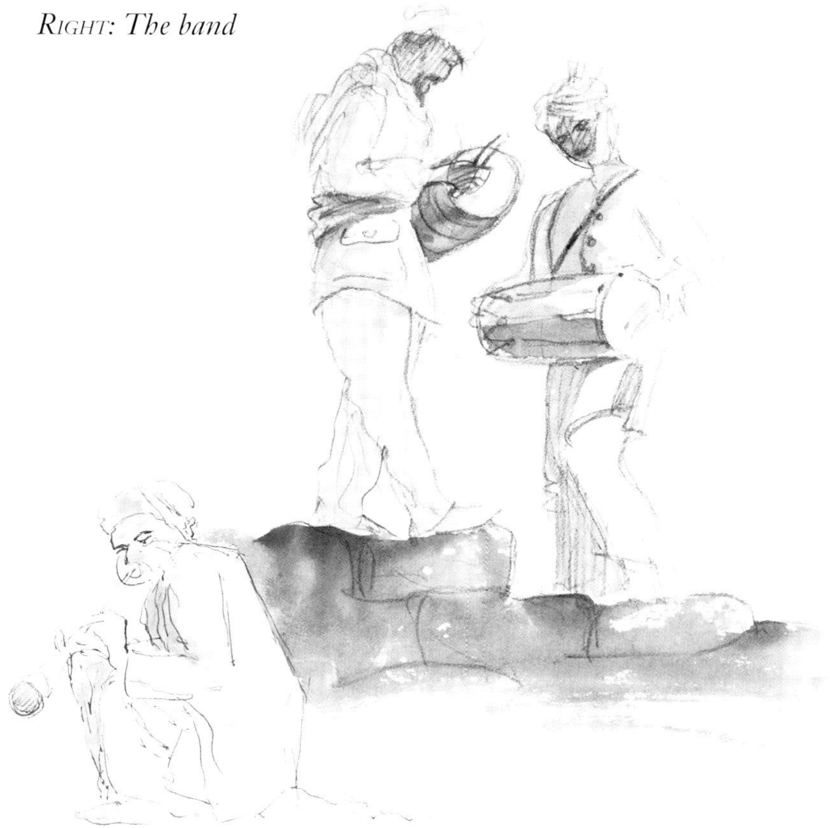

That day we completed our concrete roof in record time. Some 2,500 cubic feet of concrete had been mixed by hand and with one concrete mixer, poured down shoots or carried in small baskets and placed in position, tamped and troweled off smooth by about 200 coolies in just seven hours. All the labourers were on their way home by 5 o'clock! In other words, the band idea was a roaring success and we had created a landmark in the annals of concreting in the North West Frontier with unskilled labour.

The band had a stimulating effect on everybody. The music sometimes worked up to a high pitched frenzy, which had the effect of working the coolies into a frenzy too! They passed their buckets with ever increasing speed and every now and then one gifted member of a gang would break away and perform a dance, much to the delight of his colleagues who would cheer loudly. A great shout from a hundred throats would go up sometimes out of sheer joy and appreciation of the music. But what music. I went to bed that first band night with the squealing, high-pitched pipe still singing in my ears. It was rather like a bagpipe without the bag; some of the deeper notes were quite melodious, but on the whole it was not music to my ears.

From then on we always made roof concreting days band days, and I believe the coolies actually looked forward to them

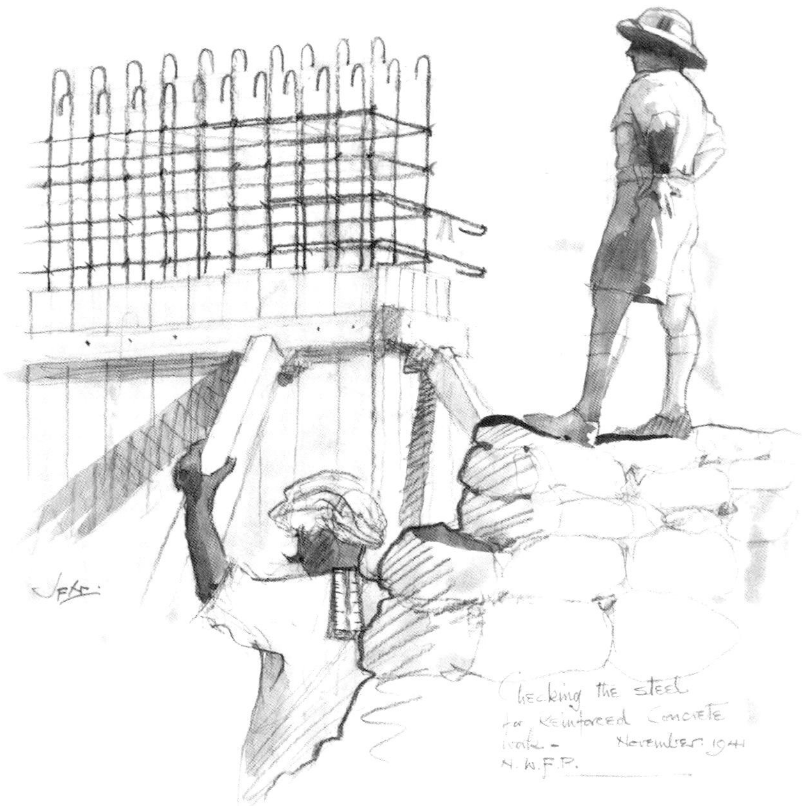

Above: Checking steel reinforcing rods

instead of dreading them as they must have done formerly on account of the late working hours. The general shindy created on these occasions was pretty terrific and when the Colonel arrived on the site while the performance was in full swing one day he was quite amazed at it all, but perfectly agreeable. Fortunately he did not ask any awkward questions.

The Colonel was a slave driver, as I have already mentioned, but managed to impart his tremendous enthusiasm for getting the job done quickly to all officers under him. Our own little set of four were particluarly infected. We each had a similar job of work to do and it was a question of who would finish first. We had all started about the same time. Methods and labour problems were discussed over the dinner table and bright ideas were exchanged. The band idea, for instance, became quite popular and the musicians were in great demand before long.

But we were rather reticent about progress of work and did not 'let on' just how far each particular job had gone until a surprise announcement could be made one day that it was finished. One became quite skilful at this game of bluff and it had its uses when stores were getting low. It was most unwise, for example, to announce that one was running short of cement on a job as there would be an immediate rush on the cement stores. It was far wiser to quietly acquire stores first and talk about them afterwards.

During these hard-pressed months we talked of nothing else

Right: 5 Pouring concrete

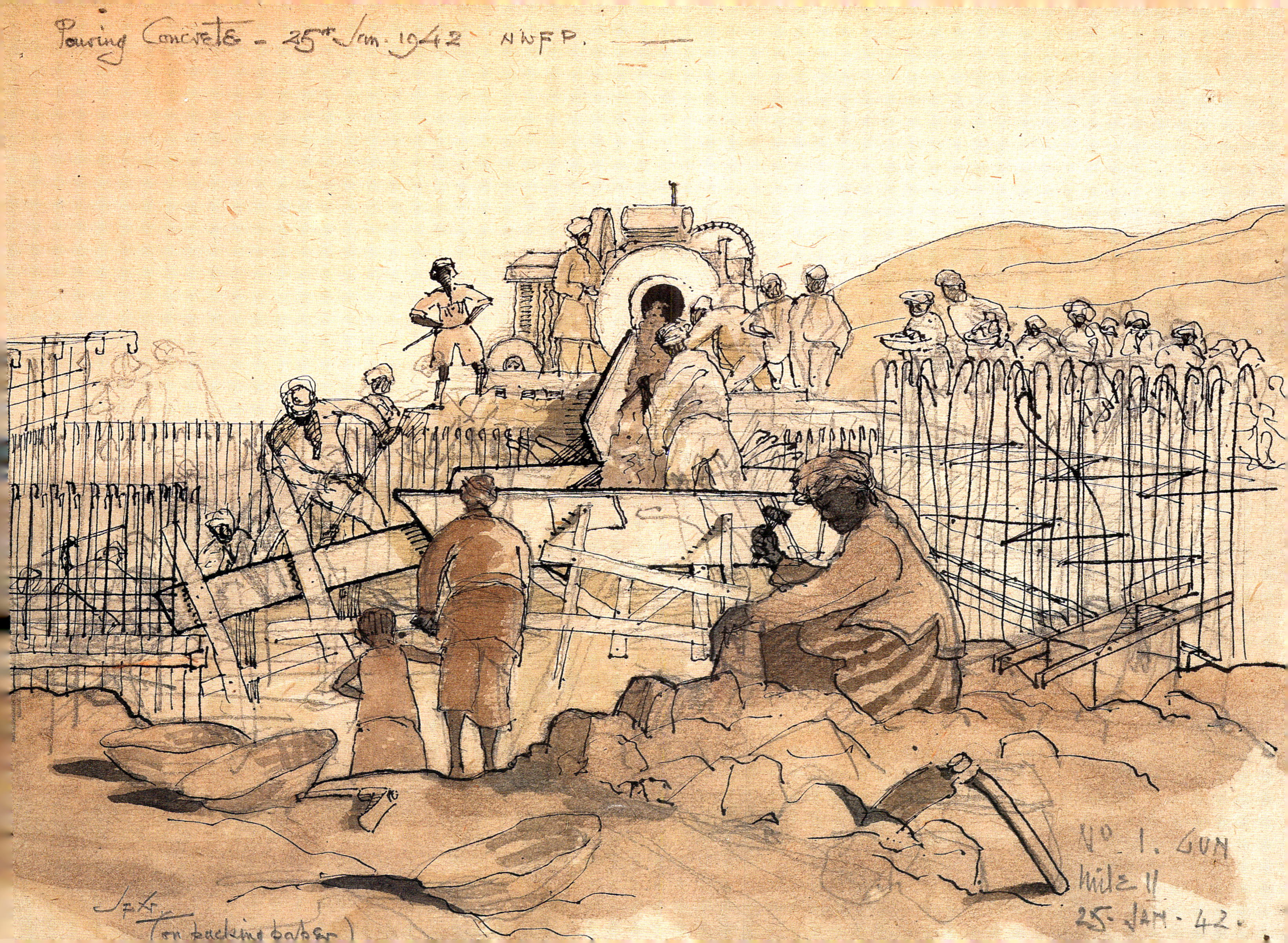
Pouring Concrete - 25th Jan. 1942 NWFP.
No 1. GUN
Mile 11
25. JAN. 42.

but concrete. Our uniforms were covered in concrete, we dreamt about concrete, we almost ate concrete – at least we swallowed a lot of cement dust. Speaking for myself, I learnt a lot about the practical application of reinforced concrete construction. One could not rely totally on a local overseer to arrange reinforcing rods in the correct positions; the only way was to do the setting oneself. Looking back, it strikes me as a very marvellous thing that we got the results we did with what amounted to a group of undisciplined villagers who had no building knowledge whatsoever. They had to be trained up as we went along.

The drawing of 'pouring concrete' was made very hastily one morning on the back of a piece of packing paper found on the site. It was all right for pencil but when I tried to put a wash of colour on afterwards in my room, it sank in like blotting paper. By persistant dabbings and lots of water, however, I managed to get some sort of tone on to it.

There were many problems to overcome almost every day. Building materials were not always forthcoming at the required moment; the water supply system would often stop functioning; our own staff car would break down and we would

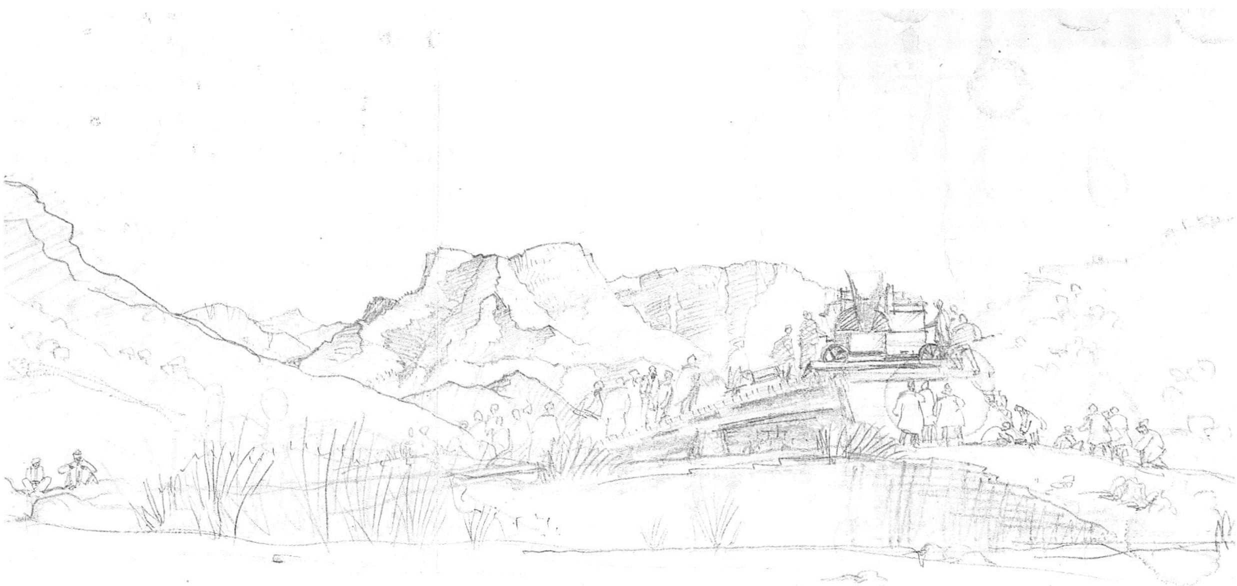

LEFT: Pencil sketch of the Bride and Bridegroom mountain

RIGHT: 6 The Bride and Bridegroom mountain and concreting work in progress

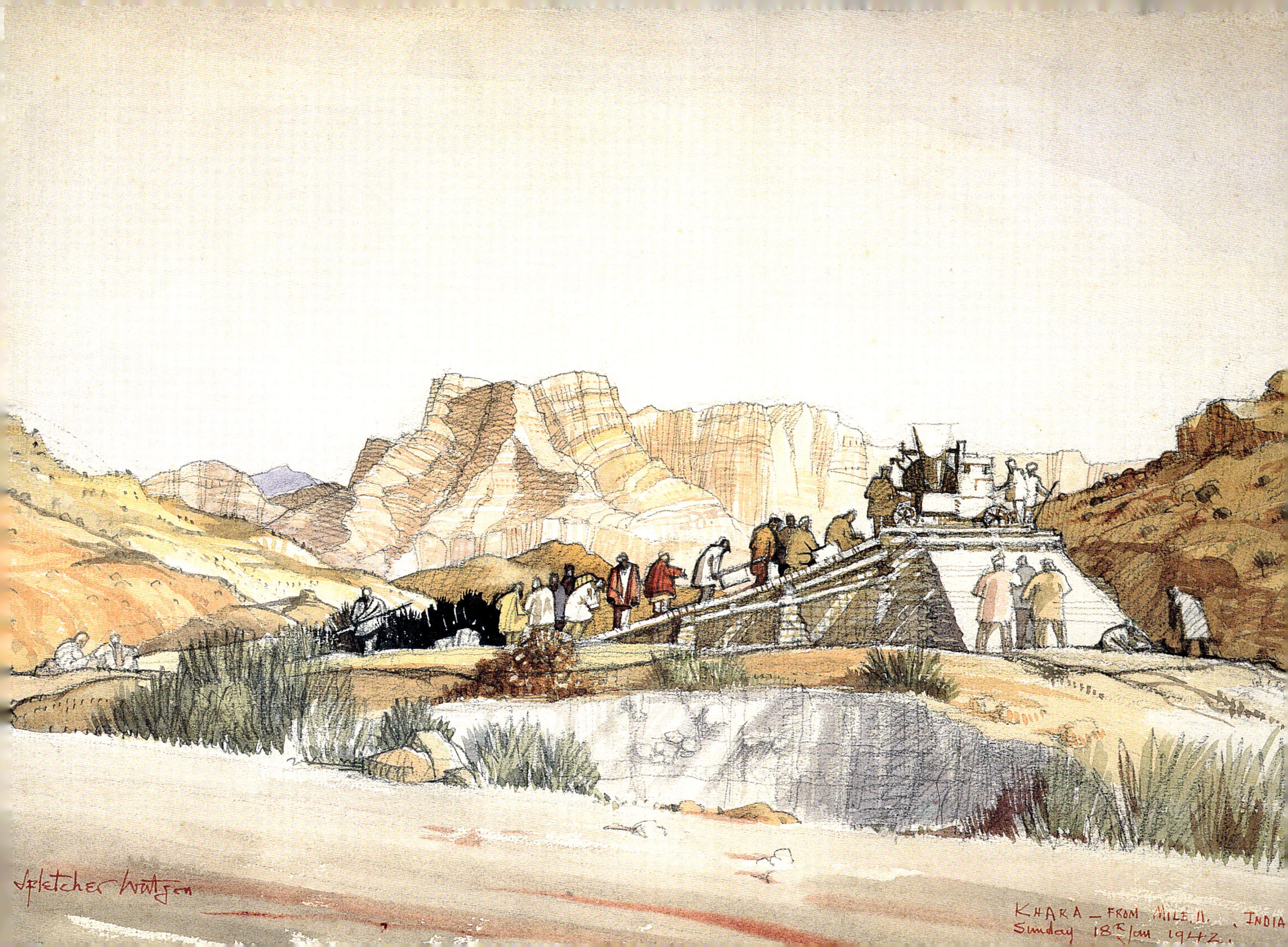
JFletcher Watson
KHARA – FROM MILE 11. INDIA
Sunday 18th Jan 1942.

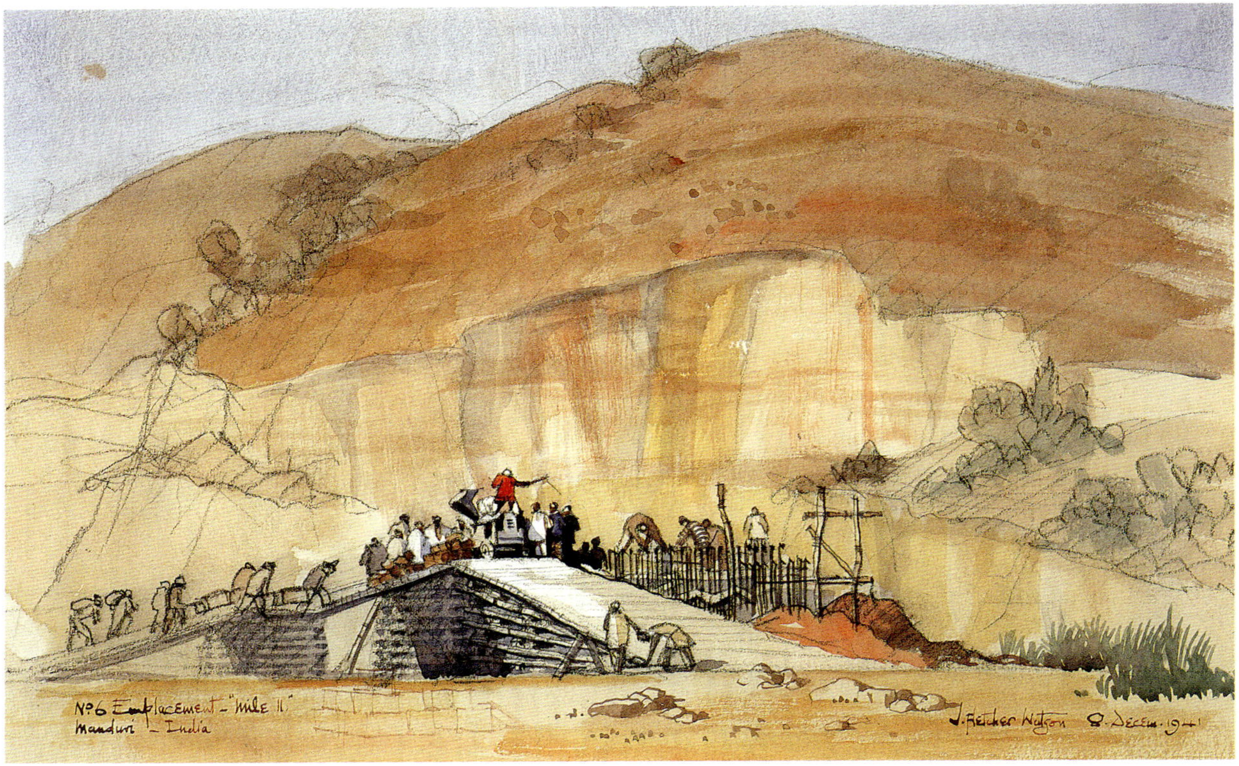

LEFT: 7 Another gun emplacement

have to walk to the job. But in spite of all the setbacks there were compensations. We were working in the midst of wonderfully impressive scenery. The sketch of the Bride and Bridegroom mountain gives an idea of the sort of background that existed to most of our works. The pencil sketch was made on the spot on the back of a working drawing and I made the coloured picture soon after in my quarters. The great craggy pink mountain in the background became a familiar but always satisfying sight to me. One could find some new features on its rugged form every day that one had not noticed before, and the ever-changing lengths of shadow and tones of light gave constant cause for admiration. In the early morning the colour was often grey, changing to sepia at high noon, and a brilliant rose-pink by sunset. Finally, as the sun went down, it assumed a deep purple, looming up in silhouette against the fading sky.

Later on, when the work had really got a grip and could be safely left to run itself for twelve hours, we managed to get an occasional day off. One of our happiest trips was a day to Parichinar. This place lies close to the Afghanistan border and is about sixty-five miles up the Kurram Valley from Manduri. The first time I went there was with three others, one of them being an Indian officer who knew the district and was showing us round.

We left early in the morning by car and as it was my first change of scenery for four months I was fairly straining at the bit and was fully equipped with pencils and sketch book. The road climbs very gradually all the way until it finally reaches a height of 2,500 feet. The villages become more like fortified castles as one goes on. They are each surrounded by a high wall with a tall Malikh's tower in the centre. The Malikh is the headman who owns the village and always has a two-storey house with a tower in the midst of the more lowly one-storyed buildings (built of 'mutti' or mud) of his retainers.

The sketch of Kurram Valley, which I sent home to England, and the picture of Shama Village, show typical 'mutti'

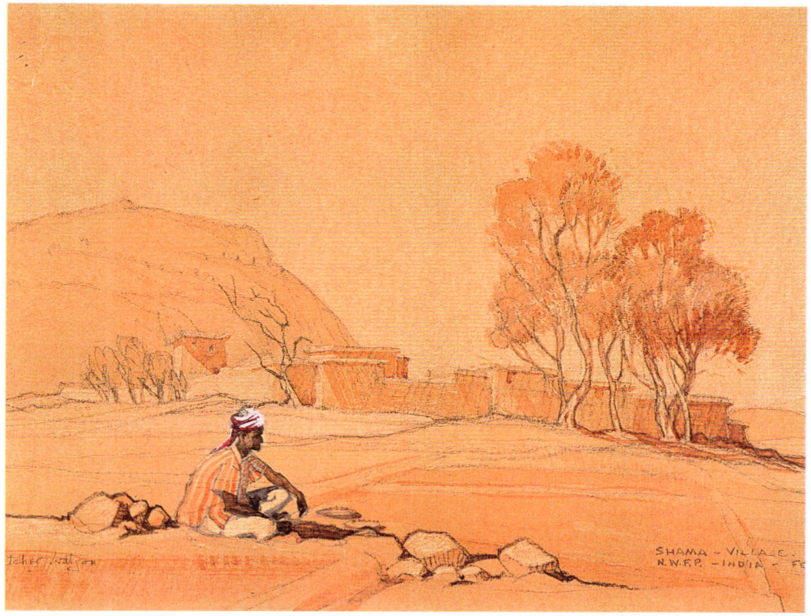

Above: 8 Shama Village

villages. The construction of these buildings is not just solid mud, of course. Walls are strengthened with a core of sticks like the old wattle and daub cottages in Norfolk or Somerset and other parts of England. Some walls are of stone laid in mud instead of mortar. The variety of beautiful scenery on this trip was quite breathtaking, changing from vertical cliff edges along the Kurram River to flatter and more open plains dotted

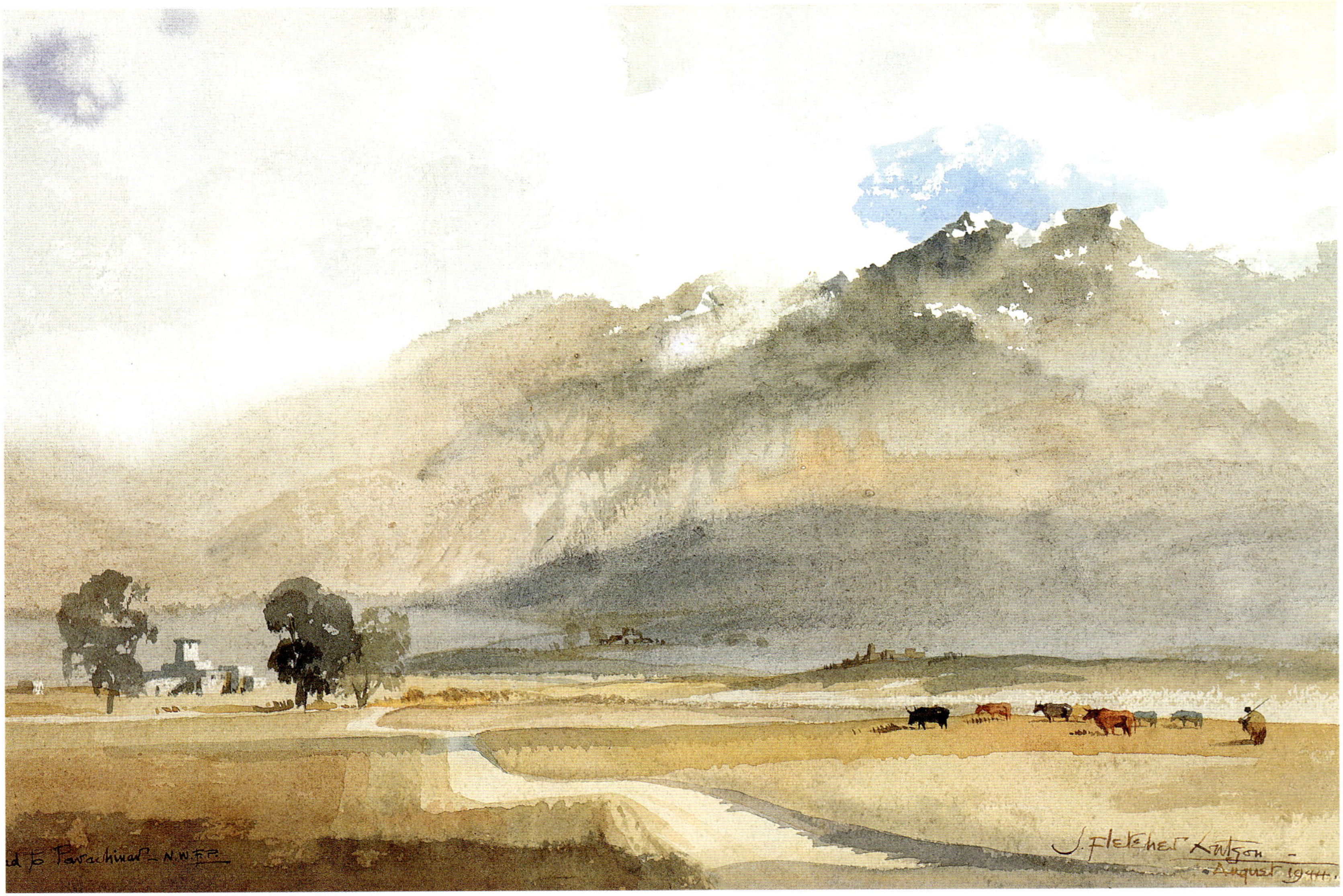
d to Parachinar – N.W.F.P.
J. Fletcher Watson –
August 1944.

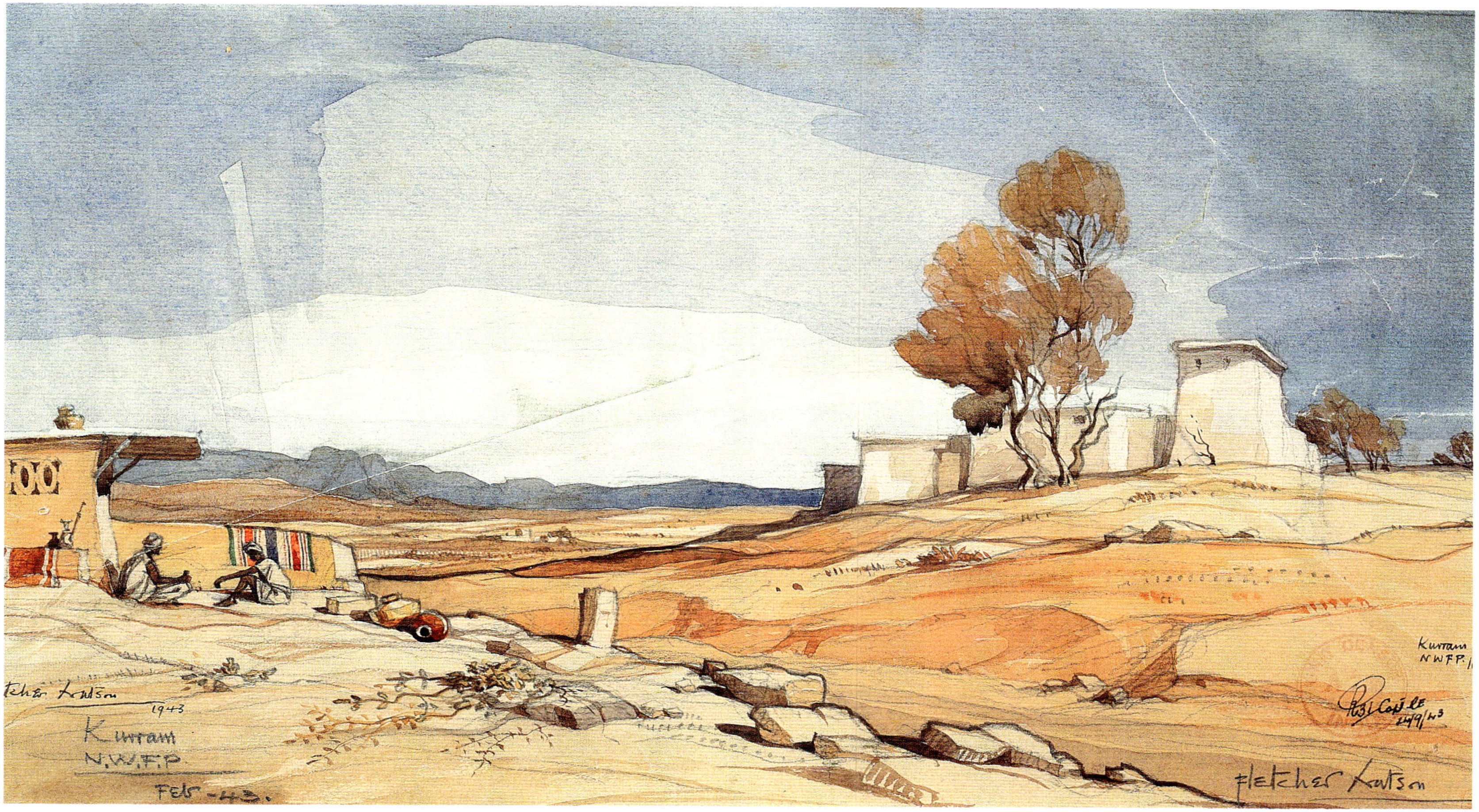

Left: 9 The road to Parichinar

Above: 10 Kurram Valley

with villages and clumps of tall trees. That was the most refreshing thing: the trees. And gradually the land became more barren as we approached the foothills of the mountain range which marks the border of Afghanistan and joins the western end of the Hindu Kush.

The colouring this day was superb: clouds with gaps of blue letting through shafts of light which would flood the snowy tops of the mountains in a sparkle of sunshine. Villages would light up for a few moments while the sun caught their cream walls with a warm glow, and then the light would go out again as the clouds rolled onwards.

The country around Parichinar was a sepia landscape, ranging from dark grey-brown in the hills to yellow-brown on the plains. Even the people were sepia coloured – their faces and their home-spun coats and rugs.

We passed on to Tori Mangal on the border itself, where two forts stood, one British, the other Afghan, and I did a pencil sketch, making notes about the colouring. Here again the colours were all browns and yellows.

Another memorable day was a shoot with the Malikh of a village called Ali Zai, ten miles up the valley. Budi Saman was the Malikh's name, and his village was one of six situated near the river in a close group. From a distance, they were like a young city, with a tall tower and very high perimeter walls. The further up the valley one went, the more hostile the country became and the more defensive the design of the villages. Big studded doors barred the main entrances which were securely bolted every night.

None of us had guns of our own, but we were fortunate in having an excellent head clerk . In this instance, he was asked to produce sporting shotguns which he managed to do – two of them. One more was lent to us by the Malikh. All three firing pieces were objects one would not be seen dead with at home, at least, one probably *would* be seen dead with them as they had extremely loose breeches and were, I should think, quite capable of exploding in one's face. But we were not to be deterred by such troubles. We were six guns in all and beaters were almost in their hundreds, it seemed. After walking two or three miles we crossed the river Kurram. Crossing the Kurram was easier said than done, however, as at this time of year it was high and running pretty fast. Budi Samar had very thoughfully arranged for three ponies to take the party across in relays. Some of the men shied off as they did not like the look of a bare back pony ride through a swift current and a rather rocky

Right: 11 British and Afghan frontier forts

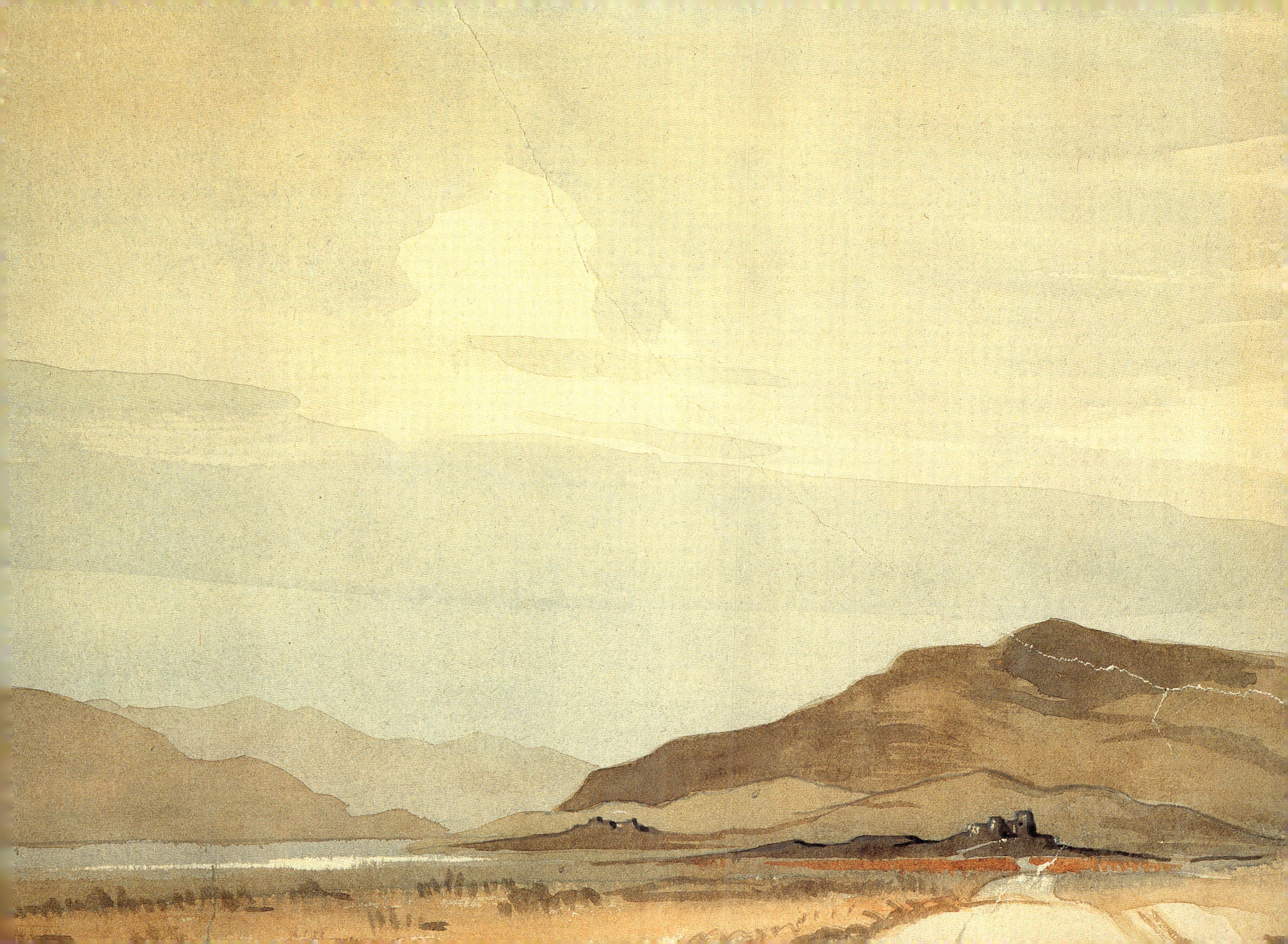

foothold. It was quite an anxious manoeuvre but I preferred it to wading or piggyback as some of them did. One of the party distinguished himself by falling in after wading three steps, much to everybody's amusement – except his own.

Considering the great army of beaters and the enormous mileage we foot-slogged, our total bag was extraordinarily small. But then we lost a lot of birds in the impenetrable Mazri undergrowth, and having no dogs, the birds were quite irretrievable – at least that is my story and I'm sticking to it! We actually brought home one hare, a brace of black partridge (a very pretty bird with a scarlet feather), two brace of chikore, and a pigeon. The bag also included a wild cat, a menace to local villagers. She was spotted in the fading light, peering at us from behind a rock above our heads, a great strong-looking creature, as big as a jackal. She was left to the vultures.

On our return to the Malikh's house, he insisted on feeding us with very tough roast chicken. Dish after dish was brought in, no vegetables, just chicken and rice. Everybody started off in fine style, taking a big helping, but their faces soon changed from smiling, hungry anticipation to anxiety, mingled with a smile for manners' sake. One by one, they realized what they had let themselves in for with those big helpings. Fortunately, I had started off with a modest leg, but a leg never to be for-

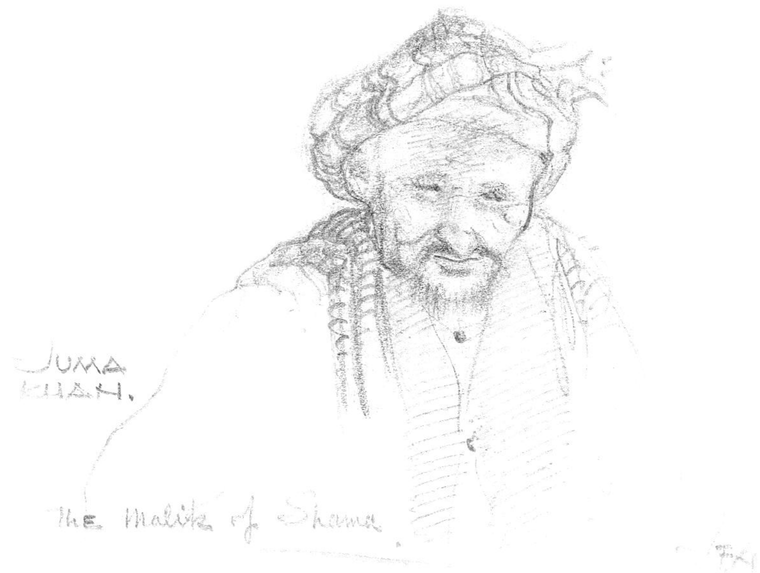

gotten. One simply chewed and chewed at rubber and nothing seemed to happen; it just bounced back at you. There were a lot of half empty plates with half chewed chicken hidden beneath the remains of the rice. After the meal, old Budi Seram kindly insisted on our taking the bag with us and we parted excellent friends.

I wish I had had enough time to make a series of pencil studies of some of the many fine faces amongst our labour gangs. So many types there were, with well-proportioned heads and sharp features of great character. The Mistries – carpenters, joiners, blacksmiths or stone masons who were more permanently established on the work – were mostly men with interesting intelligent faces. Their work was so far unspoilt and untouched by the soul-destroying mass-production industry in the West. These men still took a pride in their work, even in building a plain stone wall. There is an art to doing just that, and to well and truly laying a stone was enough for them.

However, some of them deserved more scope for applying their individual skill, and I got one mason on to carving a foundation stone. We had the names of various officers put on it in the best V cut Roman lettering which I sketched out on the stone first. It was laid in a building of a special nature which will have to remain unnamed for security reasons. We built a cash below it containing a few coins and newspapers, and had a short laying ceremony at which two officers were presented with trowel and hammer respectively. The finished article was quite a masterpiece.

I discovered one old joiner who could make awfully good wooden toys. So I got him to make all the toys he could think of, in his spare time, for me to send home to my small son, Michael. The first thing he produced was a marvellous mouse carved in wood taken from a broken pickaxe handle. When you pulled a string the mouse's mouth opened and shut, and its tail wagged. It was some time before I could bring myself to part with this fascinating toy. He also made a wooden ball built of many small rectangular sections of wood. This ball is a well-known Indian puzzle but not an easy one to make and I was informed by the Mistrie that the method of taking it to pieces was a closely-guarded secret known only to a privileged few. He would only tell me this secret in the privacy of my tent where no other mistri or coolie could see the demonstration. He had a long white beard and looked very benevolent. We became firm friends and he was always suggesting new toys for the 'Chota Sahib'. Amongst his other creations were a camel, a top and a snake.

The tools these people use are very interesting. The adze is the most well known; it is an instrument that was widely used in England in the Middle Ages and is still used in certain districts. A wood panel which had been adzed rather than planed has a rippled surface which is very pleasing in appearance. The Indian joiner uses the adze with great skill and accuracy considering its massive size and weight. Another Mistri carpenter collected a whole set of tools for me. He gave me his own ancient adze which he had used for the last twenty years in exchange for a new one which I bought him. They used a form of bradawl for boring holes which is made to revolve by means of a piece of string and a long stick. When sawing wood, they hold the timber with their feet, and the teeth on the saw are arranged so that the pull and not the push is the stroke which does the cutting and receives all the energy. Altogether I have some twenty tools, complete with the box, all made by this Mistri, except for the chisel which a blacksmith made from scrap metal ends of reinforcing rods. In other words the Government has a small claim to my tool box!

So many things are the reverse in India to what they are in England. Apart from the language which is, to us, spoken and written backwards, Indian craftsmen love fixing locks on doors the opposite way round to us so that the key has to go in upside down. I should say the key went the wrong way up into quite twenty per cent of all local-made cupboards and drawers in India!

We had the usual difficulty with contractors offering 'gifts' or 'bribes' as they should really be called. I was given a carpet soon after I arrived and as I wanted a carpet I decided to buy it. But every time I asked the price, I was told by the contractor, 'It is as you like' or 'I will give it to you, Sahib'. In the end I forced a large sum of money on the man, probably far more than the carpet was worth, but the only safe thing to do.

One bright young officer I heard of got over the problem in this way. He was presented with a beautiful carpet by each of three contractors as soon as he arrived at a new station. He wanted the three carpets but could not possibly accept them as gifts from building contractors, all of whom were eligible for future works, so he carefully selected three pocket watches costing approximately the same as the value of the carpets. He than got all the contractors into his office one by one, thanked each one very much for their lovely carpets and presented them with a watch which he felt sure they would be pleased to accept from him as a present. There was an understanding from that day forward between the officer and local contractors, and he never had further troubles with offers of 'gifts'.

There was no lack of choice if you wanted to buy a carpet. We had camel trains of carpet traders coming through Maduri almost daily on their way to Rawalpindi, Lahore, and even further south to do trade in the towns and villages of the Punjab. Some of them would travel many hundreds of miles before starting their return journeys back to Afghanistan and Persia. The rate of progress of these camel trains was much faster than one might suppose. The camel, with his lolloping gait and big stride, gets along at around five miles per hour and can do a lot better than that if pressed. He can keep it up, moreover, for many hours. But they do have their bad moments when they sit down, refusing to budge and making loud groaning noises. I do not know enough about camels to say whether this is a serious sign or if it is simply the camel's way of taking a rest and getting his breath. But we often passed a moaning camel with a driver tugging at him and doing his best to get him moving again. On some days, we would pass a large train of about twenty heavily-loaded camels just arriving through the village in the morning and by the time we returned home at 6.00 p.m. the whole outfit would have pitched camp by the side of the river: camels sitting on their haunches comfortably munching, fires going, cooking the evening meal, and everybody looking for all the world as if they had been dug in there for a month.

They were fine-looking men, these Afghans: big, sturdy, black-bearded fellows with leather belts and swords or knives swinging from their sides. They had reduced travelling and camping to a fine art after many generations of the life of touring traders. They often chose the same spot to make camp, a flat area of paddy field along the river bank, close under the little village of Chahar Khal, which towered above on a rocky eminence of its own, one mile out of Manduri. The view from the main road running along the hillside, sixty feet up from the river plain, was indeed a stirring one and cried out to be sketched.

In those January days of 1942, the camel trains were passing through in large quantities but I had no time for sketching. However, the memories live vividly with me and I have not given up hope of putting something on paper yet. The tents were made of dark brown or black blanket material and were an interesting oblong shape, having two main supports in the middle and smaller ones at the edges. Contrasting with this sombre colour would be an occasional scarlet or veridian garment thrown over the corner of a tent. One or two Arab horses, wild and vigorous looking creatures, with long manes and tails, would be tied up to stakes. The general colour scheme of the encampment with its haphazard but naturally artistic grouping made tempting subject matter for sketching. The setting of river and hillside village was beyond criticism. There were the dark tents, the camels, the large water pots and the much earringed and bangled women and children in long black-and-red skirts. The men in their coloured turbans, dark waistcoats, white shirts and baggy trousers. All contributed to the formation of a brilliant and inspiring scene, enough to send any painter off his head with an enthusiasm and urge to 'get busy' with the paint box without further delay.

One had to remind oneself on these occasions that there was 'a war on' and give oneself a metaphorical dig in the ribs in order to come down to earth and get on with the job. The sad part is that when the war has ceased to be 'on' it is very unlikely that I shall ever return to the North West Frontier. That is, I think, one of the underlying reasons that prompts me to make sketches, however rough, whenever the opportunity arises. These precious chances may never occur again.

I managed to pay occasional visits to these people and was shown carpets and knives for sale. I liked walking into history. The camels, the people, the tents, the rugs, were all exactly the same as they had been a thousand years ago. Even the paddy fields were the same: little rectangular plots twenty yards long with mud bund walls three or four inches high dividing them off from each other. There is something about bargaining for a carpet which is spread out on the ground and bathed in brilliant sunshine, arguing with a spellbinding figure in a pink turban, that 'gets you', as the Yanks say. It is at once intriguing and romantic, a carpet which is acquired in this way is surely never forgotten. I fell victim to buying one rug at any rate and no doubt, in years to come, my friends in England, looking down at a small rug in front of my dining room fireplace after dinner, will be bored with hearing the stories of Afghan camel trains and carpet traders. They would not be able to visualise the wicked glint in the eye of the trader and the curl of his big black moustache or the brilliant effect of a red and black carpet laid flat on the light brown earth of the North West Frontier of India. All the more reason, I say, to get these wonderful scenes on paper in their true colours.

Our normal routine existence in the N.W.F. (North West Frontier) was quite a happy one all things considered. Spending all day long in the burning sun did take it out of one but the dry heat was much better than the humid heat of other parts of India. We were very short of transport the first three months I was there, and four of us had to share one car. It was a big grey Chevrolet saloon and would drop us off one by one in the morning as we passed the different sites of work. It was always a great moment of the day coming home in the evening at half past five or six. As the big car swung into the quadrangle formed by our mud hut dwellings, all four doors would burst open and out would climb four ravenous officers, parched and thirsting for tea and toast. 'Bearer' would be the cry from four hoarse throats which had been shouting all day. Bearers arrived and each man retired to his little den and sank onto the bed, and if his bearer was well trained, had his boots taken off! From then on, the ideal was to relax completely while one's bearer fussed round with hot tea, toast, buns or anything he had managed to scrounge to satisfy the Sahib's

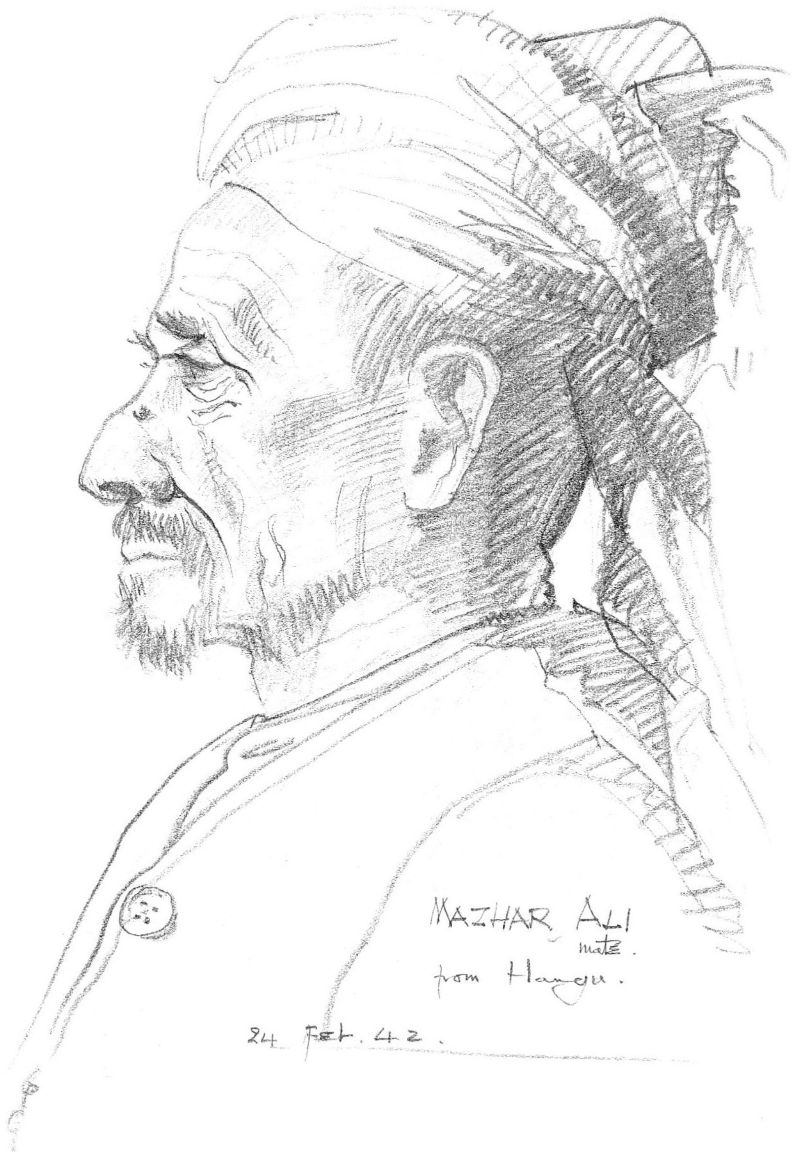

furious appetite. My great friend in those days, a brother architect, usually had tea with me in my room. I had got a slightly bigger room than the standard one and as it was adorned with sketches and tools such as adzes and knives on the walls, and rugs on the floor, it did have something of the atmosphere of a homely furnished room. I had also one or two items of furniture made by my favourite Mistri: a very nice folding table with a carved centre leg and four carved feet at its base; also, a long low stool modelled on the local charpoi (ie. bed) design with a grass string seat.

We had a walking stick craze for a spell, during which time I collected at least eight fine specimens of local stick ranging from a twisted, knot-ridden, club-like object, to a highly polished silver-mounted, ebony-handled article. All these were hanging on nails on the wall, so that the room became a mixture of art gallery and museum. A 'mate' of mine from Hangu had a magnificent stick about five feet tall with a big iron knob at its top which I am sure he must have inherited from his great grandfather at least, and I asked him one day if he would part with it. He said he would but at the same time was very fond of it, so I relented and let him keep it as it seemed a shame to deprive an old man of a treasured possession.

Great was my annoyance therefore when a few days later I

discovered one of my stick-collecting rivals was in possession of this fine specimen. I said that was carrying his enthusiasm a bit too far but he said the old boy was very satisfied with the handsome sum he had paid him for it and so I had to admit defeat. A stick was a very useful and almost essential accoutrement in our job. It was useful when walking over rough stony parts of the site, and one could poke it into fresh concrete to test the consistency. I met a Brigadier who used to carry a most ingenious stick. He used it for pointing out landmarks which he wished to discuss with you. It had a spike at the end and a metal sight on top similar to a rifle. The sight could be bent over into a horizontal position and then the stick was driven into the ground and twisted in the desired direction to pinpoint the object under discussion.

In December we started fires, a great luxury. But we had snow that year and the nights were very cold indeed. One wanted at least three blankets and a great coat on one's bed.

A typical day usually ended up as follows: From 7.00 to 8.30 p.m. would be spent in the office dealing with correspondence, paying labour, telephoning to the C.R.E.'s office and instructing overseers about work for the following day. Then there always seemed to be some domestic trouble to deal with. Either somebody's petrol lamp would not work or the bearers wanted warm clothes, and so on. At last we had dinner about 9.00 p.m. and finally a very welcome bed at 10.30.

We started Manduri mess nights to which we invited officers from their highly civilized mess in the fort at Thal. They came rather reluctantly at first to our uncivilized village, thinking that 'those poor chaps out at Manduri' would not be able to provide much of a show, but their tune soon changed after the inaugural night. The cook came right up to scratch and put through a magnificent five course dinner. We did our share by providing beer, liquors and for those who fancied it a communal hooka (pipe!). We supplied Balkan Sobriani tobacco for the hooka which made it a popular novelty. It was the locally-made earthenware type of hooka, with a reed draw pipe, not the superiour brass or silver affair, but it was nevertheless quite appreciated. We finished a bottle of Drambue and many a bottle of beer, too many to remember, and everybody went to bed singing.

These evenings became popular events, especially when the fruits of a successful day's shooting were part of the board, and we had several more shoots now that the state of work allowed for an occasional day off. Chikore, black partridge, snipe, or

Right: 12 View from the Thal-Manduri road

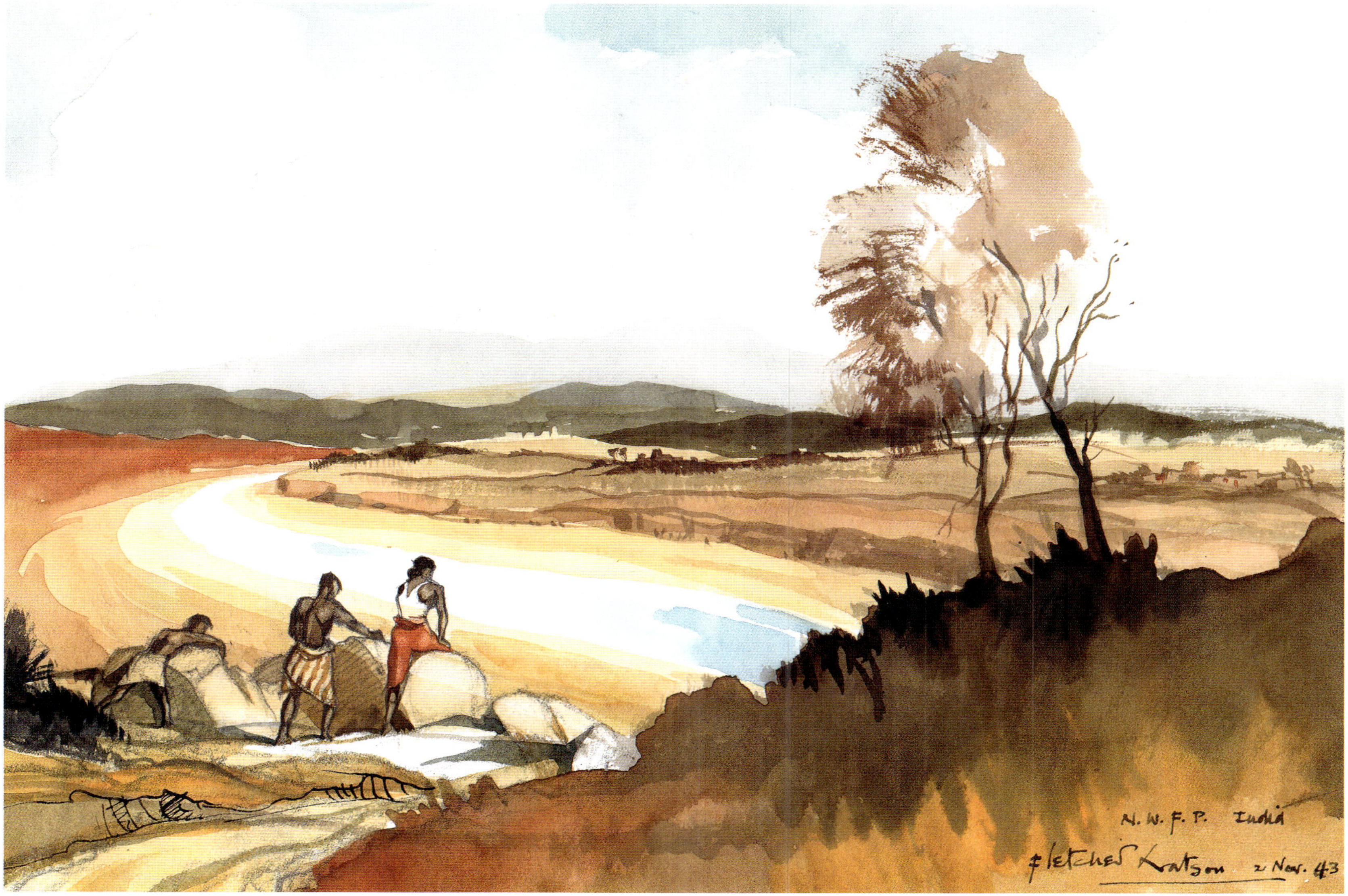
N. W. F. P. India
Fletcher Watson 2 Nov. 43

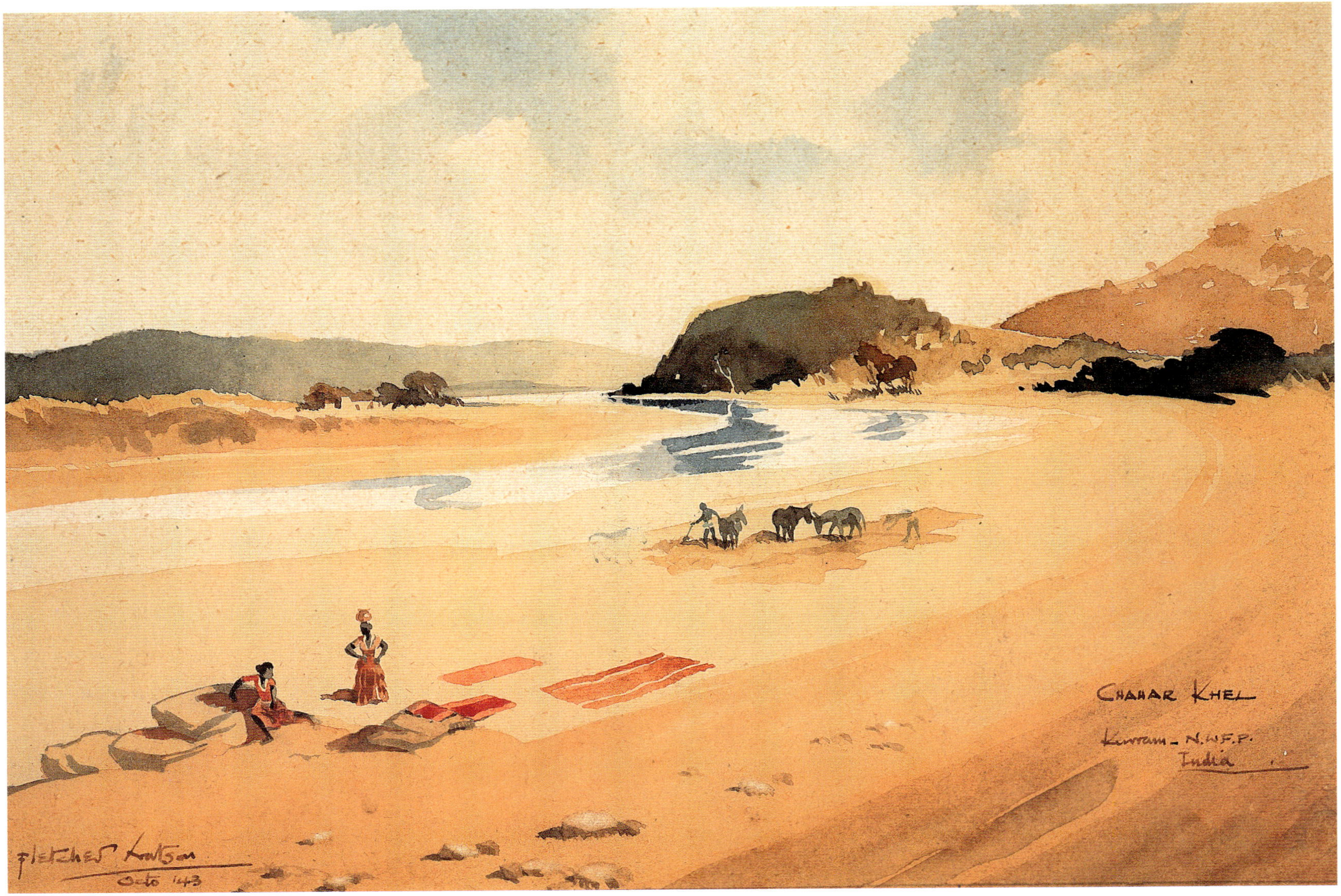
Chahar Khel
Kurram – N.W.F.P.
India
Fletcher Watson
Oct '43

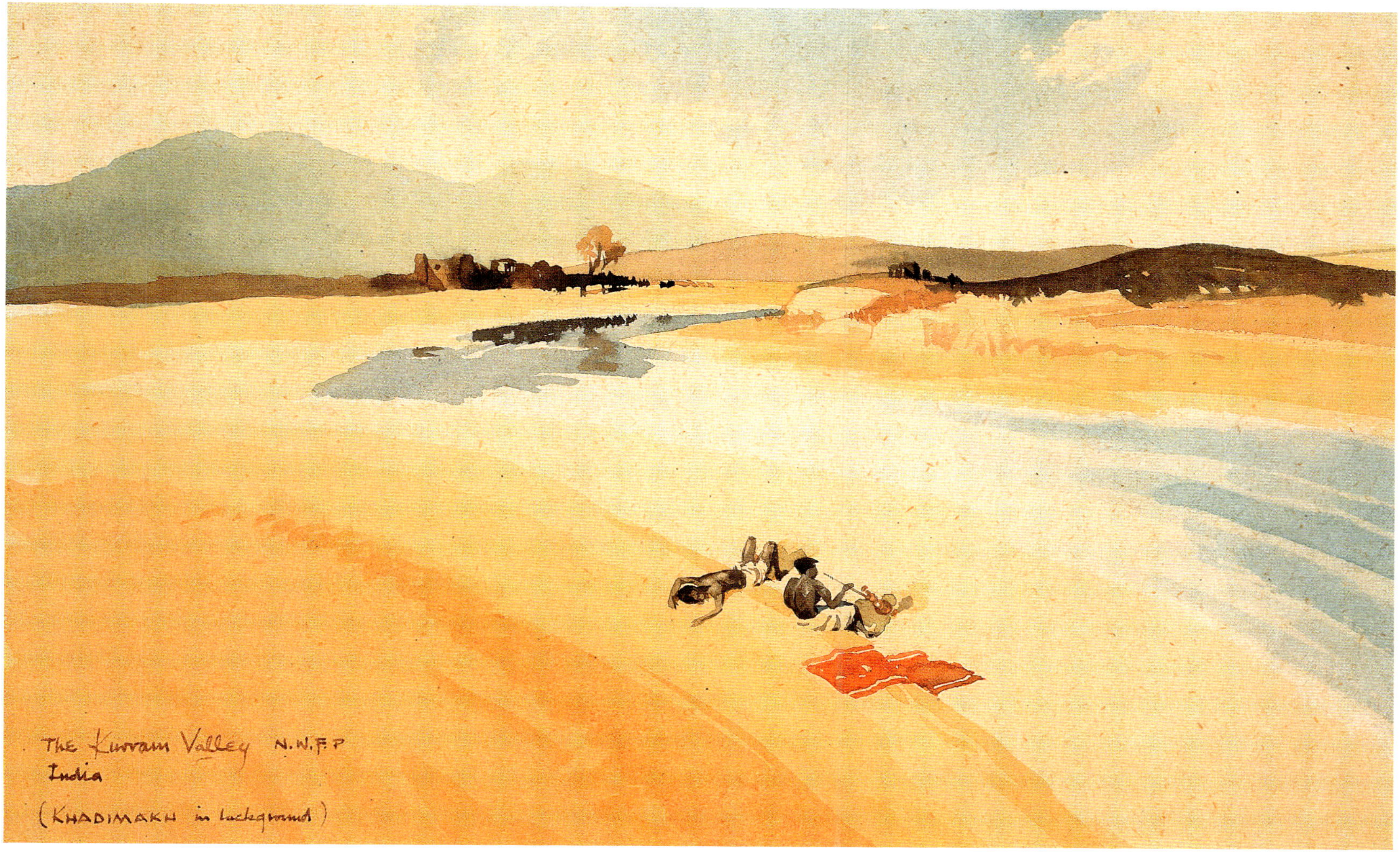

LEFT: 13 Chahar Khel

ABOVE: 14 Kurram Valley scene

hare were quite frequently on the menu. It always meant stopping a night and this was one of the attractions to the chaps from Thal who welcomed any break from the routine existence and officialdom of Brigade Headquarters. The Political Agent of N.W.F.P. (the North West Frontier Province) dined with us one night and in return sent us all a present of a walking stick made in Parichinar. This was enormously appreciated by our enthusiastic collectors.

Just before Christmas I narrowly missed an encounter with our friends, the tribesmen. A copy of the newspaper description of the occasion is reproduced here. It is typical of the sort of mischief the tribesmen like to get up to.

BRITISH OFFICER AND FIVE INDIANS KILLED

Hostiles Wound Two and Kidnap Three

PESHAWAR, Dec. 23.

One British officer and five Indian other ranks were killed, two wounded and four kidnapped when a military lorry, proceeding from Thall to Kohat on December 20 at 4-30 p.m. was ambushed by a gang of hostiles near the 38th mile.

Later at night, pickets of the Frontier Constabulary and police had a brush with the retreating gang and secured the release of one of the kidnapped persons. Three persons still remain in tribal captivity.—A.P.

I was taken ill with malaria and it was decided, after I had spent two days in bed at Manduri, that I should be moved to Kohat hospital about seventy miles away. An ambulance collected me at about 2.30 p.m. on 20th December, the day of the 'shoot up' and we looked in at Thal hospital before proceeding on. The M.O. (Medical Officer) changed his mind and decided I should be the first B.O. (British Officer) to remain in Thal hospital for treatment. Previously all B.O.s had been sent to Kohat. Although I felt very unlike travelling, I was a little disappointed at not going to Kohat where I should at least have got a change of view of life for a short time. However, if we had gone on we should have run right into the ambush and I would have been a gonner. The tribesmen's usual game is to block the road with a few stones placed in a line across it. A car then has to slow up to see what it is all about and then out come the cut-throats from their hiding place.

They looked after me beautifully in the hospital and by Christmas Day I was well enough to sit up in bed and put away a bottle of beer which was brought in to me personally by the M.O. himself.

CHAPTER THREE

THE TAJ IN SPLINTS

I was sent on a camouflage course at Poona on 30th March 1942. On my way back to the N.W.F. an architect Sapper friend from the course and I arrived at Agra late one Sunday night in May 1942. As we had to break our journey back to Rawalpindi at Agra, we were determined to see the Taj at whatever cost. The people in the hotel told us it was disappointing at the moment as the dome was covered in scaffolding. But dome or no dome, we realised it might be the only opportunity of a lifetime and off we went in a taxi early next morning.

A drive of some fifteen miles of dusty road was necessary at the end of which we were both impatient to bring our critical architectural eyes to bear on this daunting wonder of the world. We were not disappointed, however, in spite of the scaffolding and even that had its interesting aspect. So much has already been spoken and written about the beauties of the Taj Mahal that I won't indulge in a long string of rapturous sentences. As a matter of fact, I am not tempted to do so anyway. I don't mean that I disapprove of the building itself; it is a wonderfully proportioned piece of geometric design. But I did sustain a certain shock with regard to its setting. The photographs one had always seen at home showed a Taj Mahal closely hemmed in by big dark trees and tall Cypruses leading up to the central arch in impressive perspective. None of these now exist. I believe the Preservation of Ancient Buildings people cut the vegetation down considerably during the Viceroyship of Lord Curzon and consequently all we have today are lines of very thin young Cyprus trees only about eight feet high. A few larger trees do remain in the grounds, of course, but to my mind there are not half enough. There is a cold feeling of nakedness about the whole setting.

The scaffolding on the dome is quite the most amazing that I have ever seen. A veritable forest of wooden poles completely obliterates it. An interesting 'switch back' effect is formed by

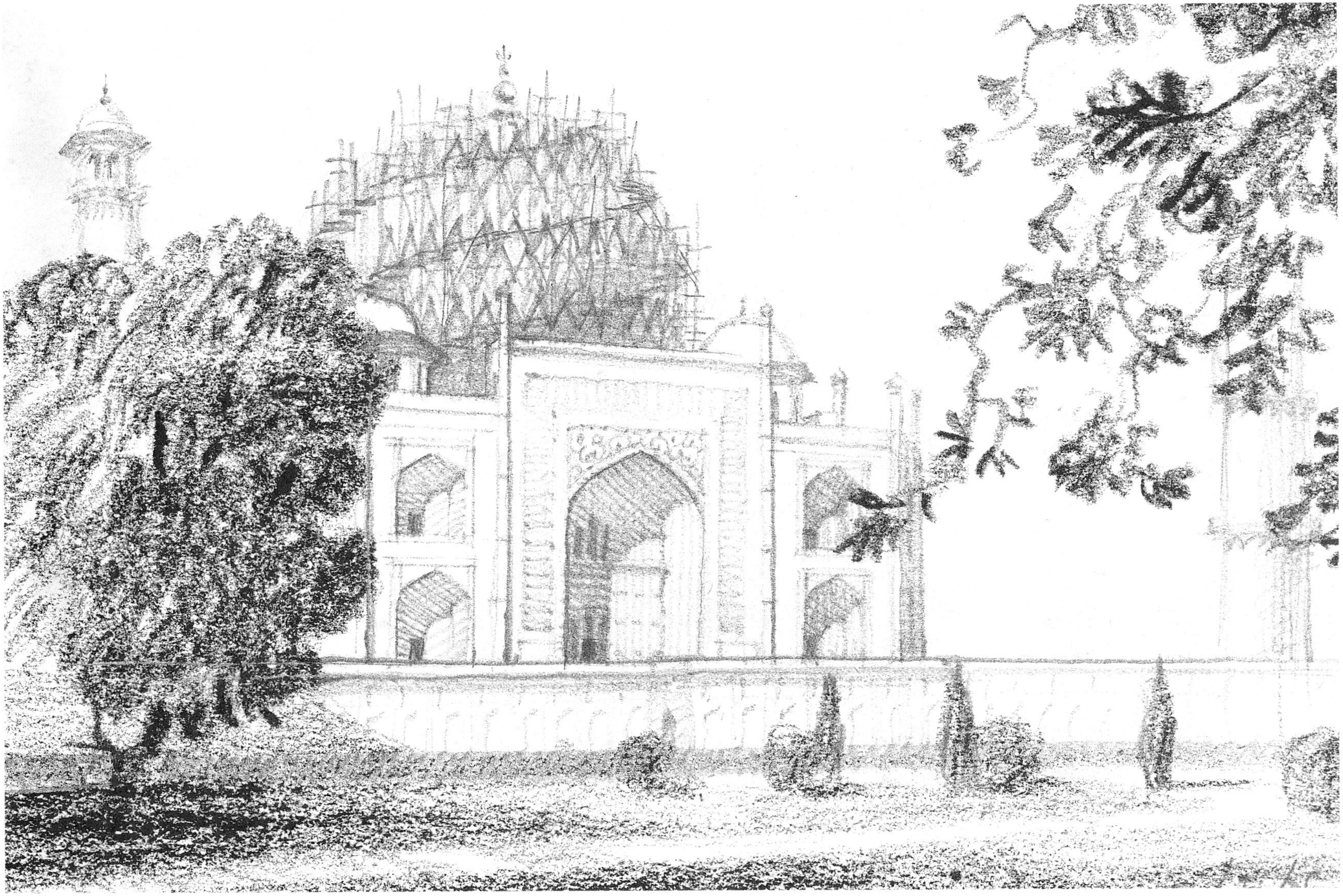

the galleries made with planks to give the workmen access to different parts of the dome.

The first impression I had when I looked at this mass of scaffolding was of fine rendering of Gothic architecture, like some lavishly ornamented Early English arcading in grey stone. It really was not an unpleasant sight at all, throwing the white marble wall surfaces below into strong relief.

We had no time to sit down and browse, but had to rush round and see all we could, rather like the worst type of tripper who thinks that the more 'sights' he can see in the day the better he is doing. I did find time for a quick pencil sketch, however.

The reason for all this scaffolding, by the way, was to re-set a large number of loose stones in the dome before they fell through into the inner dome and did untold damage. One stone weighing about a quarter of a ton had already done this. I think the presence of this scaffolding helped one to appreciate what a tremendous achievement it was to build this great marble structure. One could visualise the entire building as it must have been three hundred years ago, when twenty thousand workmen took over twenty years to complete it. Solid blocks of white marble were swung into position from wooden derricks by masons who had spent half their lives on the job. Specialists in filigree and inlay work toiled on the pierced marble screens and decorative wall designs in precious stones. The best building experts of the time were collected together in order to accomplish the task. The great Mogul emperor, Shejahan, must have been fond indeed of his young wife, to spend the remainder of his life after her death in building this great mausoleum to her memory.

Left: 15 The Taj Mahal under scaffolding

CHAPTER FOUR

MOUNTAINS, CAMOUFLAGE AND CARPET WALLAHS

In the middle of August 1942 I was moved to Quetta as a Camouflage Officer.

I suppose one judges a place in India by the climate, the people one meets and what one does in that place. At Quetta I met few people but as the climate was almost perfect and I had a number of opportunities for sketching, my judgement of it is an extremely favourable one. I will even say it is the best station in which I had the good fortune to be quartered during the whole of my three years of moving about India.

The work on camouflage took me into many remote parts of the surrounding mountainous countryside. Photographs had to be taken and sketches made of certain secret localities before effective camouflage schemes could be planned. What more perfect an opportunity could there be, therefore, for including, during these periods of sketching, views that could later be made into watercolour pictures? I hastened to make the most of this marvellous opportunity, and during my all-too-short stay of only two months, I completed twelve watercolours and a large number of pencil studies (some of which are illustrated within this chapter), not to mention a useful collection of photographs. There was no end to the sketching one could do in a place like this with mountains near and far, rivers, villages consisting of thatch-covered or flat roofed 'mutti' huts, and clusters of mango or neem trees in some districts. Barren, dried-up stretches of country with no vegetation contrasted with more fertile green strips along rivers and streams. The colouring compared with the North West Frontier Province is more varied. While the N.W.F. mostly consists of mountainous landscapes of yellows and browns, Bulachistan has more blue and purple in the distant mountains and the rocky foregrounds have a reddish hue.

One day I was talking to the manager of a photography shop in Quetta, who also sold paintings, most of them prints, and he asked me to give him a few sketches to sell. I gave him eight and they had a little exhibition. I am very sorry now that all the pictures got sold. I do not keep records in pencil of every subject I paint and some of them were very pleasant views which I shall not be able to recall and paint again. All this was very amusing as far as it went, but enquiries for more started to come in and one good lady even applied for sketching lessons. The idea was attractive but it was beginning to stretch the point a bit too far. I had got a job to do other than painting unfortunately so I had to wave aside such temptations accordingly.

My mode of arrival gave me a dramatic first view of Quetta from the air. I had been ordered to go from Karachi weeks before my actual arrival in Quetta, but the Indus had burst its banks and both railway and road were completely washed away at Sukkur. This flood looked like a pretty serious obstacle to my ever getting to Quetta before October. It was most annoying of it to come just as I was given the one job I had been wanting to do – camouflage. But there is usually a way where there is a will, and in this case the Airforce came to the rescue. They got me into a transport plane which took food supplies for stranded towns in the flooded areas. 'We can get you to Jacobabad' I was told, but I might or might not get a lift in the Quetta mail plane from there. At Jacobabad I was lucky; I did get my lift as there were not too many mail bags so there was weight enough to spare. We flew up the Indus for many miles and had a wonderful view of the floods – one of the biggest they have had for years. A sheet of water stretching for miles and miles was broken up only with little black spots of villages like small islands on a vast lake.

The Indian villager, when he lives in a low-lying district liable to flooding, always builds his village on a small self-made eminence of earth. He makes several rectangular excavations ten to twelve feet deep in order to obtain soil for this purpose. These excavations are known as tanks; they are usually full of water and serve as drinking places for domestic animals. Tanks are a regular feature of the more fertile districts of the Indian landscape.

The cleanliness of these tanks varies considerably. Some are comparatively clean: drinking water is sometimes drawn from them and only the odd bullock has a paddle and the village children a bath. But others are decidedly dirty; one is left in absolutely no doubt about this if one makes an approach from the leeward side. Everything seems to happen in these dirty tanks, from the villagers washing their dirty clothes, to the water buffalo washing themselves, the depositing of unpleasant village refuse and the breeding of mosquitoes.

The country for the last fifty miles to Quetta became very mountainous. Strange formations of bare rock would break out at the summits with their strata almost vertical. One could see clearly from this aerial view how the once horizontal strata had been hurled into unnatural positions by violent earthquakes of many centuries ago. A geologist would no doubt be able to make many interesting deductions from such an aerial reconnaissance, but with my small knowledge I admired it all from an aesthetic point of view only. We finally ended up by flying low along a valley following the railway line, with forbidding cliffs on each side of us narrowing sometimes to a gorge and then opening out again to some thousand yards in width. This flight more than any other I have experienced made me sensitive to the fact of being in the air. At great heights one loses all contact with the ground and the sense of scale is gone. But when great rocky craggs and cliff faces are whizzing past you on either side it is altogether much more exciting.

We came suddenly upon Quetta as we rounded a bend in the valley, a long straggling mass of low one-storey buildings. Unlike most Indian towns, however, at least half the buildings had sloping roofs, being the new earthquake-proof designs put up since the devastating quakes of 1935. There is something that sounds rather magical in the word 'earthquake proof' but the facts are quite simple really. I took the trouble to investigate the design of these buildings while I was there. The principle, to put it simply, is that of a cage where the house is built with a frame of reinforced concrete. The spaces between the framework are filled in with a thin, light building fabric which would not do very much damage to anyone if it did fall in on them. All chimneys are built out of asbestos pipes and not out of brick which would tumble down and do damage. There had been at least one major earthquake since the one in 1935 and the new buildings stood their ground firmly without exception. The mud and brick type of house in the old town would come down like a pack of cards of course, especially if they are two-storeyed, as a good many of them are, or rather I should say, were.

Quetta aerodrome has been built on a very marked slope which, unfortunately, falls in the opposite direction to the prevailing wind. Consequently pilots have to choose between landing down hill against the wind or up hill with the wind. We chose the former as the wind was quite strong. Added to this snag is the fact that Quetta is 7,000 feet above sea level and therefore you require more than the normal sea level length of runway. However, the aerodrome has not got this extra distance as its situation amongst the mountains does not allow for it. We were a comparatively light type of plane, however – about a fifteen-seater – and my Indian pilot made a perfectly happy landing.

I lived at the Chilton Hotel while I was in Quetta, but I was away on tour quite a lot. From my room in a little annexe hut I had the most marvellous view of Murdar, which is the second highest mountain near Quetta and dominates the town. Its characteristic shape and ragged skyline together with its varying tones of brown and yellow made it an impressive sight. This mountain was always changing colour according to the time of day and type of sky, cloudy or clear, just like my pet mountain in N.W.F.P. It would look quite brick-red on occasions and at other times blue or grey. Having Murdar just outside my front door, so to speak, again gave me ample opportunity for studying her in different moods. Adopting a mountain was becoming quite a habit of mine. I sketched it from my door on one of its brown and yellow days and tried to capture the warm dry heat with the sharp clear atmosphere that pervades Quetta.

It was sitting in my door starting this sketch one evening that I made my second carpet purchase in India. The usual carpet wallah came up with an enormous pile of carpets across his bicycle and asked me if I wanted any. I said 'No' as a matter of course – one always did this, whether one was interested or not, as it was part of the bargaining ritual. Naturally, he was not going to take 'No' for an answer, like all true carpet wallahs, and proceeded to lay them out in the sunshine where they looked very lovely and colourful. I found that I was in a really strong position for bargaining, being fully occupied with the business of sketching and just sparing a casual glance at the carpets every now and then. I gave him a little encouragement to keep him interested, and after about half an hour I agreed to examine some, showing most interest in the ones I did not want. Eventually, when I had offered him one third of what he was asking for two prayer rugs and a small carpet six feet long, I said I did not really want any at all as they could not be packed, and so on and so forth. His last act but one, rehearsed so many times, was to roll all the carpets up except the ones I wanted and ask me once more to accept his bottom price. This is where you have to show complete disinterest, however much you want them. Sketching hard I found I could do this very effectively. Then his final act began: that of putting all the carpets onto the bicycle and moving away slowly. 'What is Sahib's last price?' I stuck to my guns and he relented. 'Alright, Sahib, I am a poor man who want money today otherwise I not give you.' I try to put on my most disinterested expression and after

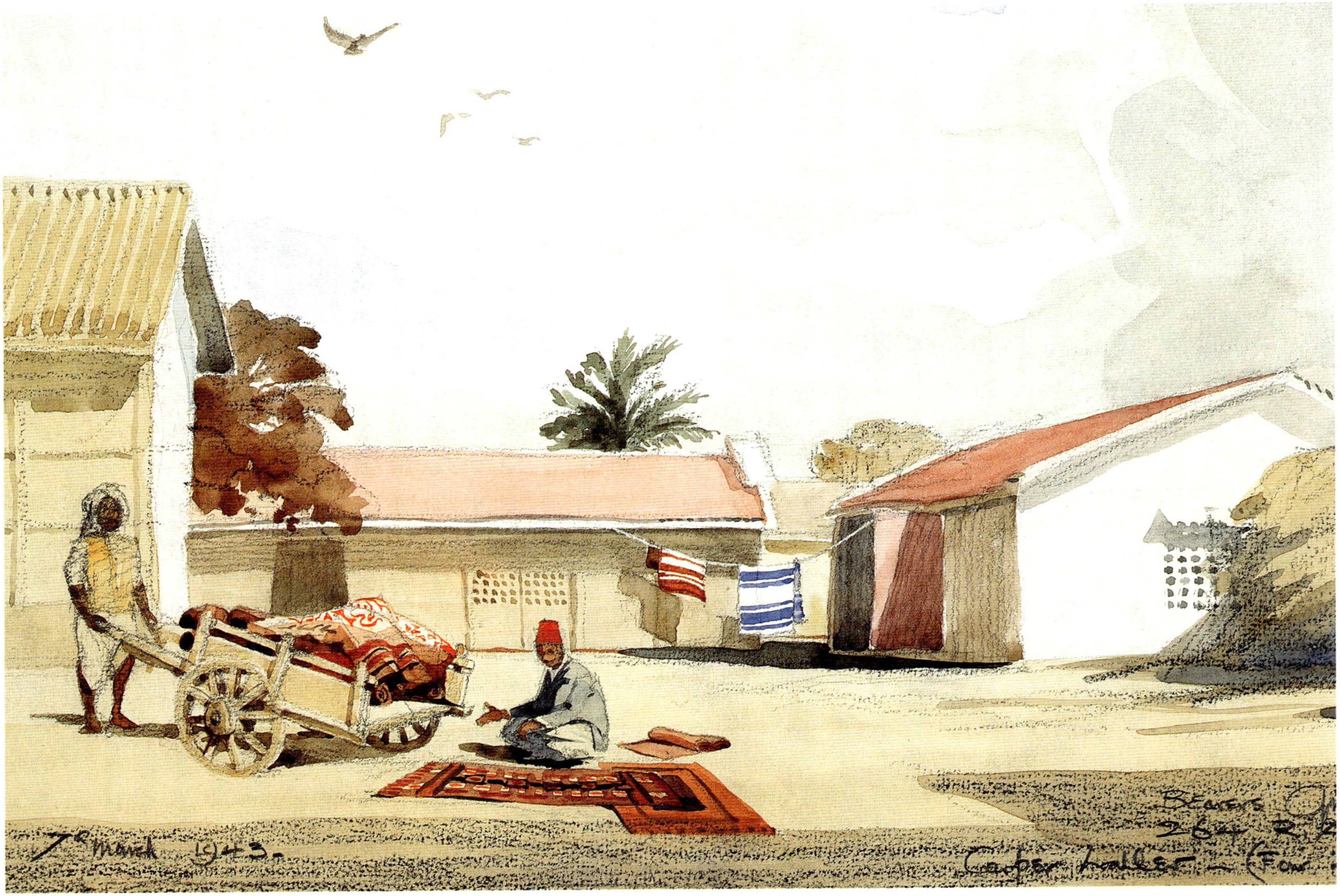
7th March 1943.

some more sketching, which by this time has become a mere fiddling with a paint brush, I am much too excited to paint, and go inside to write a cheque.

One always has such mixed feelings after concluding a bargain with one of these crafty salesmen – you are pleased with your purchase but you wonder how much less you could have got it for. He is probably wondering how much more he could have made you pay and has almost certainly made you pay a good deal more than you should have. In this case I think I got an extraordinarily good bargain. My two Baluchistan prayer rugs and one larger rug are rough and hard, but a close small weave and genuine enough if not very old. The characteristic of the Baluchistan carpet is its dark red and black colour with a thin white edge pattern. The rich deep red of these three is what attracted me so much.

One of my tours of duty from Quetta took me to a little place called Killa Abdulla where I had to stay for four days. I stayed with the Garrison Engineer, Khojak; the Khojak being the great range of mountains separating Quetta on the East and Chaman to the West, situated on the edge of the broad plain which follows along the Afghanistan border. The

LEFT: 16 Carpet wallahs

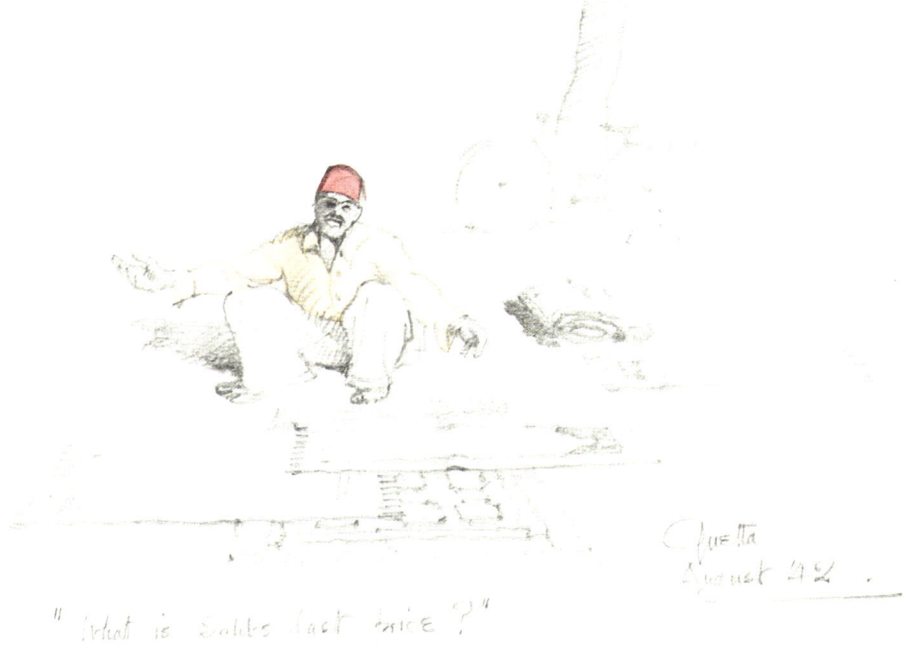

Garrison Engineer and his three assistant G.E.s lived a lonely life in this wild and desolate place. It is a hard monotonous life these young Engineers endure and they are faced with many difficulties every day, both in their work and their domestic arrangements. Indian coolie labourers are not the same as English navvies by an awful long way and all problems arising during the building of aerodromes, roads, or block houses, however small, have to be settled by the G.E. or A.G.E. Getting up stocks of cement, sand, stone, or building brick kilns and making bricks are major problems in themselves

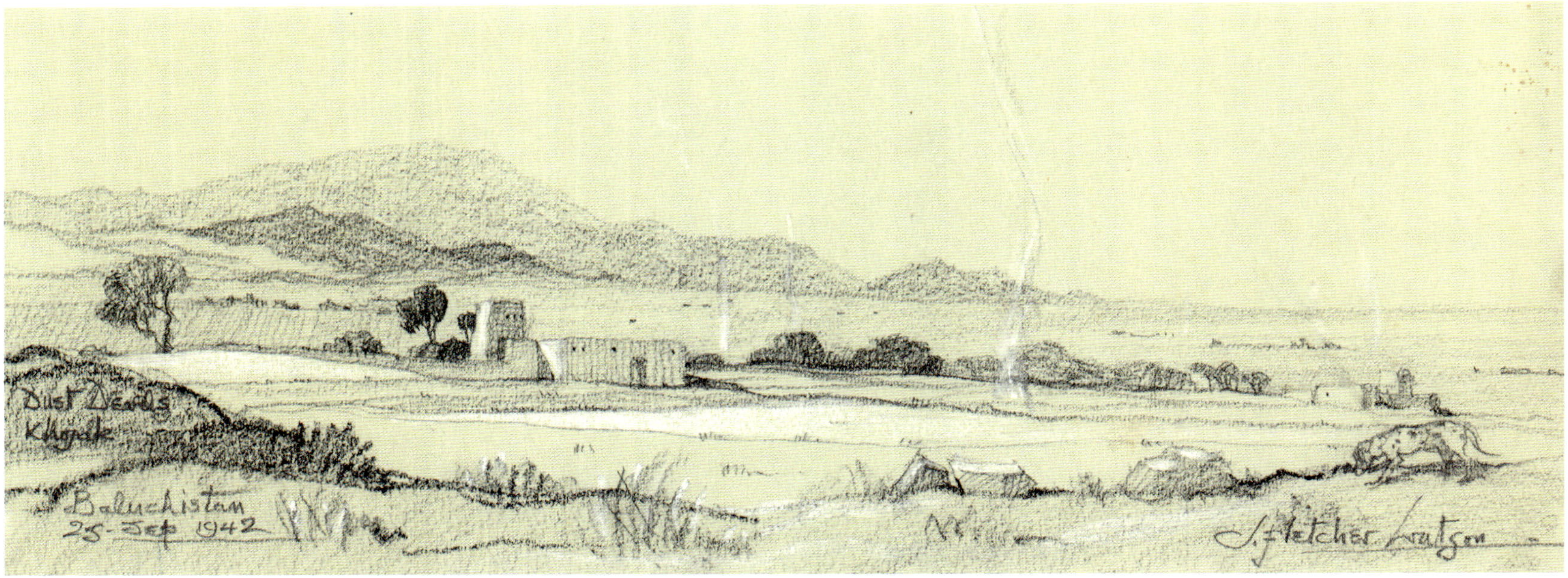

Above: 17 Dust devils, Khojak

when transport is scarce and labour and time is short. Finding supplies of water to meet large demands is not an easy matter in an arid country .Thousands of coolies have to be fed and huts built for them to live in. All these responsibilities fall on the shoulders of the G.E. or his staff. He must also attend to his own food supply and health matters.

The G.E. of Killa Abdulla was a good organiser and he did not neglect personal health. A P.W.D. (Public Works Department) Sectional steel water tank was built to serve the office buildings and quarters in case of fire. The buildings were all of wood construction, some of them having mud and plaster walls and others only chatti matting. All of them were very inflammable and a good big fire tank was essential. It so happened that the tank also made an excellent swimming pool, it was a nice oblong shape allowing one to do four or five strokes and had been built on the ground, a few yards away from the

G.E.'s quarters. One of those happy little coincidences in fact that the Garrison Engineers know so well how to 'engineer'! I enjoyed a number of cool bathes in that tank and blessed the P.W.D. organisation many times.

A most precipitous road leads over the Khojak Pass to Chaman, and the sketch I did of the Pass indicates the twisting mountain road and the steepness of the surrounding terrain.

My car very nearly had a fatal accident here one day. The driver, all on his own initiative, thought it would be a good idea to turn it round after it had been parked. It should be mentioned that we all drove ourselves when touring these switchback mountain roads, preferring to have our lives in our own hands rather that those of a Sepoy driver of not very long standing. The driver chose one of the hair-pin bends where there was a little more breadth of road, to turn in. But unfortunately he did not quite 'make it' and the two near side wheels went over the edge. When I walked back to where I had parked it, to my horror I suddenly saw the thing half over the edge of the road at the dangerous angle of 45 degrees. The edge of the road was soft and had caused the trouble in the first place but actually saved the car in the end as the wheels dug in and stayed put. But it looked like toppling over at any moment. Having developed the sort of press photographer's mind from taking photographs of camouflage so much, the first thing I did when I had ascertained it was moderately safe, was to stealthily pick the camera out of the car and then photograph it from four different angles. The prints came out very well and are a most startling and amusing record to look back on. But it was not really amusing at the time. If the car could not be budged it meant a ten mile trudge home along a very stony road. I eventually decided not to try to pull her back, a thing the coolies were longing to do, one could see that plainly enough as they crowded round her. I was almost certain they would start her slipping further over and it only wanted another six inches and she was gone. So I started to foot it down the road to an English store, three miles away, where they might have a lorry, and a tow rope.

Great was my surprise and relief after two miles of walking when the car caught me up, safe and sound. The only damage was to the exhaust which was bent and made a loud popping noise. About a hundred coolies had eventually lifted it bodily onto the road, so the driver told me. I think he was very anxious about his future prospects as a staff driver and was prepared to risk all in getting the car on the road again before my wrathful return.

Before I left Killa Abdulla, I had an afternoon's shoot with

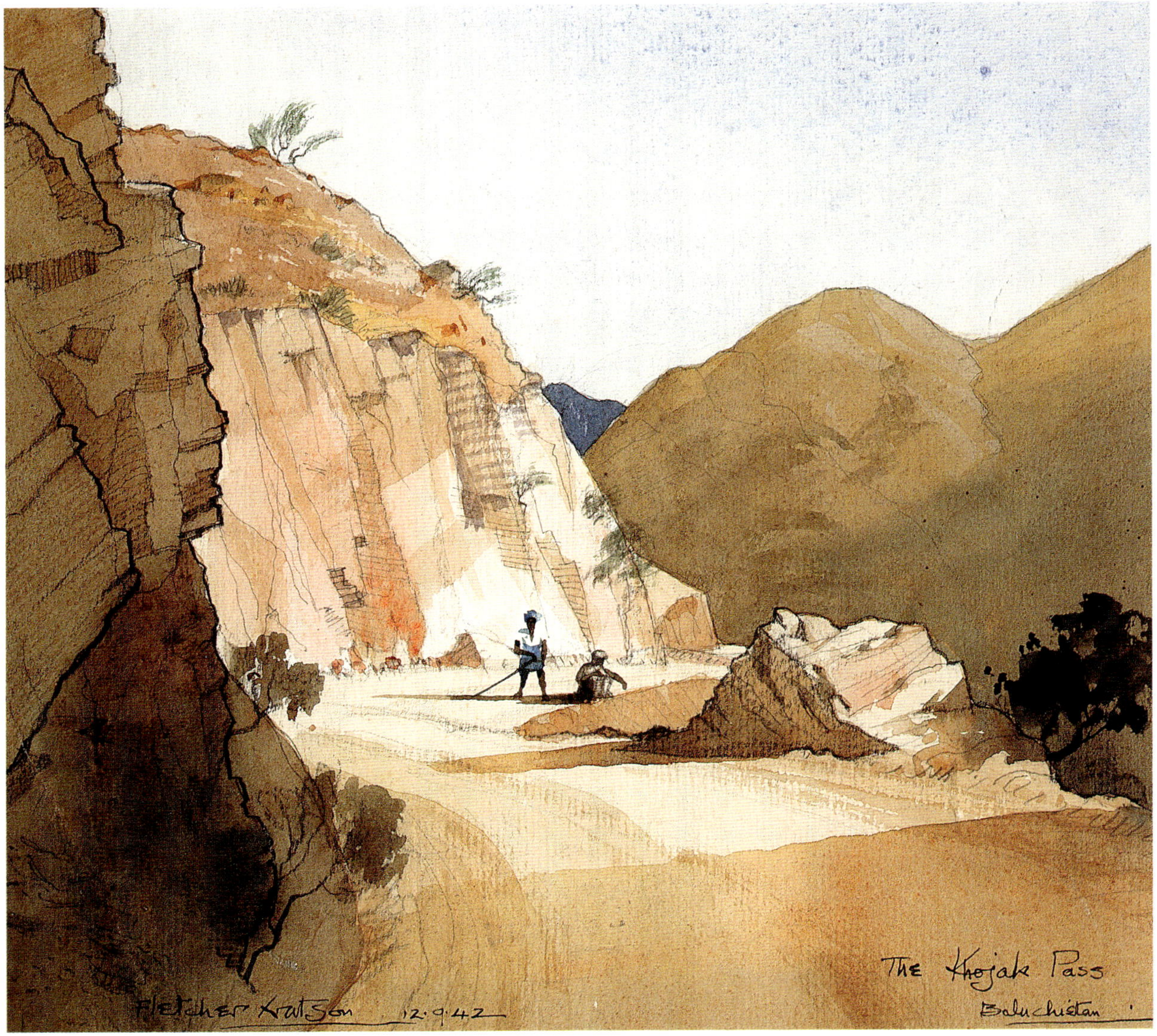

Left: 18 The Khojak Pass

one of the A.G.E.'s on his day off. He borrowed two 12 bores and we set out to a place where there were high bushes which offered considerable cover and hopes of finding chickore. We walked for about two and a half hours through this thick bush country and put up a number of quail. One or two beaters assisted but in the end we only got a brace and expended nearly all our cartridges. At about 6.00 p.m. the beaters were dismissed and we started back for home with about three cartridges between us. It looked like being a pretty poor day. My friend suggested a slight digression along a river bed with high cliffs each side. It had the slightest trickle of water running and plenty of green grass and weeds. To our amazement it proved to be an absolute hot bed of snipe. One bird after another got up; they were sitting very tight and we should have made a good bag if we had only had some ammunition left. We brought down two and then ran out of cartridges, but I counted easily thirty birds.

I became the owner of the Dalmation which I have already referred to, in rather a hasty and spontaneous manner – not at all the correct way to acquire a dog, but fortunately it turned out to be a good partnership. I had seen an advertisement for the dog on the Quetta Club notice board a few days before I came to Killa Abdulla, and finding I practically passed the

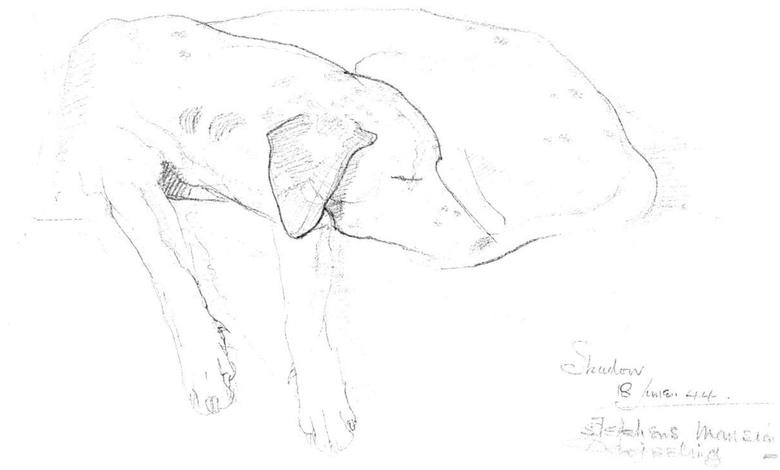

house of the owner on my way out of Quetta, I called in and took her away there and then. I think the owner – one of those dog-loving horsey women – was a bit surprised at such a speedy deal and not a little sorrowful at having to make such a rapid farewell to the little puppy. Shadow, as they had named her, was not a little surprised either at being whisked away in a large army car which swayed and bumped disturbingly over the rough road. We had not been going for long before the poor pup wanted to be sick and I popped her out of the car just in time. This was a trick she took a long time to throw off, which was bad luck on her and me as we were destined to make many journeys by road, rail and even river together.

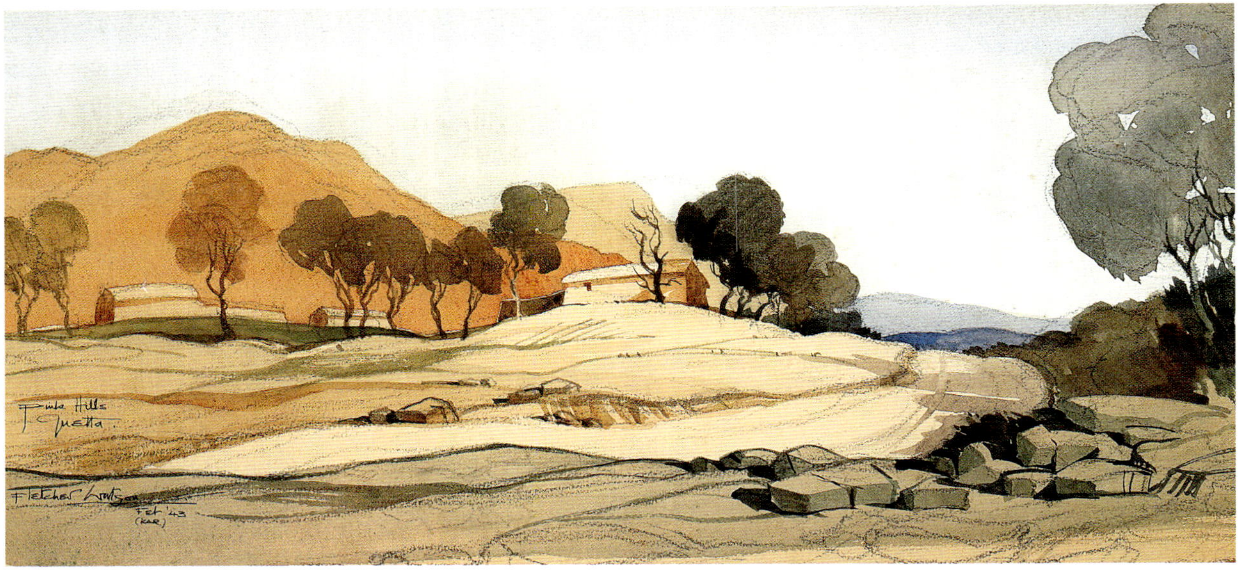

LEFT: 19 Pink Hills, Quetta

RIGHT: 20 The road through Pink Hills from Quetta

The road to Killa Abdulla went through a district that is known locally as 'Pink Hills'. For three or four miles one sees nothing but small cone-shaped hillocks, literally pink in colour as in the picture 'The road through Pink Hills'. They are volcanic formations but I do not pretend to know how or why they are formed. Pink rocks also appear in the form of vertical cliffs edges. The colouring in this part of the country is really most unusual and very pleasing. Thin lines of brilliantly green grass growing by the side of small streams contrast happily with the pink rock formations and blue hills beyond.

I had a surprise in store for me that evening when I arrived home at Sheilla Bagh, a few miles beyond Killa Abdulla where the road starts to climb steeply to get over the Khojak Pass. It is a small military station and I had to call on the adjutant of the Punjab Regiment stationed there. I did my business with him, and as we were parting I just happened to mention my coming from Norfolk. At the mention of Norfolk his whole countenance changed. He also came from that blessed corner of England. We immediately found that we knew the same places and the same people. That delayed me another hour so

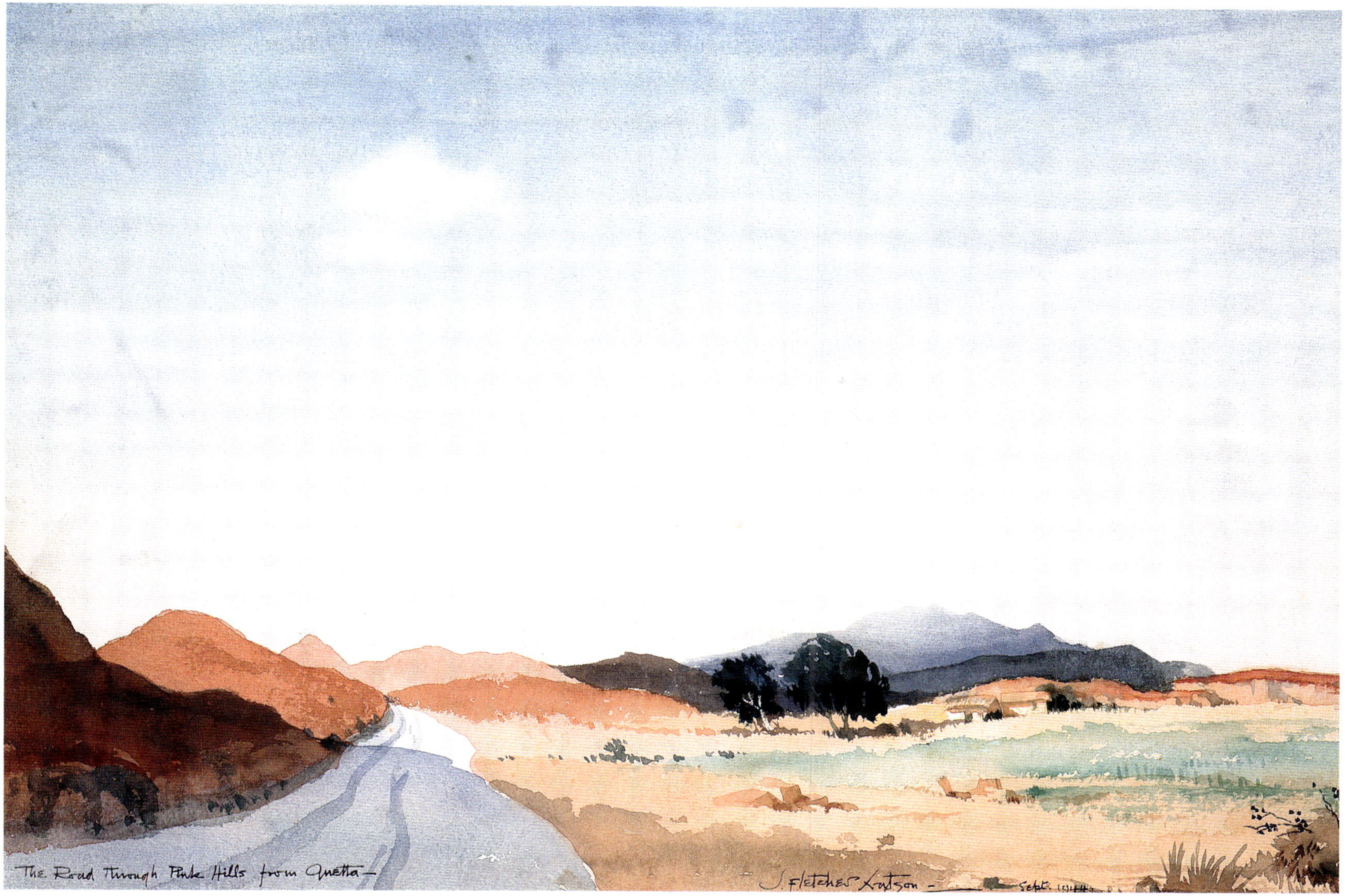
The Road Through Pink Hills from Quetta –
J. Fletcher Watson –
Sept.

it was completely dark by the time I reached the G.E.'s bungalow at Killa Abdulla, and little Shadow was looking extremely hungry.

Christopher Perks, my Norfolk friend, was a real breath of fresh air and we met as often as possible. He was an enthusiastic watercolourist too, and had done dozens of very good sketches of the hill country surrounding his little camp. It was a great relief to meet someone who really spoke what I call painting language. We discussed watercolour techniques: the use of white paint (should one or shouldn't one use it?!); scratching out; sponging out; total immersion in the bath tub; graduated washes; pencil outlines; types of paper; and many other 'trade secrets' *ad infinitum*. The paper problem was getting acute and we could no longer buy our favourite Whatman or David Cox papers but had to put up with cheap cartridge. We talked of Cotman with his flat slabs of colour and precise rendering of architectural detail, of Crome and Constable, all geniuses from East Anglia. Architecture ran pictures a close second. My friend was surrounded with copies of *Country Life* newly arrived from England and we spent some enjoyable moments admiring photographs of Georgian houses and discussing the future of architecture in England after the war.

I did the sketch with Takatu in the distance on my last evening before returning to Quetta (see picture No.21). I very nearly did not bother as I said to myself I can do that some other time. One says that about a good many things. However, I am glad I did make the effort as I never had a chance to return before I left Quetta.

The war had failed to stop racing at Quetta. It must be one of the prettiest race courses in India. Green grass, trees and a background of mountains, all the excitement and colour of an Indian racing crowd, the scene was worthy of Frith or Brangwyne, or even Munnings might go for it. Bright sarees worn by Indian women, of every conceivable colour, red, orange, green, yellow, blue, and so on, gave a sparkle to the less brilliant but never-the-less interesting tones made by service men in bush shirts and topis, and civilians in grey or white linen suits.

Another gathering having a rather more limited type of crowd was the Handy Hunter Trials organised by the Quetta Hunt. The course included several fearsome dry ditches, serious obstacles on account of the hardness of the rough soil each side which had to be cleared in one by a horse jumping them, although they were not very wide or deep in themselves. Other nasty places were typical of what one meets out hunting in this part of India, mud walls and a small bog included. The usual

Right: 21 Takatu

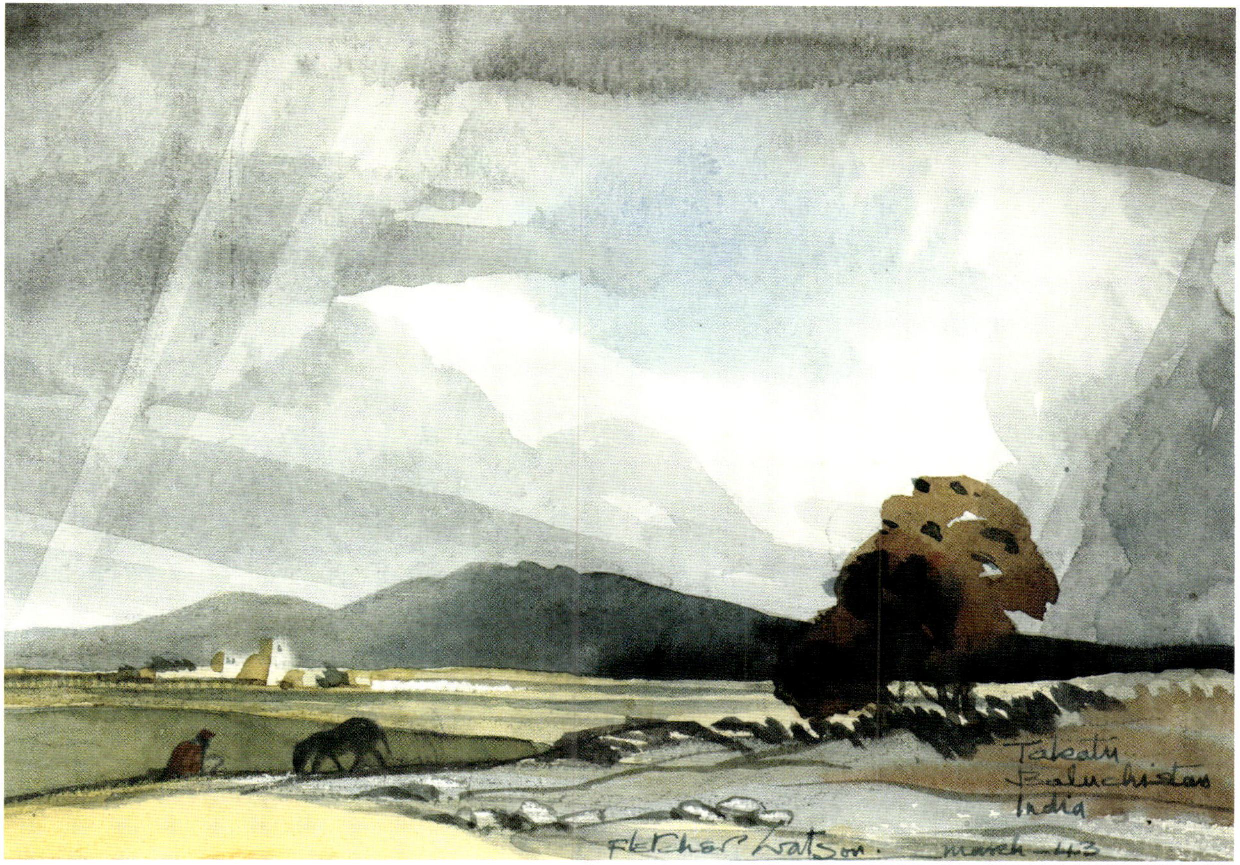

bush fences, styles and 'In and Outs' were also provided and the whole course was one which would be viewed with misgiving if not a certain amount of horror by a hunting man from home. The real unique obstacle of which the Quetta Hunt boasts was not present, I am glad to say. This is a long line of enormous holes about ten feet in diameter, called 'Carazes'. Mr Jorrocks would, I am sure, describe them as 'the most awful place that ever was seen'. They are very close to one another

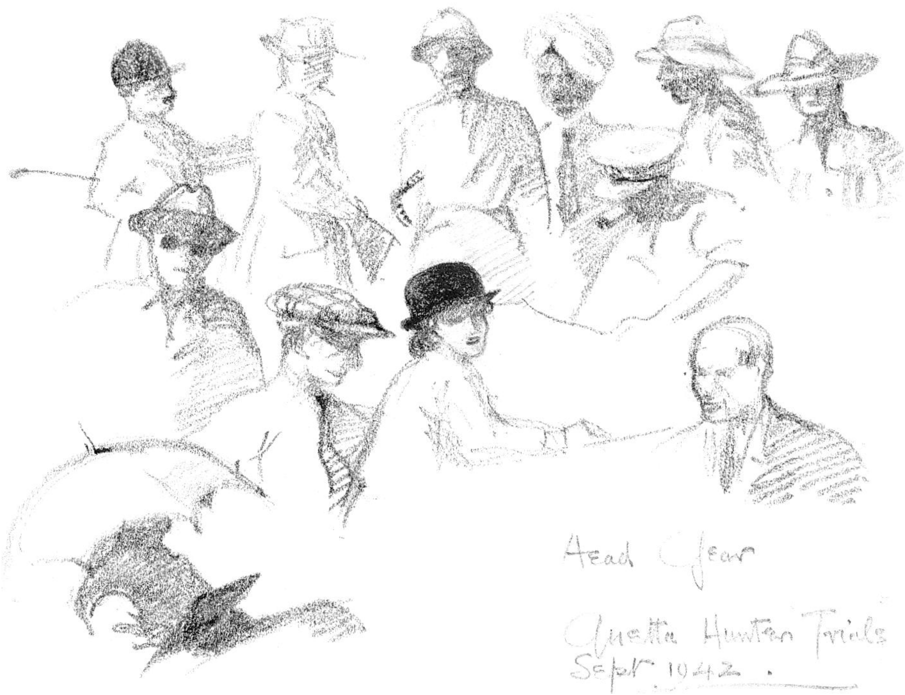

and it is not easy to ride between them. Beneath these holes or wells runs a great underground drain about seven feet in diameter. The wells are made to give access for mining the tunnel, and also to allow surface rain water to run in. The idea is a special form of irrigation peculiar to Baluchistan and no other place. The men who make these drains are specialists in the trade, and their skills have been handed down from one generation to the next. But to return to our point, imagine yourself suddenly coming upon one of these on a horse, no half measures, you are either over or in! Many people jump them out hunting, but it is possible to go through sometimes. It has been known for man and horse to go in and stay in unnoticed, his cries unheard. Heaven knows how you get out as there are no moving staircases up from this 'underground'.

This Hunter Trials crowd was quite suggestive of an English point-to-point: the shooting sticks were abundant and so were the breeches, the riding boots and the horsey talk, but there the similarity ended. Sunglasses, topis, short-sleeved shirts and silk dresses are hardly comparable to macintoshes, overcoats and umbrellas. The style in hats was interesting and I have drawn a few of the many varieties.

I cannot leave Baluchistan without mentioning the London Road. I had to visit certain Military projects in the vicinity of a small town called Nushki, eighty miles from Quetta, quite frequently. About ten miles out of Quetta a large signpost stood at a fork in the road, the right hand arm of which announced in bold black letters 'London 5877 miles'. When we passed this in the staff car I always had a comfortable feeling that now I was heading for home. It seemed quite fantastic to see a London signpost in the heart of Baluchistan, but plenty of people have made the trip, and apart from crossing the Dardonelles and the

English Channel, one can do the entire journey by road.

I departed from Quetta in a very different fashion to that in which I had arrived. It was by train and in the evening at 6.00 p.m. on 10th October 1942. The sun was just sinking as we rattled our way down the mountain valley, the same beautiful valley up which I had flown only two months before. Shadow and I felt a distinct pang of sorrow and regret at having to leave a country so rich in fine scenery and beautiful colouring, just as I was getting to know it. But the army had decreed that I should take up duties in Karachi and needs must obey.

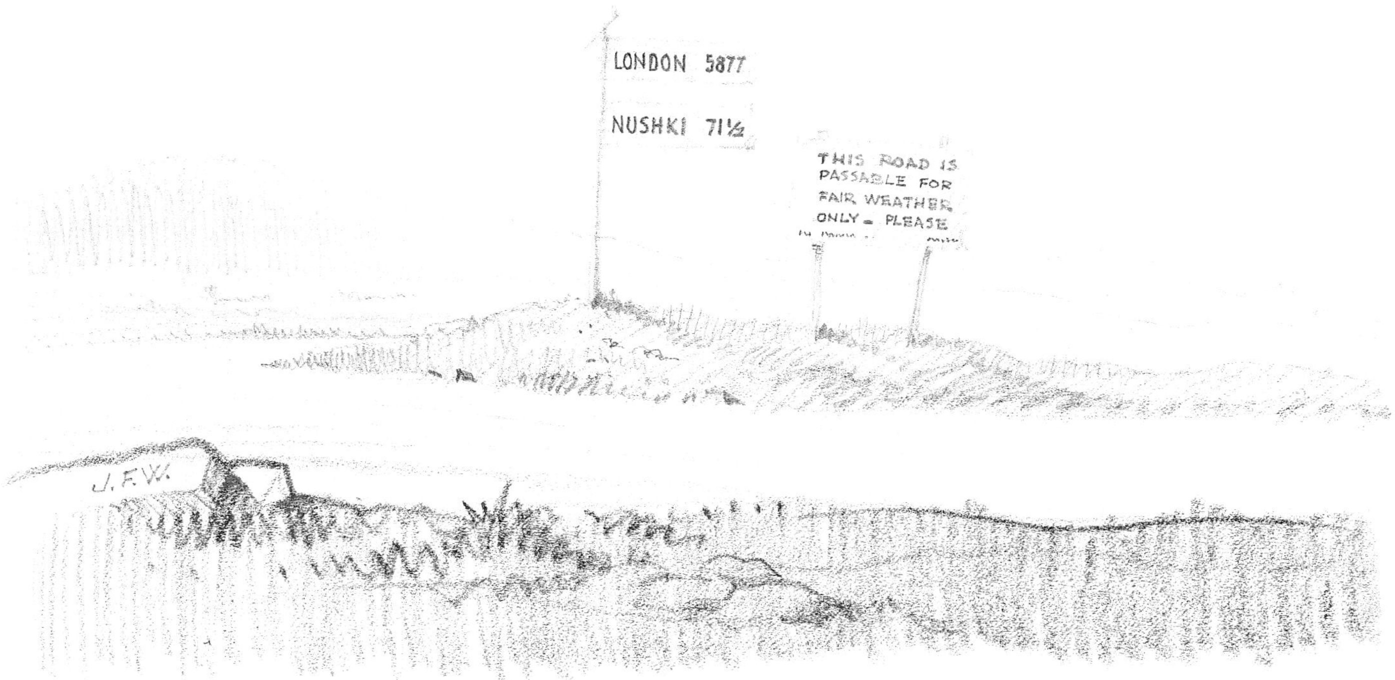

CHAPTER FIVE

THE HOUSE THAT JACOB BUILT

In spite of the fact that India produces over half the world's tea, the Indians cannot make a decent cup to save their lives, not by Western standards at any rate. Either they don't use freshly boiled water or one is given a re-hotted-up pot, but one way or another it usually tastes like strong stew. In the waiting room of Jacobabad Railway Station at 5.30 a.m. on Sunday 11th October 1942, I was provided with a cup of tea in the best traditions of Indian tea brewing. In other words, it was mahogany in colour, it smelt like a floor cloth and tasted like nicotine. But it was hot and anything hot at that hour of the morning is helpful. The brain is not properly functioning and the body, in this case, was craving to go to bed having been rudely turned out of a comfortable bunk in a railway carriage a few minutes before. In other words, I was not in the best of moods on arrival in Jacobabad, but I felt better after my second cup, for all its shortcomings, and could now contemplate my surroundings a little more clearly.

Jacobabad, named after the renowned General Jacob (of whom you will hear more later in the chapter), and also famous for being the hottest place in India (the temperature often rising to 126° F) was not very hot at that hour of the morning. October was not, fortunately for me, the hottest month of the year. When the hour became a little more civilised, I decided to sally forth in search of the Garrison Engineer whom I had come to see. I had only got my valise with me and, of course, Shadow. My bearer had gone on to Rohri with the luggage by another route, to wait for me there.

It was still quite cool an hour later when I took a tonga and set out to find the G.E. bungalow. We passed down a few silent, narrow streets with shops that still had their shutters up and from thence along wider roads with gardens on each side and white bungalows. It was beginning to get lighter now and the driver pointed out the bungalow I was looking for some way ahead. Shadow and I decided to walk the rest of the way so that we could stretch our legs. Flights of small green parrots swooped low across the road between the palm trees, letting out high-pitched screeches and the abundance of broad-leaved shrubs and, in places, very thick undergrowth gave the whole place a very tropical atmosphere.

Shadow drew a good many barks from stray pie dogs who rushed out at her from drive gates as we passed. We were well out of the town here and the soft damp brown earth at the side of the road held many enticing smells which she enjoyed, stopping occasionally for a sniff and then galloping on again.

We finally reached the right bungalow. Sticking up on top of the flat roof was a large white mosquito net covering a bed on which, as I rightly supposed, the G.E. himself lay soundly enjoying his beauty sleep. I found a bearer preparing his early morning tea so I sent up a note with it and an answer came back asking me to join him in a cup on the roof. This I did and incidentally it was a very much better brew than the cup at the station.

I stayed with the G.E. for five days during which time we travelled many miles of hot dusty road, inspecting his far-flung and varied works, all of which had to receive a camouflage plan. What an enormous amount of work now falls on a G.E. who, in peace time might only have a total of a couple of small stores to build, a few potholes in the road to repair and a few door knobs and W.C. plugs to renew. Now he might quite easily be responsible for constructing runway taxi tracks for two or three large aerodromes, as well as the workshops and living quarters for hundreds of personnel covering acres of ground, a hutted camp somewhere else and stores depots, gun emplacements, recreation halls and canteens and about ten miles of road building in other places. To mobilise local resources of labour, building materials, water and transport, called for a man of action and a hard worker. This particular G.E. had a task equally as big as this with only two Lieutenants, young and inexperienced Lieutenants at that, to help him. Added to his worries were people like me who came round and demanded 'camouflage', of all the unreasonable things! Lorries must travel along given tracks only, otherwise their tracks would show from the air and give away positions. Buildings must be erected only in certain places and be painted in certain colours, and plenty more stipulations besides sufficient to give the G.E. many headaches. But I had been a G.E. myself and knew what the difficulties were, which made it much easier to know what should be insisted upon and what was unreasonable.

With camouflage one had to weigh the likelihood of the enemy paying you a visit by air, which might demand a hundred per cent concealment of the ground projects, against the reduction of the working efficiency of those projects caused by the imposition of heavy camouflage measures. G.E.s very often and rather naturally made a big case for the 'curtailing efficiency' argument.

That evening, the head policeman of Jacobabad brought some of his horses round to the bungalow and we all three had a most enjoyable ride. He took us over the race course which is used once a year when Jacobabad had its annual 'week'. This I gathered, is a show rather like an old English fair. Horse dealers assemble from near and far to exchange bargains and to make use of the carefully selected Government stallions. As well as a horse show, there is also a cattle show, a ploughing competition, police sports and an industrial exhibition to show new farming methods and devices. Not that very many new methods seem to get adopted; I think the method of tilling small fields thirty yards square with a wooden plough drawn by bullocks has been going on without change for the last two thousand years, in spite of all new suggestions made at Jacobabad Week. On the last day, the excitement mounts when the races are held. The horses are ridden bare-back except the police race. There are camel races too, where the camel kneels at the start with the rider standing beside him. When the starting pistol is fired the riders leap on, some camels refusing to move, others lollopping off in the wrong direction, and a few staying the course. I should very much like to have been present at this unusual race meeting. Our policeman friend said it was a wonderful sight with crowds of country folk clad in colourful garments who had travelled from many miles away. Some came on foot, others on horseback and in carts, and some on camels, where whole families – women, children, chickens and luggage – are all crammed onto one camel.

One day, we were asked to tea at the Residency, Jacob's House, as it is called locally. This was the first really interesting house I had been into in India with a real history attached to it. It was built by General John Jacob just under a hundred years ago.

Directly the Superintendent's wife heard I was interested in buildings she said she would show me around the house, which was just what I wanted. She certainly knew her Jacob's House history well, from the life of the great General himself to the pistols and other relics hung on the walls. I am not going to attempt to write everything she told me on my long conducted tour, and I cannot remember half of the details anyway. But one or two items are worth relating. The General appears to have been a bit of an old martinet.

Apparently he would not allow whist to be played in the Mess because he could not play it himself and he ordered that only English should be spoken in the Regiment as he did not like learning languages. Jacobabad was, in those days, the Headquarters of the Sind Horse which Jacob commanded.

Some peculiar types of rifles hung in the hall and dining room which were Jacob's inventions. One of them was a double barrelled four grooved rifle, another had a rapier-bayonet attached, but they were never taken up seriously by the army.

The most interesting item in the entire house is Jacob's famous clock. He made it with his own hands out of local materials: brass, iron and wood. It stands about six feet high and I made a rough sketch of it there and then. It is an amazing piece of practical mechanics: the pendulum weight is made from a round shot taken from the battle ground of Miani where Sir Charles Napier with 2,800 men defeated some 22,000 Baluchi troops.

The clock, in addition to telling the ordinary time, tells the days of the week, the date, month and phases of the moon.

Outside the building, an inscription on the central portico says in Urdu and English 'In this house lived and died General John Jacob, Political Superintendent and Commandant, Frontier of Upper Sind, 1847-50.'

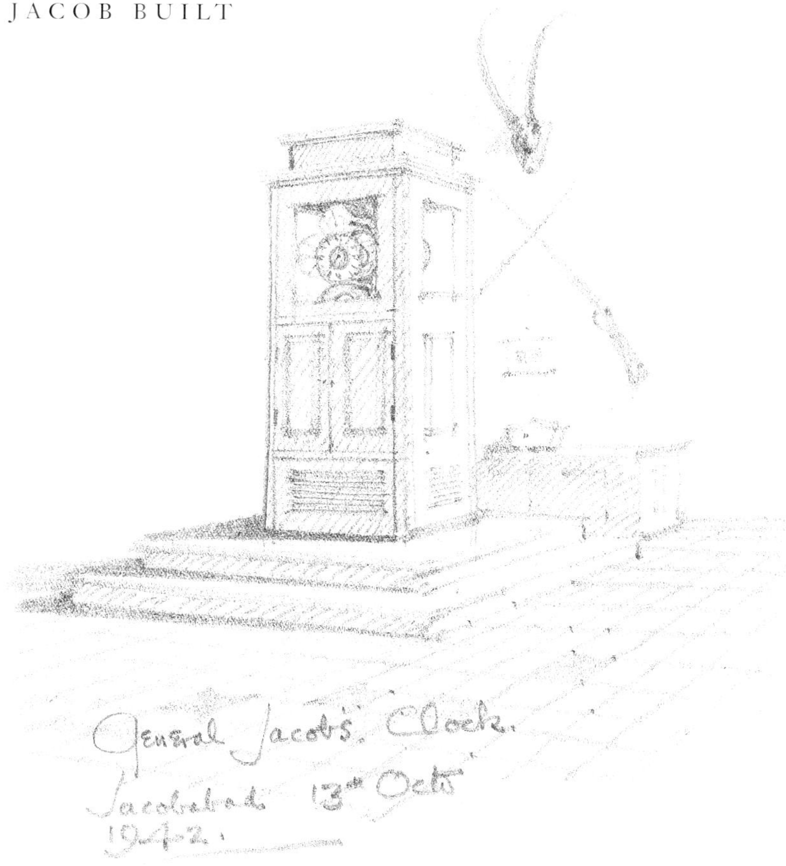

We had tea on the lawn with a really delightful view of the house – quite the most English scene I have experienced in India. The trees somehow looked English and the beautiful mown lawn certainly did. The turf was in pretty good condition and so was the rest of the garden which Jacob planned himself. When I asked the Superintendent if he would mind if

I did a sketch of the house from where we had tea, he was delighted at the idea as he said the house was in a very serious state structurally and it might not stand up very much longer, so any record of such an historic place was very welcome. The walls were of solid mud construction, a form of half baked clay lump as far as I could gather, and about three feet thick which made the rooms very cool inside. The timber beams spanning the two big rooms – the dining room and the drawing room – had been vigorously attacked by borer beatles and were in a very precarious state. A number of the walls were crumbling and it appeared to me that nothing short of building an entirely new inner shell of brick or stone against all the main walls would save the old place now that it had been allowed to deteriorate so far.

Next day I managed to finish my work by early afternoon and do a watercolour of the house. I had with me my compact paintbox which holds sixteen colours, two brushes and also water in the hollow back of the box. I take this everywhere 'just in case' an opportunity crops up. The sketch I did on this occasion is not the one reproduced in this book; I sometimes do a rough colour sketch on the spot as there are often too many irritations sketching out of doors in India for doing finished works. The colour nearly always dries too quickly; almost as soon as a loaded brush is drawn across the paper it is dry on a really hot day. Then there are usually a variety of flying pests that settle on the white paper and interrupt the application of a wash. Flying ants are among the chief offenders. On the whole, one's patience just does not run to a finished painting out of doors. But if one knows that it is only rough then it does not matter if an ant gets mixed up in the blue sky and causes a dark blot where it is not wanted.

While I am on the subject, I should like to warn anyone who is thinking of taking up watercolours in India not to leave his or her paint box open in a room over night. If ants are about, especially the big black variety about quarter of an inch in length, they will lap up colour out of the pans like nobody's business. I have lost whole pans full of some of my best colours through the gluttonous activities of these ants. They seemed to favour crimson and ultramarine particularly and there is nothing more annoying than to wake up one morning and find that these colours have been eaten out of one's box. They are also fond of white paint, and will actually take it off the paper itself.

I don't often use white paint, but I did need it for a map which I included in one of my pictures. The morning after I

Right: 22 Jacob's House

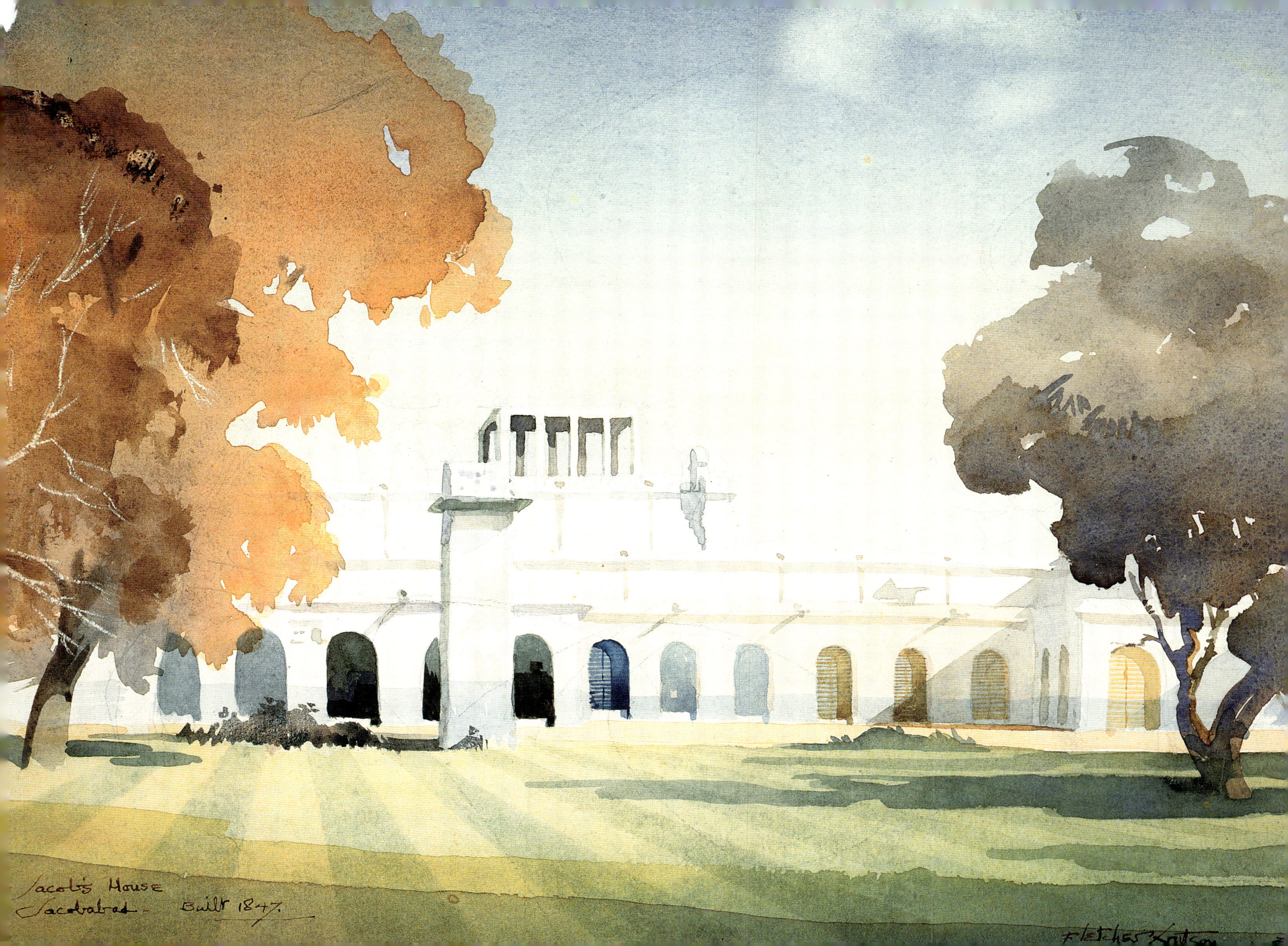
Jacob's House
Jacobabad - Built 1847.

had completed this picture there was no white map but instead a yellow-grey one. The little brutes had eaten every bit of paint off the paper and it was down to the background colour again! I adopted new tactics in order to get my white map, but I won't go into further details as this is not supposed to be a book on how to paint.

On my last evening, we had the policeman in to dinner together with the assistant G.E. and a touring officer from H.Q. at Quetta. The policeman brought two bottles of port with him; these were not intended for consumption by the general company but for one man only, the G.E. The two men had had a bet, the G.E. boasting of being a two bottle man and the policeman betting him the cost of the two bottles that he was not. As soon as dinner was over, the G.E., a man of about forty-five, set to work slowly and methodically to try and win his bet.

Glass after glass was poured down while we were quietly drinking beer and watching for any signs of his weakening. Well, the second bottle never had to be opened; after growing redder and redder and talking less but grinning more, the G.E. finally slid back in his chair, nodded his head forward and relapsed into complete unconsciousness. He had only just managed to finish one bottle, so a one bottle man he was and owed the policeman the price of the two Indian ports which he had purchased in the bazaar. Drinking an Indian grocer's port is not the same thing at all as drinking vintage port, and that gave the G.E. a certain excuse, I think. However, it was an interesting evening and one which I shall not forget. We carried the body carefully to bed where it remained in peaceful oblivion until well into the next day.

I left Jacobabad early next morning so I am unable to say just how late my friend did sleep. When I tried to thank him for looking after me so well during my stay, there was absolutely no sign of life, so I left a suitably worded message and departed.

CHAPTER SIX

BOATS, BULLOCK CARTS AND TONGAS

Journeys in India often involve travelling in a quaint variety of transport before destinations are finally reached. My trip from Jacobabad to Rohri included quite a representative selection of Indian vehicles: taxi, country boat, bullock cart, tonga and train, not to mention quite a lot of foot slogging into the bargain.

Of course, our taxi had to have a puncture on the dusty road from Jacobabad to the Indus; it would not have been normal not to have one. We were supposed to connect with our boat at some lesser known jetty on the river at 11.00 a.m. on 17th October and we did not have too much time in hand, what with a driver who only 'thought' he knew the place, a road with a surface covered in four inches of dry powdered mud, and now a puncture. However, wonder of wonders, there was a spare wheel, quite an exceptional occurrence for an Indian taxi. The change over was effected so quickly that I did not have time to finish the pencil sketch I started to make. The next hold up was caused by Shadow, poor girl, who thought it would be a good idea to be sick on my lap while I was busy looking at the scenery. She certainly put a fast one over on this occasion, as she was sitting half on me and half on the seat so it was easy work to be sick into my lap without having to move (I can usually detect it coming and manage to stop the car in time). She looked very guilty and one could not punish her for something she could not help. In any case, it was only a minor hold up of two or three minutes.

We eventually arrived in tact at our rendezvous on the Indus. It was a small landing stage where an old Dhow, the local name for this Chinese-looking sailing craft, was tied up waiting for us. Incidentally, this was not the recognised route on which to travel from Jacobabad to Rohri and on to Karachi, where I was finally destined, but I decided to accompany a Staff Officer from Quetta Headquarters who had come down to investigate an alternative route. The damage at Sukkur to rail and road caused by the Indus overflowing her banks was still far from being repaired and it looked like taking several months more before the breach would be mended, so a different route was required. A stretch of railway embankment had been completely washed away for several hundred yards at Sukkur and the road was under water. People were taken off the train on one side of the gap and paddled across in flat bottomed boats with all their baggage, then they boarded the waiting carriages again on the other side. A very long and tedious business.

The next little incident we had involved my dog Shadow again. During the excitement of getting the luggage carried on board, she had slipped off, probably to investigate a nice smell somewhere, and before I knew where I was, we had pushed off without her and were already about fifty yards from the bank. Frantic signalling and shouting ensued, which eventually stirred someone on shore into activity. Shadow was bundled into a canoe which came paddling after us. Her expression was a mixture of hurt feelings and utter relief to be with us safely again. She did not think she deserved to be left behind, even if she had been sick on my lap.

We then spent five solid hours creeping at snail's pace down the Indus. A certain amount of punting was done with twenty-foot poles. In addition to this, two men – wading when it was shallow enough and walking on the bank when it was not – towed us along by ropes which were fastened to the masthead. Our captain did not seem to think there was enough wind to make it worth while hoisting up a sail.

Sitting in a cane chair and drifting down the Indus is a peaceful occupation and I had plenty of time to make pencil sketches of sailing craft of all types. The thin distant lines of the flat land broken only by occasional clumps of palm trees provided a fitting background to river craft, plenty of which we passed on our way. Flat country has always appealed to me; there is something about the great distances one can see with the feeling of openness and the wide expanse of sky which has a great fascination. Perhaps coming from Norfolk where there are so many varieties of flat countryside – the Broads and the mud flats of the North Norfolk coast – has given me an inherent liking for flat landscapes.

This painting of Dhows on the Indus was done afterwards, from pencil drawings.

When our sluggish craft at last brought us to a point about ten miles down river where we were to disembark it was getting late (about 4.30 p.m.) and we were getting very hungry. My Staff Officer friend, being an old soldier and experienced

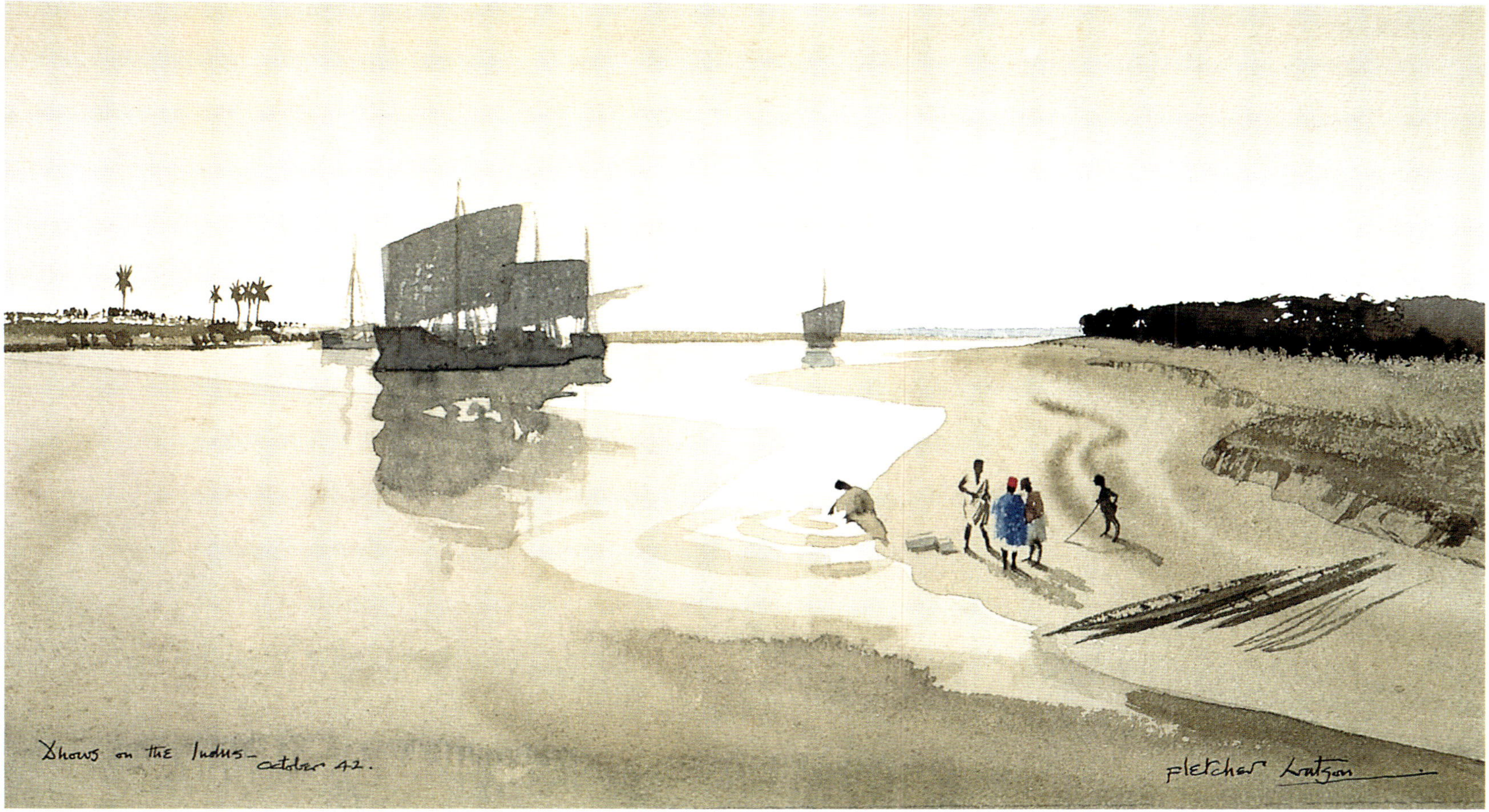

ABOVE: 23 Dhows on the Indus

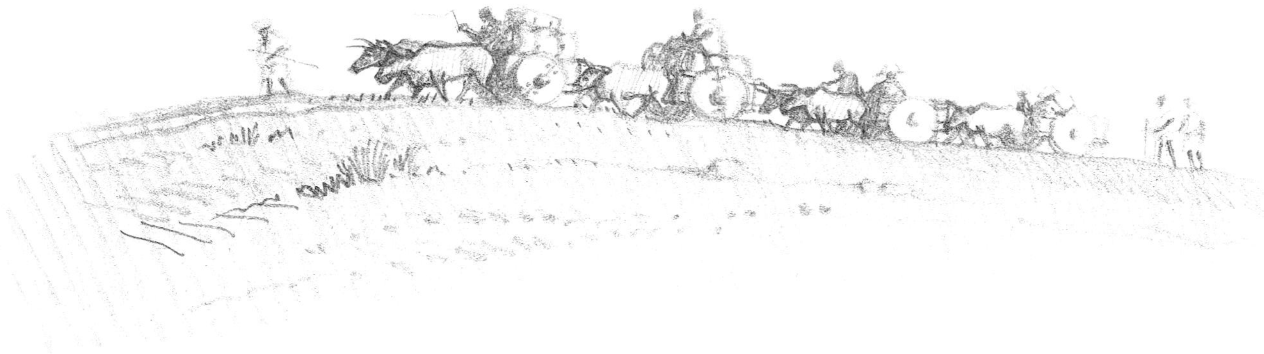

Left: Our bullock train transporting all our luggage

in travel in India, had produced bully beef and bread for lunch which had filled our bellies adequately enough; Shadow had her share too. But now we felt empty again. However, we were doomed to emptiness for a great many hours to come. Fortunately, we did not know that our next meal would not be until breakfast next morning. Quadirpur was the name of the place we had reached, but it was hardly a place in the sense of a town or village. Just a few huts and not even a jetty — a plank served to get us ashore.

After waiting for an hour and sending many messages to the mud hut village, where they were slow movers, we were eventually rewarded with four bullock carts. The average Indian bullock cart is a strange vehicle, very heavily constructed with thick squared timbers on sides and floor. The clumsy wooden wheels sometimes have spokes and sometimes they are solid wood. The worn down hubs fit loosely onto the axles allowing the wheels to slant inwards as the cart goes along, creaking and groaning under its own great weight. The actual carrying space is comparatively small and quite out of proportion to its strength. However, I would not have the design altered for the world as they are the most artistic looking objects.

Our luggage went in two of these carts, and we travelled in the other two – but not for long, as we decided it was more comfortable walking. After travelling a few miles across fields and cart tracks we reached a large village where slightly more modern conveyances were procured in the form of tongas. They were drawn by skinny-looking but very active ponies. We just managed to squeeze ourselves and luggage into two of these and off we went. It was dusk by now and it soon became completely dark. Fortunately, our guides knew the road to

Ghotki like the back of their hands, which was just as well on a black night. The route was full of hazards such as narrow portions of banked up road with irrigation canals and ditches at the sides, and we seemed to go along a great many bye-lanes and lonely tracks that only an experienced guide could follow in the dark.

We passed through one large mud hut village. The very narrow main street, with only about twelve feet between the walls of buildings, was lined with small shops selling food, drink, cloth, 'any old iron' and other stalls displaying interesting junk always to be found in Indian bazaars. They were dimly lit with oil lamps, wisps of smoke and smells of cooking drifting across our path. Dogs barked at us and children shouted as we rocked over the uneven road nearly knocking people down or bumping into open stalls and shop counters. We were eyed with curiosity and suspicion travelling at such a late hour. At long last, after what seemed like miles of total darkness, we pulled into Ghotki. The ponies looked hot and tired and we were cold and hungry.

As a matter of interest, this route was never adopted as an alternative to the way across the flooded area at Sukkur. My fellow traveller made sure of that in his report. Even if fast motor boats and steamers could have been made available for the ten mile river passage, the dusty badly surfaced and narrow roads would never have stood up to the heavy military and civilian traffic that would be expected of them, without a vast amount of construction work being done first.

We dossed down that night in Ghotki Station waiting room and caught an early train for Rohri, but not before we had scrounged some bread and eggs off the station master. They were more than welcome as we had not eaten anything since our bully beef the day before.

CHAPTER SEVEN

BAD SMELLS AND GOOD VIEWS

Fate had decreed that my journey from Jacobabad to Karachi was to be no picnic. The first half to Rohri, as I have already described, took over twenty-four hours, during which time we had not eaten one proper meal. The second half was all right as far as sustenance was concerned, but I was destined to sleep in another waiting room as I had just missed the Karachi mail train, so had to wait twenty-four hours before catching the train at nine the next morning.

This at first seemed to be a ghastly prospect: the station and what I could see of the town appeared to be dirty and uninteresting. But it turned out to be a blessing in disguise. I decided to explore this dirty-looking town and was rewarded with one or two architectural specimens worthy of considerable notice together with a fascinating collection of old warehouses, temples and tumbled-down boat houses, characteristic of an oriental waterfront. As well as the dirt, there was a smell of a most pungent nature. The stench is an ever-present feature of any oriental town or city, a point which must often be forgotten by people at home when admiring some picturesque painting of a native city. The artist has often had to sit in the midst of a really bad odour which, to the average man, would outweigh any desire to stop and appreciate the view. In this case, I sat on a box amidst the stench of bad fish and the town drain, which emptied itself into the Indus at various points. Diseased pie dogs came up and sniffed me, and unhealthy old men peered at me, naked children ran about on the shore and a few vultures were clustered around the carcass of a goat. But in spite of all this, the view still remained interesting and asked to be sketched. Yellow and pink washed buildings with overhanging balconies rose out of the water, small sailing boats were dragged up onto the shore and amidst palm trees was a tomb with a blue door and dome topped with a golden pinnacle. One could not pass that sort of thing by, however bad the smell! My main concern was to keep Shadow away from the

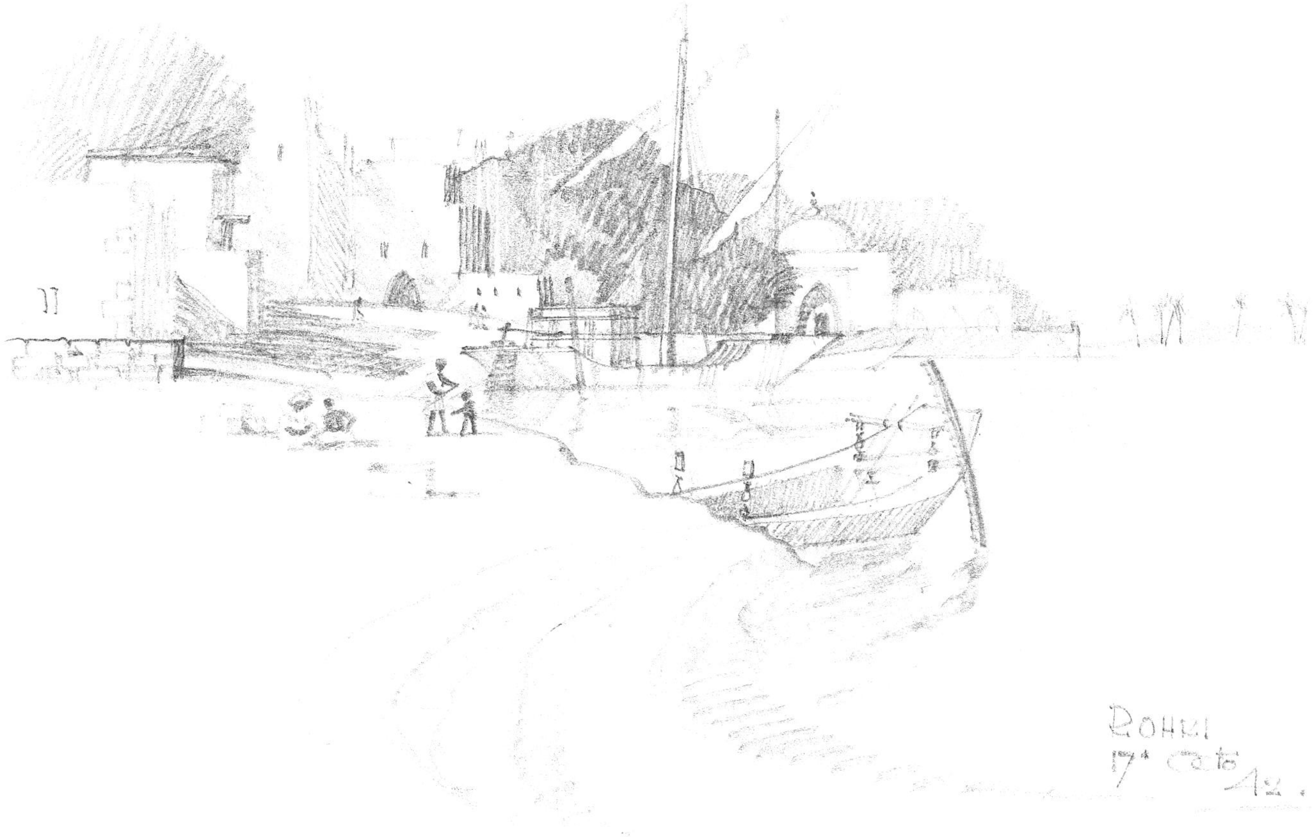

Above: The Indus at Rohri

pie dogs who were showing a lively interest in this white and black spotted apparition trespassing in their backyard.

It was on these occasions that one had opportunities to see the sort of poverty that the poorer class of Indian had to endure. Such families have only one garment each – a torn and threadbare piece of cloth about the size of a bath towel – and that is all.

I finished two pencil sketches and walked, with Shadow,

back from the river into the main street. From there I travelled in a tonga, moving slowly through the crowded bazaar where there was only just room for two of these vehicles to pass. The shops were colourful, having brilliant red, yellow, blue and green saris and scarves hanging from the stalls. Some shops were full of shining brasswork but no copper goods. I wanted to lay my hands on a plain copper tray very badly. An aunt of mine in England has several magnificent copper trays which she bought in India but I have not seen any myself yet. However, as her household have to spend a great deal of time polishing these big trays – they look their best only when they are shining brightly – it may be as well if I never do find any.

Below: Sukkur from Rohri

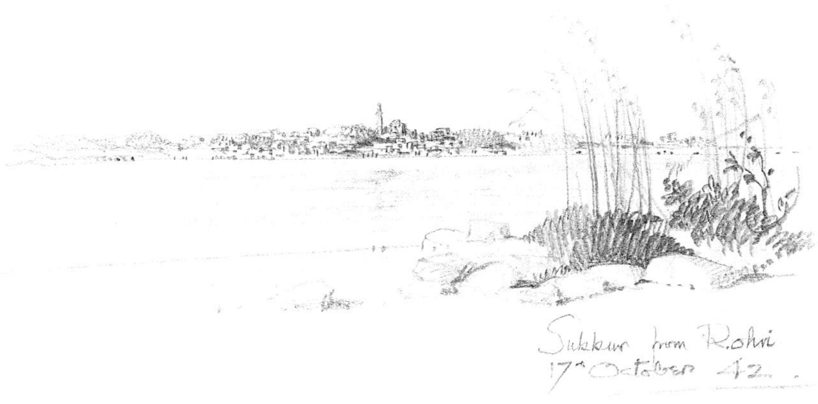

That evening, after my dinner at the station, I wandered back to the bazaar again on foot and came upon a lovely subject for a night picture. A very high building close to the water's edge with a broad flight of stone steps running round its base, and near its top, overhanging rooms built out in timber, made a skyline both medieval and romantic against the bright starry sky. Yellow lights were shining dimly through small windows here and there and the whole scene was quite irresistible. A light by which to draw was my problem, but there was a stall lit by a flickering oil lamp close by my viewpoint and with the help of this I managed to jot down enough outlines and notes in my sketch book. From these I painted afterwards 'Rohri by night'.

Earlier in the day I made a quick sketch of Sukkur on the other side of the river. About a mile out of Rohri one gets a charming river view with the tall minaret dominating the town and the long straggle of flat-roofed buildings intermixed with dark bunches of trees near the water's edge.

As my train pulled out of Rohri at five past nine next morning, I was not sorry I had been delayed on my journey and given the opportunity of seeing this interesting old town. After all, I had got four pencil studies to add to my now rapidly growing folio of views of India.

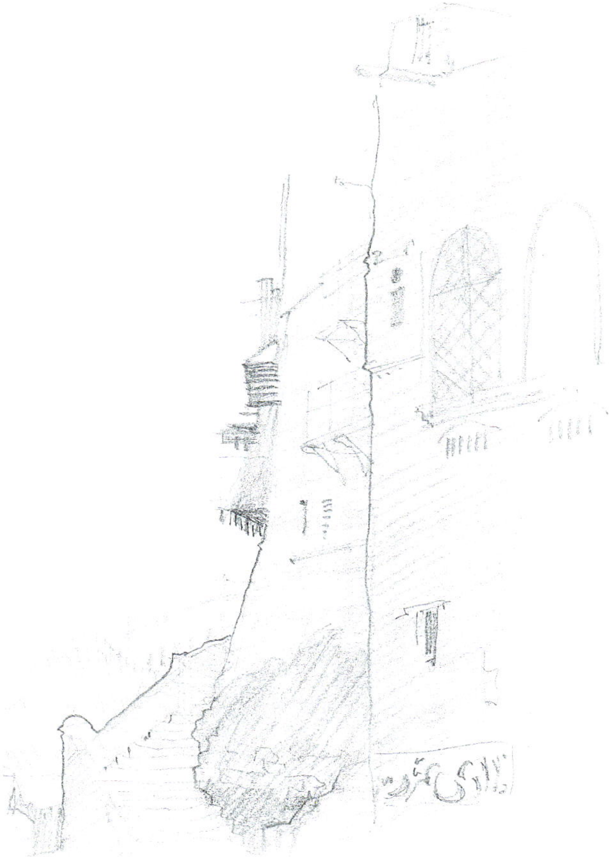

Right: 24 Rohri by night, and the original pencil sketch from which the final picture was painted

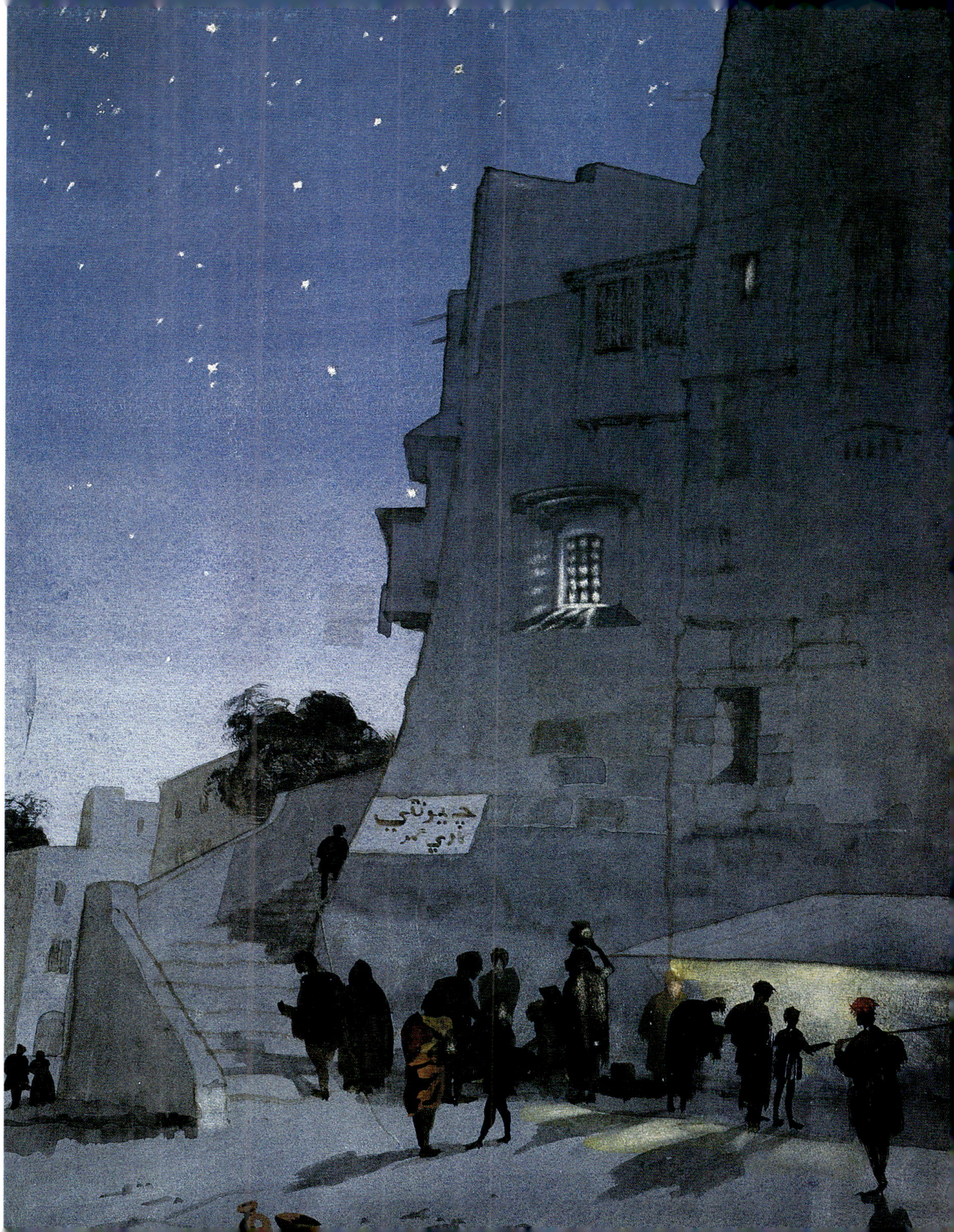

CHAPTER EIGHT

DESERT

Siting an aerodrome in a remote part of the Sind Desert does not sound much like subject matter for picture making. But it is surprising how attractive a desert can be on a day when clouds are blowing across the sky, their shadows bringing ever-changing tones of light and dark to the flat landscape. Some of the December skies over Karachi were wonderful cloudy ones. Such was the particular day I did the sketch 'Siting an airfield'.

Having left Karachi early in the morning and traversed many miles of heavily dust-laden road, at some points so much so that the road was undefinable and merged into the desert on both sides, we eventually arrived at a proposed airfield site. Six very hot engineers and one R.A.F. officer extracted their sweating bodies from two large army cars and shook quite a large proportion of the Sind Desert from their clothes. We were unlucky enough to have had a slight following wind so the windows had to be shut all the way and even then the clouds of dust thrown up by the wheels found their way in somehow. The atmosphere inside, bereft of any draught and filled with small particles of desert sand, became something between a Turkish bath and a dust storm – very unpleasant.

Filling our lungs with clean air and taking a pull at the iced water from the thermos, we soon pulled ourselves together and settled down to the business in hand. Maps and plans came out and discussions were started on the various engineering and flying problems, such as water supply, rail transport, prevailing wind direction and last but not least, my own particular subject, camouflage. My camera and sketch book were with me as usual in order to collect as much information as possible about local features and 'ground pattern'. That is a camouflage phrase which includes all features such as rivers, lakes, bushes, trees, villages, cultivated land and so on; anything, in fact, which gives a distinctive pattern to the ground when viewed from the air.

RIGHT: 25 Siting an airfield. Choosing a suitable place often involved private talks with the Malikh on the spot, to iron out local worries

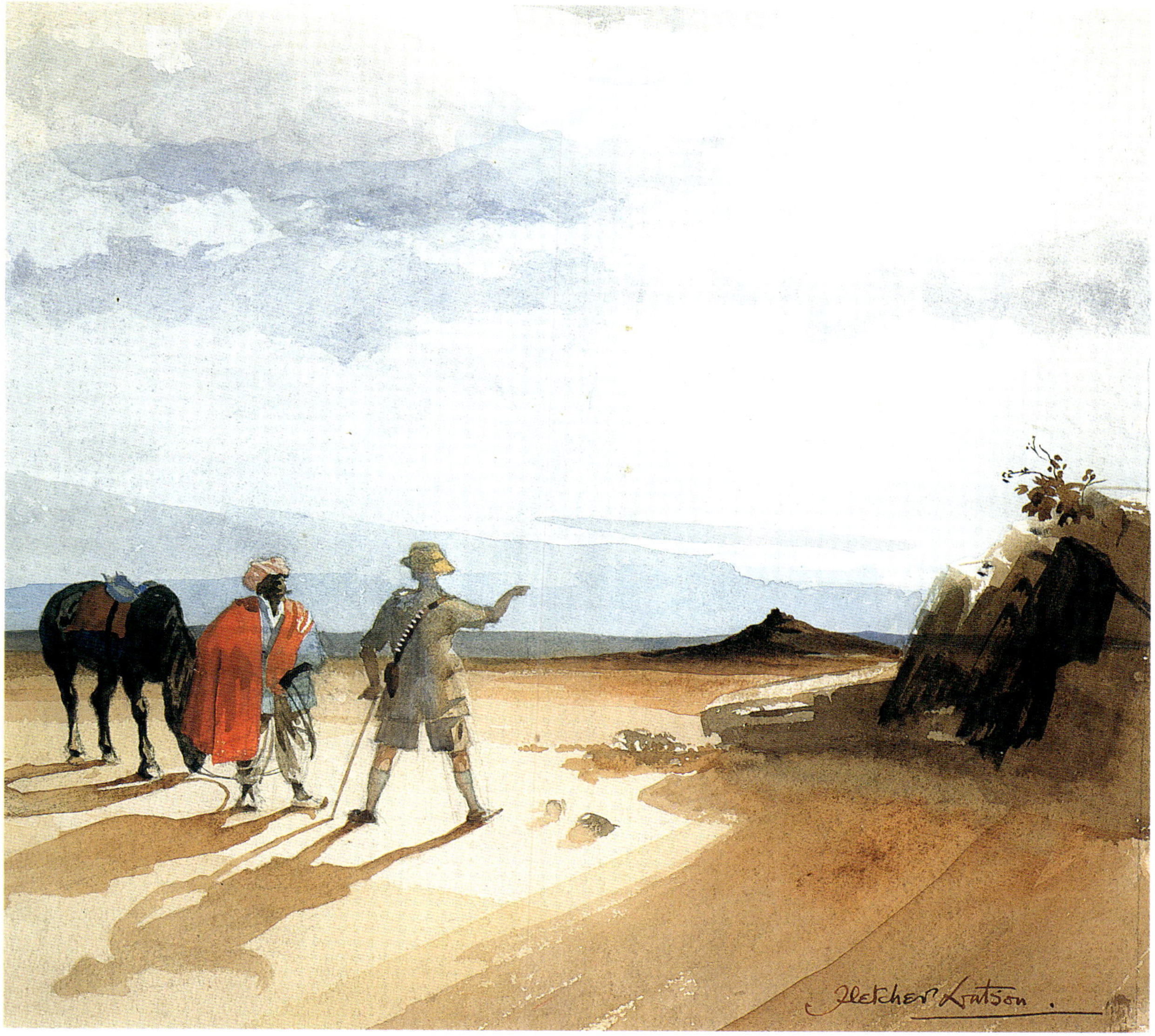

I soon collected more than enough information for doing a watercolour sketch. In this instance one needed little more than a note about the actual colour of foreground and distance, cloud shapes and shadows, and the Malikh and myself deciding on the siting of the airfield. By quarter past one the party was beginning to feel hungry, decisions had been reached on nearly all points and it was unanimously decided that the remainder of the pro-ceedings could safely be left in the hands of the Garrison Engineer!

Good old G.E., he had done most of the work anyway. It was he who had made a rough survey and drawn out a proposed layout showing positions of buildings and runways, investigating all sources of water supply and problems relating to drainage, malaria and other diseases. Railways, roads, stone quarrying and brick-making had all been considered by him. All he wanted was 'yes' or 'no' answers from the various specialists and the Siting Board. I am afraid he seldom got his answers as direct as that. But if he played his cards properly and especially if he did not ask too many questions until near lunch time, he usually got things his own way!

We ate our sandwiches with great relish. They had been wrapped in paper in a closed tin, but even then the sand had found its way in somehow. After this the party turned its head for home, all feeling rather thankful that they were not going to be the poor unfortunate who would one day have to live on this hot desert airfield. That evening I got down to working out a few desert landscape studies with windswept cloudy skies.

CHAPTER NINE

BUNDER BOATS AND AIRCRAFT

The most attractive part about Karachi is the sea and the harbour. My tours of inspection took me several times a week across the harbour by motor launch. These were pleasant moments when I got away from the heat of the city into the fresh sea breezes and the picturesque medley of shipping, both ancient and modern.

The harbour was a real sketching ground but an area where one was unfortunately not allowed to sketch. Too many wartime activities were going forward there. I must have been one of the very few people, if not the only one, who was allowed to carry a camera in these forbidden areas. Very often my official camouflage photographs of parts of the coast taken from a boat would include, by chance, or not always complete chance, a fine group of bunder boats coming into the harbour under full sail. Such photographs came in very useful when I was making memory sketches of seascapes and harbour scenes. 'Karachi Harbour' is one of these memory pictures, but security officers can rest assured that nothing of military value is portrayed. What small features there are, are by no means dead accurate. The bunder boat is a vessel which can vary in size from a twenty-foot craft with a single lug sail to quite a sizeable sea-going ship of some 300 tons, having two masts with big main sails and various top sails and jibs. Some of the latter are the most fascinating looking craft and have quite a suggestion of the Spanish galleon about them. They do extensive voyaging between Karachi and Bombay, carrying cargoes of bamboo or food stuffs, and quite a number go as far as the Persian Gulf. The principle on which all these boats are designed is interesting: the main mast leans forward at a considerable slant while it is held fast by blocks and tackle reaching from near the top of the mast to a point aft where it can be tightened or slackened according to the strain. The smaller boats all carry a plank, ten or twelve feet in length, which is lodged under a cross-bar running between the seats, and projects over the gunwale so that a man can safely squat at the end of it. I say safely, but he is really in an extremely precarious position as he sits out over the water, counter-balancing the angle at which the boat leans as she sails close hauled into the wind.

The sketch I did on airgraph paper which was sent home to England, indicates this technique fairly clearly. Sometimes several men at a time sit out on the plank on some of the longer and faster boats, adjusting their position as the breeze drops or stiffens. They have to look pretty slippy on a gusty day.

An enormous fishing fleet of no less than sixty sailing boats would leave for the open sea every evening at about six. This was a most stirring sight to watch. I was able to spend several Sundays at a most delightful spot along the coast which had a yellow sandy beach, a place where the peacetime dwellers in Karachi were wont to spend their weekends. From this point one could lie and watch the fishing boats go past the headland with their white sails, catching the soft rays from the evening sun, bobbing and swaying on the outward journey. I did a watercolour of this subject which is now in the possession of a friend in Karachi, but I still have the preliminary watercolour sketch which is reproduced here.

Returning to Karachi one day after a little camouflage

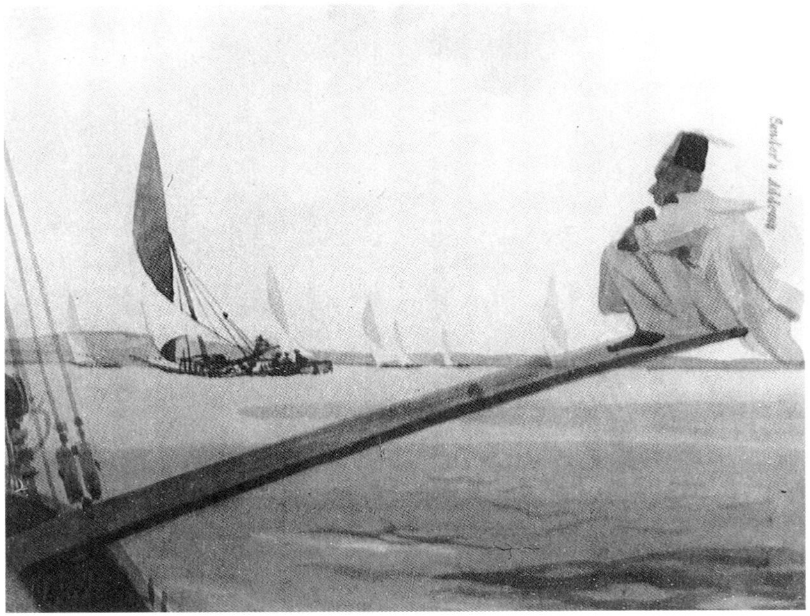

Above: Airgraph sketch

reconnaissance trip all on my own out in the Sind Desert, I passed through the village of Malir where there is a very pleasing example of Hindu temple architecture. I had passed the temple several times before, but had always been with fairly senior officers and I had never quite had the nerve to say, 'Excuse me, sir, do you mind if we stop for half an hour while I sketch that temple.'

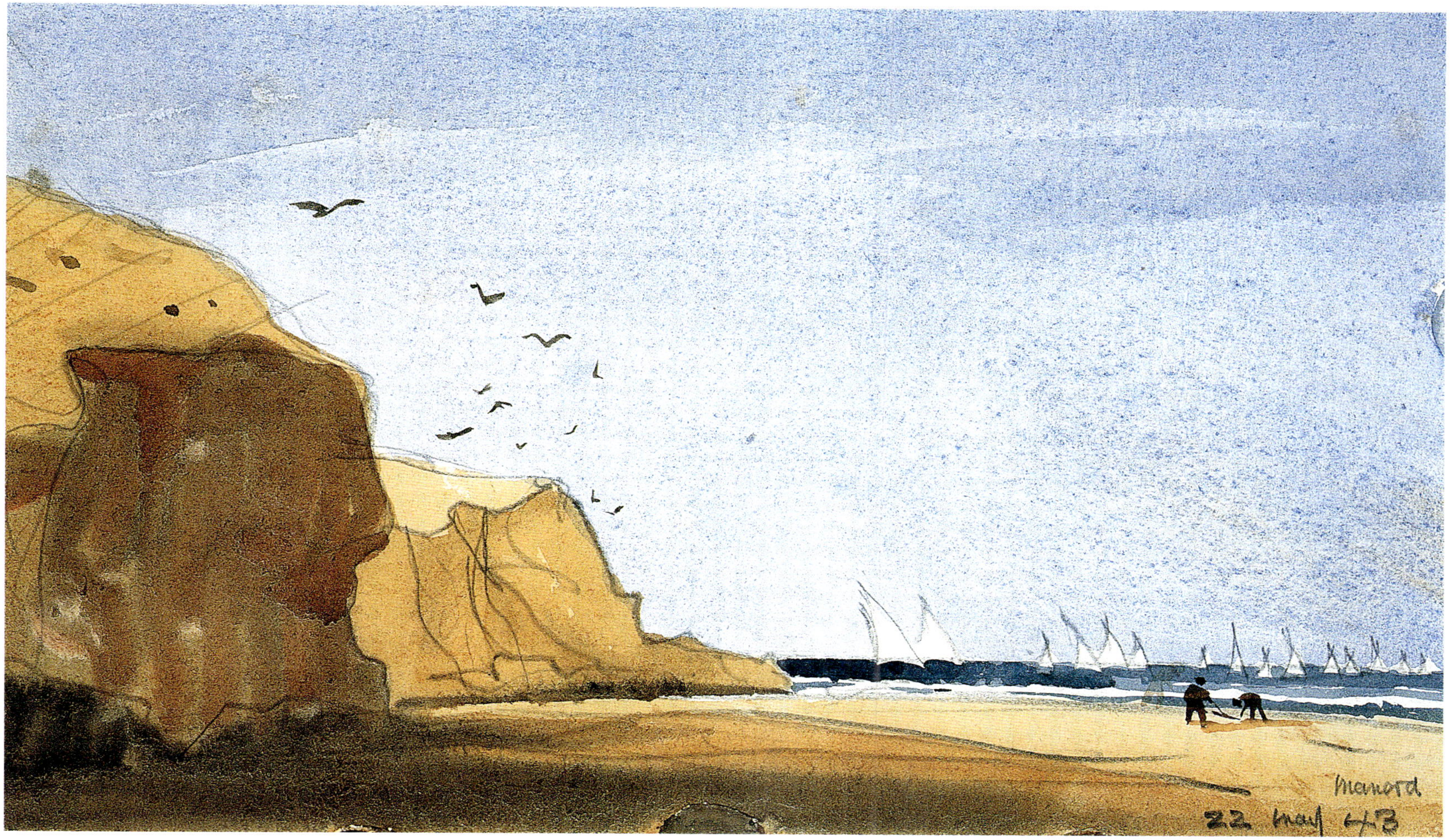

Above: 26 The Fishing Fleet, Karachi

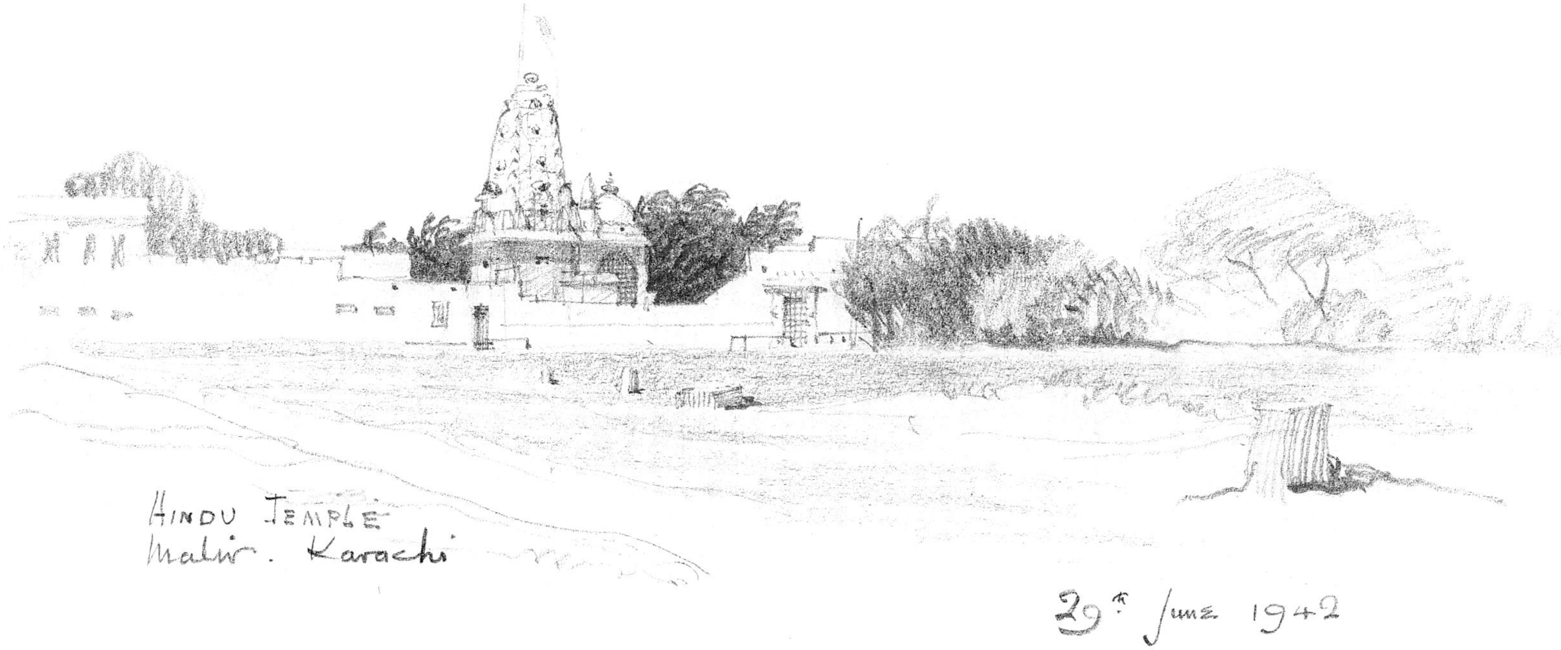

Above: Hindu Temple sketch, from which the final picture was painted

However, this time I had nobody but my staff car driver with me, so we spent a happy three quarters of an hour of Government time making a pencil sketch. The mellow-shaped dome is ornamented with heads of humans and animals and various decorative mouldings. It is all plaster relief work and one interesting fact is that there are no straight lines about it anywhere: all the mouldings, both vertical and horizontal, follow a slight curve. This gives the whole design a feeling of stability. Dates are not easy to place on some of these temples; this one is probably about a hundred years old. I have seen absolutely new temples being built, which look positively

Right: 27 Finished painting of the Hindu Temple, Malir

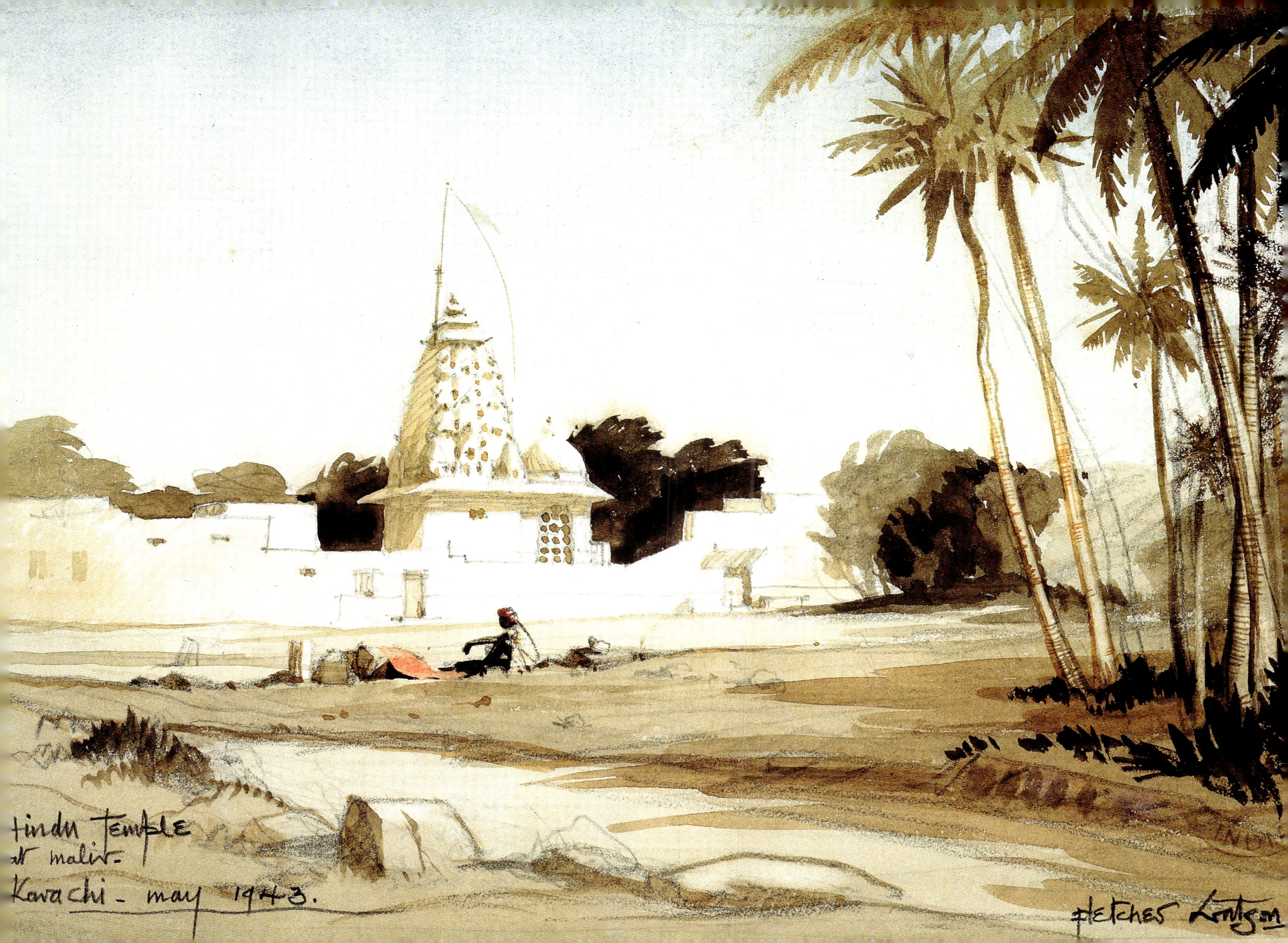
Hindu Temple
at Malir.
Karachi - May 1943.

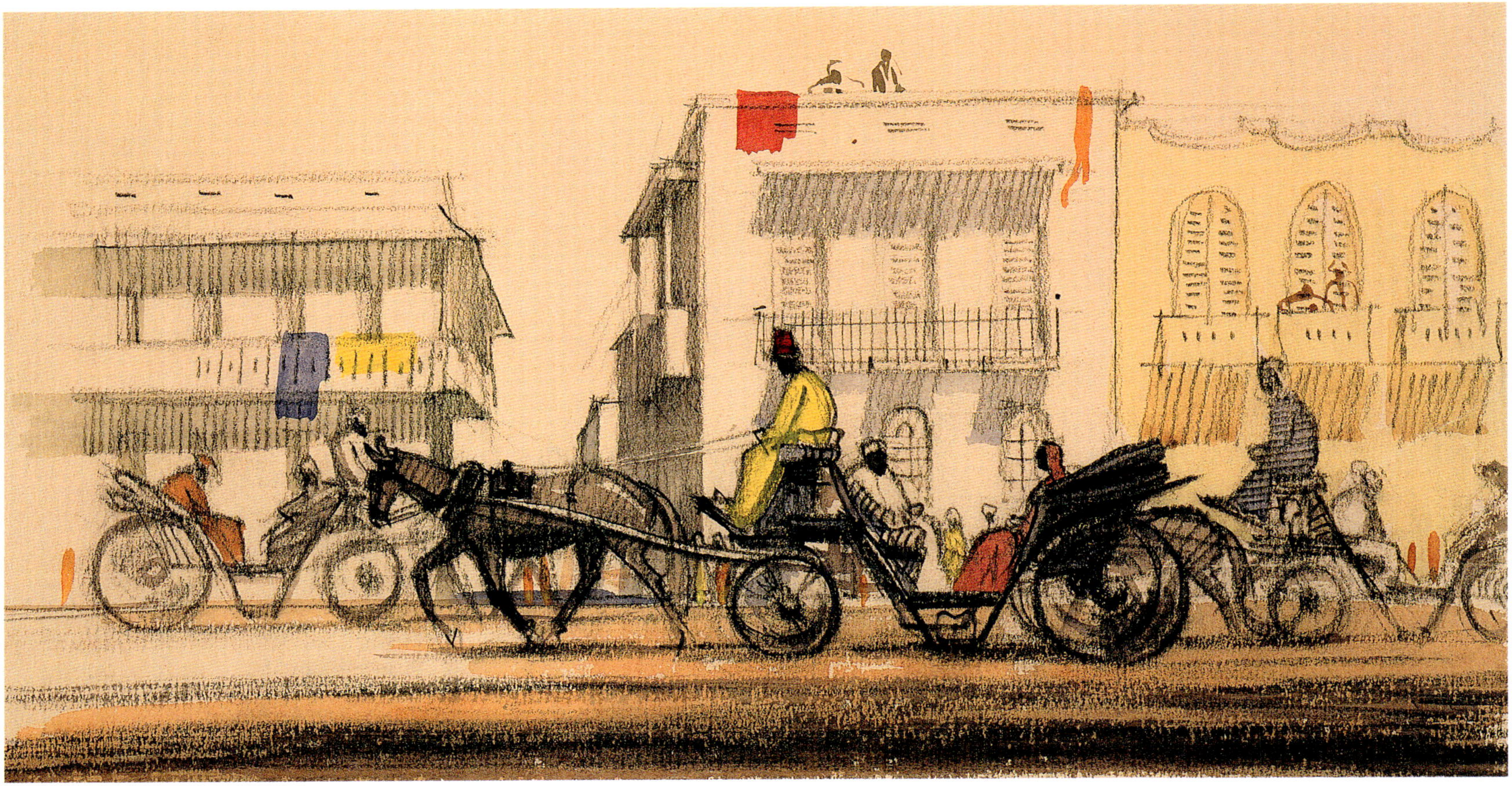

ABOVE: 28 Gareys in Karachi

ancient even while the work is still going on. It is for the same old reason, that the tools and the methods employed are also ancient, and much of the measuring is done by eye instead of by rule. In India, even the most ordinary interiors have a rather artistic ancient roughness of the plaster trowelwork and float tools. They are seldom finished with a smooth, hard setting coat, as in modern building practice. I have known people at home who have wanted the same results but have had the greatest difficulty in getting a plasterer to do a 'rough' job. In India, we have the greatest difficulty in obtaining a smooth and pukka job!

I did more flying at Karachi than at any other place, and had on average about two flights a week. The air view is of such vital importance in camouflage, and it is not until one becomes extremely expert that one can say how an object is going to appear from the air before one has flown over it. With the very large camouflage programme that I had to carry out in the Sind area, covering many outlying districts including Jacobabad 300 miles away, I was kept pretty busy with my camera and my flying, taking aerial views at different altitudes of military or R.A.F items.

I won't say I did not enjoy it. I love flying in a small aircraft on short trips. But the old soldier never says he is enjoying his work. That, as one learns from experience, is a fatal thing to admit and liable to get one put on to a less 'easy' job. I was beginning to consider myself quite an old soldier now, not old in years of service but in tricks of the trade, a highly important side of army life, I may say. At H.Q. I would announce blandly that I was off on another of those tiresome reconnaissance

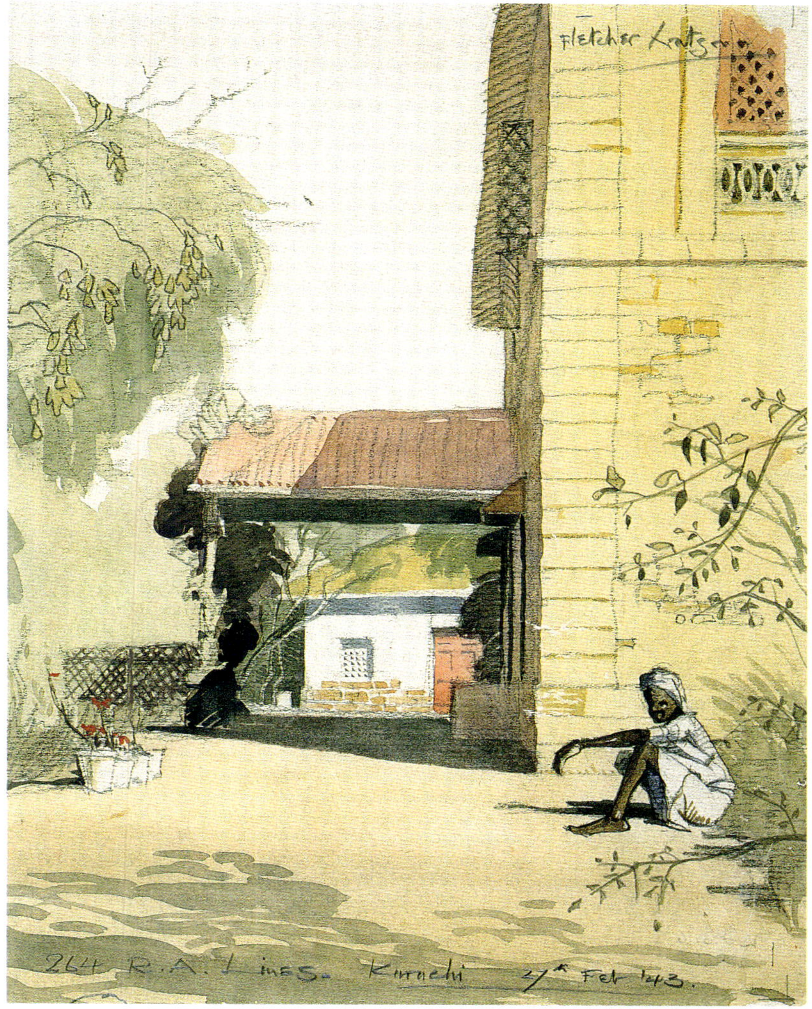

ABOVE: 29 My camouflage office, Karachi

flights. A colleague of mine would always greet me with, 'Well, where is the dizzy airman going today?' My answer to this was usually couched in terms best calculated to counteract the frivolous reference to my airborne expeditions. But on one day we were both right: the flying was both tiresome and dizzy.

On this occasion we started off with the usual understanding between me and the pilot of the Whopati regarding going higher or lower by using visual hand signs as the speaking tube never worked in this old aeroplane. I was armed as usual with the big R.A.F. service camera which weighed about as much as a portable gramophone and it was sometimes quite a tricky business handling this monster over the side of the plane in the 100 m.p.h. wind, when trying to get a verticle shot. My intention on this occasion was to get a fairly high level general view of a particular area from about 6,000 or 7,000 feet, I told the pilot. We manoeuvred nicely over the target at 7,000 feet, but at this height the objects I was interested in and which I hoped would not stand out at 5,000 feet were still as clear as a bell. I jerked my thumb out of the cockpit in an upward direction at the pilot and up we started to climb again. Observing at heights of 10,000 to 12,000 feet I was amazed to find that visibility was still extremely good and my camouflage objects were still perfectly visible. We continued to climb, and at 14,000 feet in an open Whopati with no flying tunics, it was confoundedly chilly. My Indian pilot seemed disinclined to go up any higher so I gave him the home sign ie. thumb over shoulder. It was just as well, as I was beginning to freeze, the temperature was extremely low at that altitude and it was all I could do to hold onto the big camera when peering over the side. My fingers were numb and my teeth chattering. The camera was strapped to me for safety, and I was also strapped to the aeroplane, but not with the usual straps onto the seat. The rear cockpit of a Whopati is circular and specially built for an observer.

You wear a webbed cross-bracing arrangement which has a metal attachment between your legs. To this attachment you clamp another metal socket which is on the end of a chord, and is in turn fastened to the floor of the cockpit. You are virtually free then to lean over as far as you like, which liberates you immediately if necessity requires it. Fortunately necessity never did require it.

I took about thirty-five shots on this flight and very valuable they proved to be afterwards. I could not think at the time why I was puffing and blowing so much and finding the job of turning on each film exposure such a dreadful effort, but my pilot pointed out to me afterwards that at 14,000 feet in the rarefied air one does feel a trifle weak, especially when one climbs to

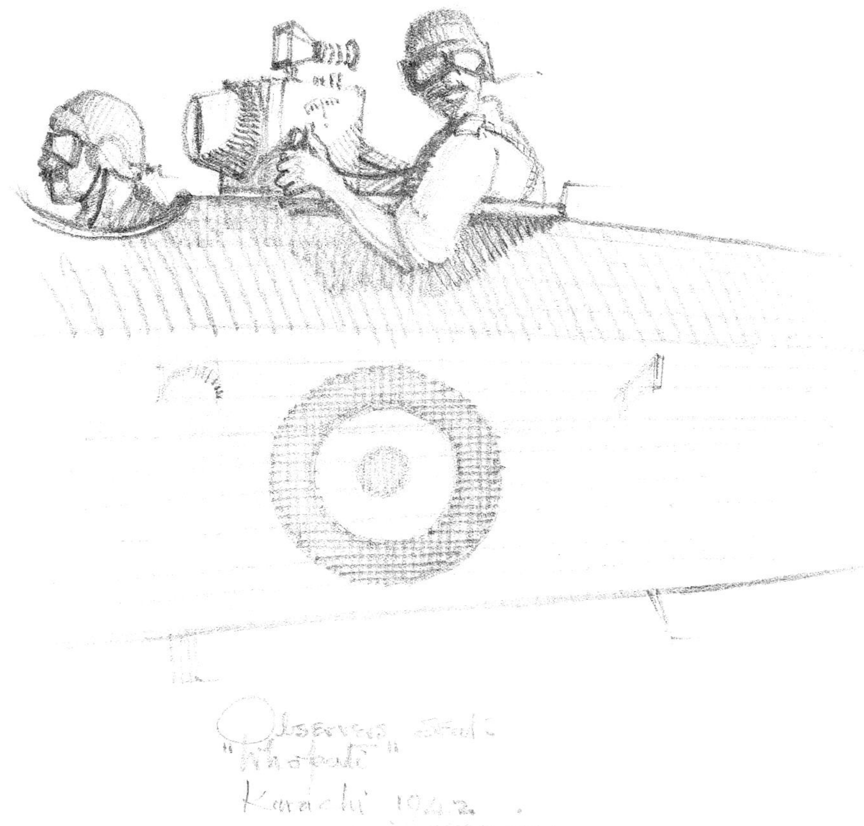

the height in such a short space of time. The only good it really did me was to get rid of my prickly heat rash for a few days. That is the highest I have ever been, and I felt confident in telling my friend at H.Q. that I was literally his 'dizzy airman' that day. It was not long after this particular flight that Whopatis were taken 'off the air' altogether, being classed as obsolete and unsafe. They are a machine which had a tremendous run of service, being first used as reconnaissance planes in the First World War.

CHAPTER TEN

BUNGALOWS, BEAGLES AND THE GANGES

I was posted to Patna as camouflage officer for the area, reporting at the end of July 1943. The district included airfields, gun emplacements and military camps. The impression that stays in my mind of Patna and the neighbouring Bihar countryside is above all else one of fresh green fertility. The rice crop was just coming on when I arrived and the various stages of growth which different fields had reached gave the acres of flat paddy land an exceptionally brilliant patchwork design in all shades of green. The very geometric shapes of the small fields, oblongs and squares, added to this patchwork effect. Some of them were almost pure lemon yellow while others with light green or dark green according to their state of growth, and a few, in an advanced state of ripeness, were a rich blue green.

There can be nothing that rivals the translucent brilliance of a new grown rice crop. Not even, to my mind, do the greenest of English lawns or well-kept golf courses come up to it. The first urge I had, therefore, on arrival in Patna, was to make a watercolour with green as the predominant factor. The thatch and rust coloured tile roofs of the village buildings with their white-washed walls made a pleasing contrast and the tall slender palms gave appropriate relief to the otherwise monotonously flat landscape.

A few miles out of Patna was an old town and military cantonment called Dinapore, which had some interesting examples of bungalow design, about eighty years old. Built with a narrow country-made brick, a mellow brown in colour, and sometimes rendered with plaster, colour washed, green and black painted shutters and country tile roofs, the general appearance of a great many of these bungalows was decidedly Dutch in character. Some other buildings of a rather later date were built in large blocks in this Regency manner in the old

Right: 30 A village near Patna

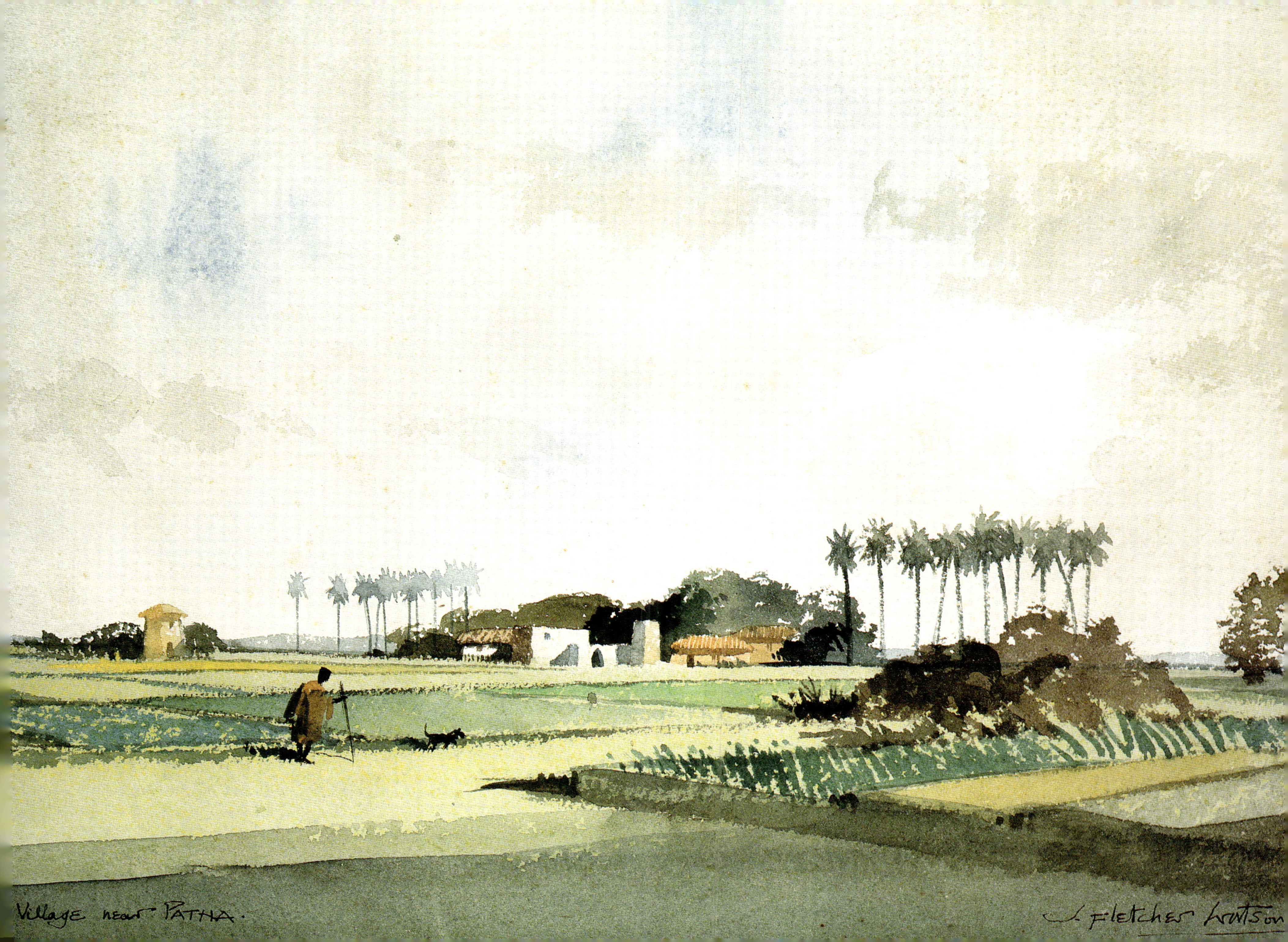
Village near PATNA.
J. Fletcher Watson

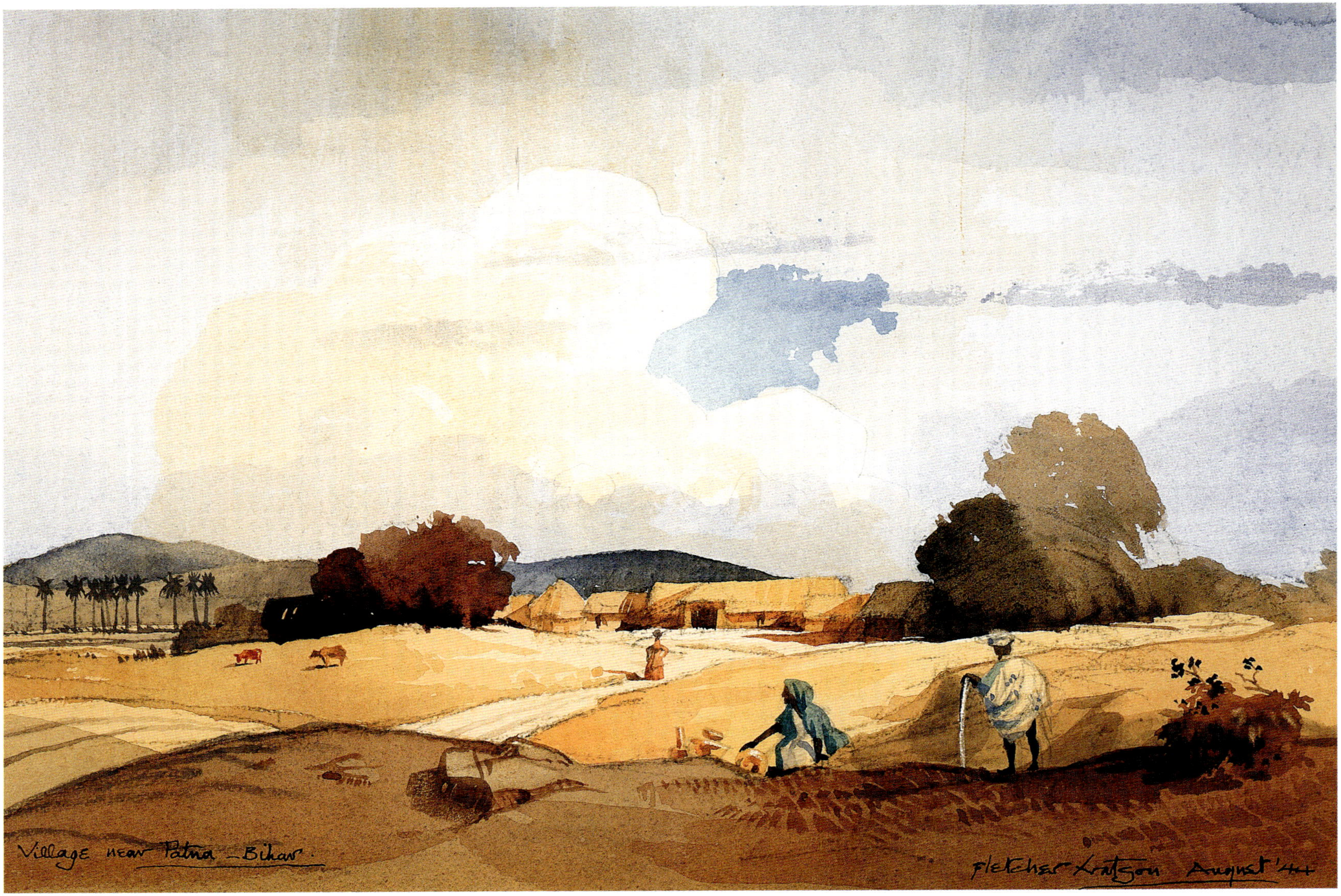
Village near Patna _ Bihar.
Fletcher Watson August '44

Left: 31 Another Patna landscape

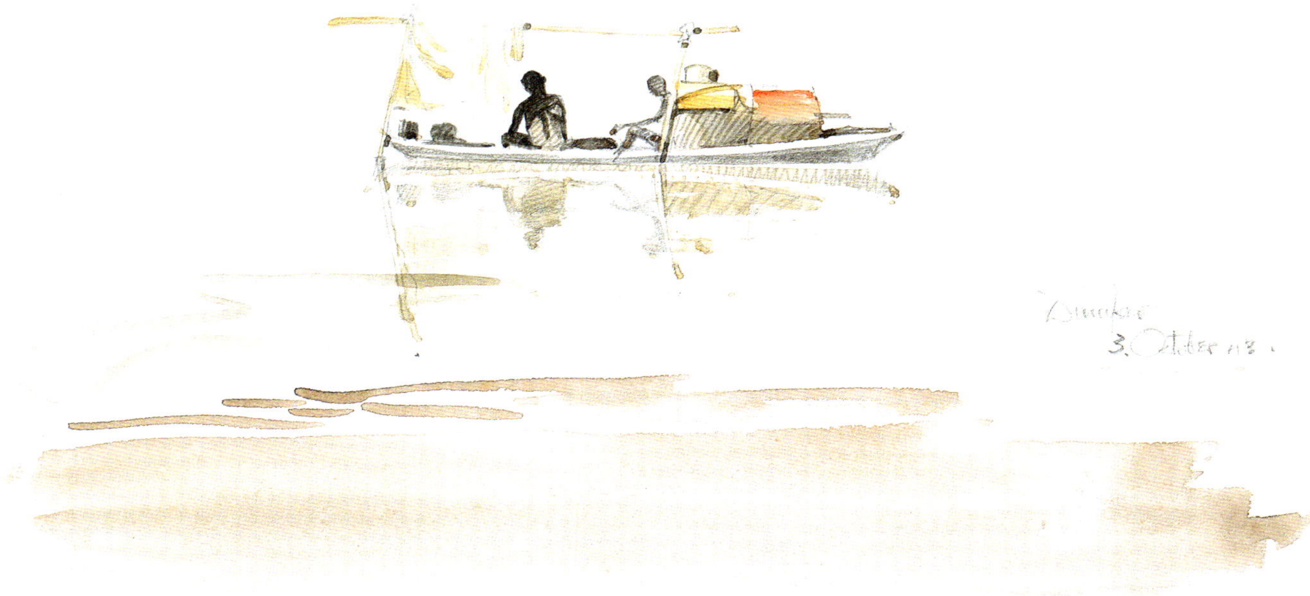

Right: On the Ganges

cantonment district of the town, and would be worthy of some architectural study.

I never had time to do any sketches of these buildings, but one Sunday afternoon when I was visiting the C.R.E. (Commander Royal Engineers) Dinapore to discuss camouflage I did manage to fit in a couple of hours sketching the truly delightful view he had from his bungalow. It backed onto a branch loop of the Ganges, with a steep bank at the end of the garden running down to the water's edge. At this time of the year it is true to say that the water runs gently past the garden but later on, when the Ganges is in full spate, the water rises some fifteen feet and laps the foot of his garden wall.

A variety of craft passed up and down the stretch of water while I sat sketching, ranging from canoe-like boats made from hollowed out tree trunks, to fully rigged two-masted sailing vessels, but always of square rig and galleon-like design, floating high out of the water.

I have come to the conclusion that nearly everything to

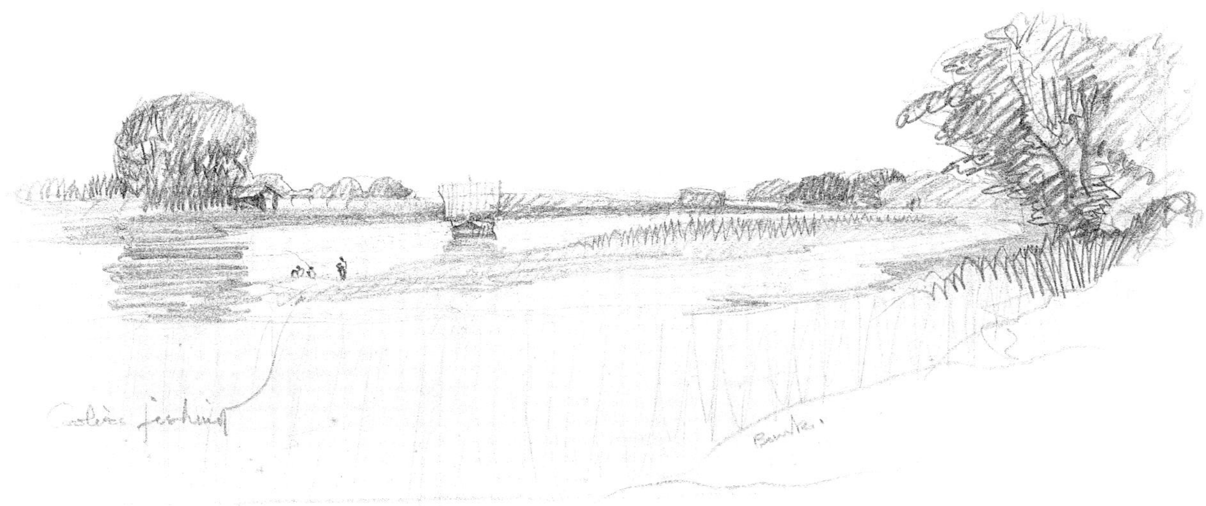

Left: Pencil sketch of a loop of the Ganges at Dinapore, later made into the painting opposite

Right: 32 A loop of the Ganges at Dinapore

which the Indian country builder or craftsman turns his hand results in an artistic creation. This even applies to the most functional subjects such as a house, a ship or a cart, and more especially when these objects have to be built with the utmost economy in labour and material. However, I am not saying that his efforts are always constructionally sound – far from it, especially where larger buildings are concerned, which have been know to fall down before they have been three parts completed. In these cases, the craftsman requires the guiding hand of the engineer. But when he is building something which tradition and experience has taught him, then the design is of a high standard and the result is sound and reliable. The very tools he uses and the primitive way he uses them make the finished result so much more artistic than the hard lines of a mass produced article. Every hand-made charpai (a bench or bed), for example, varies very slightly in design and quality because each leg is cut separately and hewn into shape with the adze; so different from legs which are turned on the lathe and produced by the thousand in a factory.

There was a pleasant little nine hole golf course at Patna where, on rare occasions, a number of us were able to take a spot of exercise in the evening. But a much more attractive

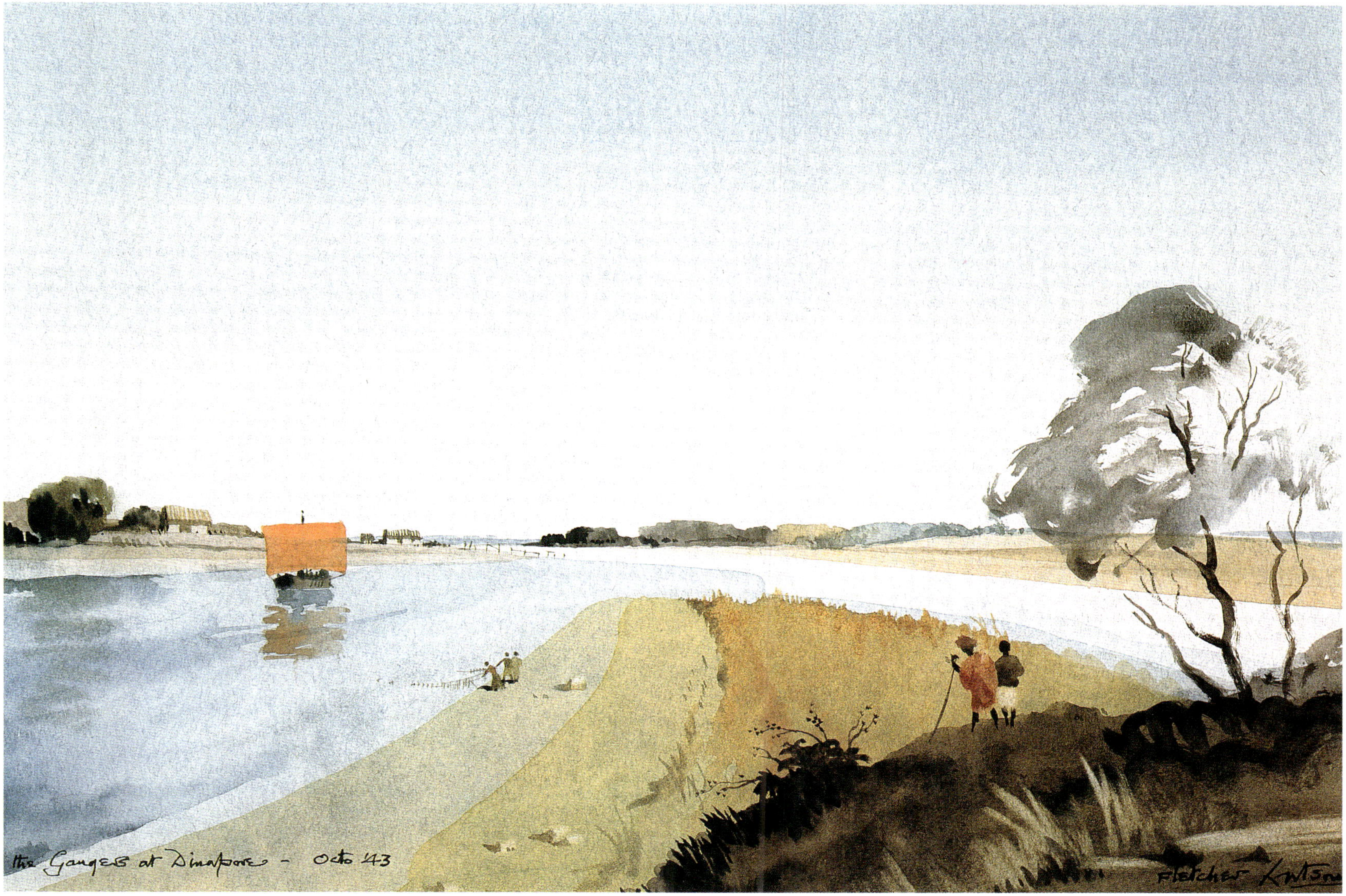
the Ganges at Dinapore - Octo '43
Fletcher Watson

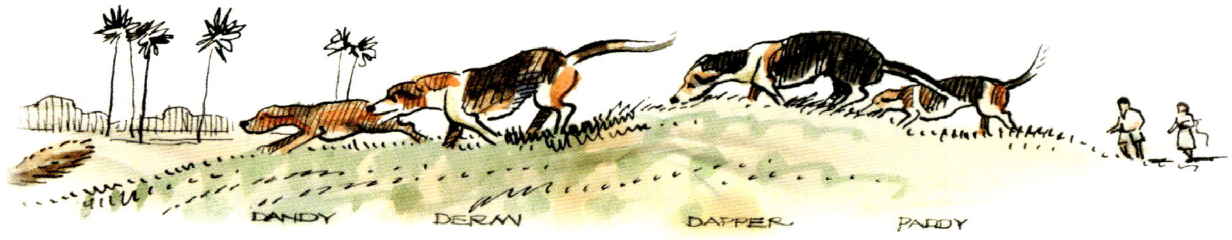

Above: General Wakeley's beagles

form or recreation, to my mind, was the Area Commander's pack of beagles. He was Secretary of the Master of Hounds Association of India and was an Irishman, with an Irish wife into the bargain, so there was absolutely no question whatsoever about his enthusiasm for hunting. He was often out in an evening with the two-and-a-half couple to which the wartime kennel had been so drastically reduced. A number of H.Q. staff were regular followers although their capabilities as runners varied considerably. Different people came out for different reasons. Some came to get their weight down. There is nothing like a ten mile alternate walk and jog trot with an occasional sprint thrown in during August in Bihar to reduce all the weight you want. Others came to exercise their dogs; the Master was very long-suffering in this respect and allowed two dashhounds and a bull terrier to participate very often, and on one occasion I brought Shadow along. But the next time I was on the phone enquiring where the meet would be, I was told that I could not come if I brought 'that spotted dog of yours'. This, I knew only too well, was due to Shadow's misbehaviour when she was out a few days before, and she simply galloped round and round at full tilt in the long grass exactly in the spot where the hounds were endeavouring to draw. Any scent there might have been was completely marred by her antics. She spent other moments bounding through groups of hounds at a terrific speed, head in air, trying to get them to chase her, but not making the smallest attempt to help with the business of hunting. Dalmations are carriage dogs, they are graceful movers and have great staying power but very poor noses when it comes to hunting. So Shadow was banned from the hunting field. She strongly resented this, of course, as she knew perfectly well, when she smelt my legs on my return from an evening hunt, what I had been up to.

General Wakeley and his wife were both busy people and it was miraculous how they managed to keep a pack of beagles going, small though this pack might be. She was a Junior Commander and head of the W.A.C.(I) arm at H.Q. Two other W.A.C.I.s were regulars with the hounds and were the owners of the dashhounds, and the bull terrior, who found a fox for us on one occasion. The dashhounds came in useful for ferreting through the thickest parts of the jungle undergrowth.

Parts of the country we hunted contained sugar crops which grow into dense thicket around six to eight feet high. Once hounds got into this, it was the devil's own job to get them out, and almost impossible to follow them in oneself. We were still calling for them an hour after dark one night, before they were all safely leashed up and we could set off for home. The little grey fox is quite a fast runner, and when he can be persuaded to break out into the open he fairly gives you a run for your money; in fact, you have got to be very fit to keep up on a three- or four-mile chase across paddy fields and ditches. Our Master was a very large man and by no means a youngster (Generals seldom are) but he had an amazing capacity for keeping with the hounds. If you wanted to take it easy the best bet was undoubtedly to stay with Mrs Master. She was adept at short cuts and had the uncanny knack of knowing which short cut to take.

Patna is one of the cleaner towns of India, rather like a miniature New Delhi. Being the seat of the Bihar Government it has a number of large civic buildings, Courts of Justice, Secretariat buildings etc. and a large Government House. These, together with a quantity of Government officials' bungalows, were built in the early part of the century with quite a useful town planning layout. Wide grass verges flank all the roads and every bungalow stands in at least five acres of garden containing a profusion of shady trees. The other parts of the town where the station, cinemas and usual noisy, smelly, dusty bazaar streets are situated, is quite apart from the new residential area.

My time in Patna certainly did not prepare me for the complete contrast of Calcutta, where I was sent in late 1943.

CHAPTER ELEVEN

CALCUTTA

The second city of the Empire does not fill one with pride on first acquaintance. Nor is one's initial impression in any way enhanced on coming to know the city better, but rather one's opinion is confirmed that it is not only the second biggest city but the second dirtiest of the Empire, if not the first. Being an architect with strong town planning tendencies and hygienic principles, one cannot be anything other than horrified at the squalor, the poverty, the stench from decaying vegetable refuse lying about the streets, and from inefficient drainage, and the general drab and shoddy appearance of the whole place. Buildings started and never finished, buildings finished but never properly started with adequate forethought as to their place and part in relation to the whole, crumbling into decay through lack of care and maintenance, and buildings which are not buildings at all but ugly temporary shacks unfit to live in.

The filthy fungoid growth of haphazard and uncontrolled development is a stain on the Empire record, a stain which can and should be removed at the soonest possible moment. It might be argued that Calcutta does not look its best at the present time owing to the war. Large buildings which were a clean white or cream colour originally, have been painted over with a dull tone as a camouflage measure and everywhere the military are making their mark, erecting hutted camps on the maiden and open spaces, and creating large stores, dumps and vehicle parks.

I am sorry to introduce a jarring note into this book, which hitherto has dealt only with the more beautiful and admirable side of this vast country. But all the more reason why India, possessing so much fine scenery and traditional architecture of great merit, should take steps to improve the living conditions and appearance of her largest town.

I reproduce below an article from a leading paper, dated 28th March 1944. It is headed 'Filthy Calcutta' and was accompanied by seven photographs bearing witness to the statements. The press photographer must have had an easier job than usual that day when he was told to find these subjects; he would not have had to look far.

> Below we illustrate sights characteristic of Calcutta. Years of public protest have made them no rarer. They are visible daily all over the Empire's 'Second City' – typical in great streets like Chowringhee (among the wealthiest and most renowned in Asia) as in the squalid by-lanes of the slum areas. Calcutta is now an extraordinarily crowded town; fighting men of all nations unused to Bengal's climate and conditions, fill its buildings and jostle in its thoroughfares; last year's famine left a terrible legacy of disease, which the city's abnormally swollen mortality figures evidently still reflect; another hot weather has begun. Yet huge open stinking heaps of garbage, whereon crows and kites and many dogs, cattle and human scavengers scramble for sustenance in swirling wind and heat, continue to be tolerated – as in the complacent days before Bengal's administrative methods won international concern.

One can only hope for a future time when there will be no more beggars sprawling across the pavements, no more rubbish littering the streets and no more houses built which have become slums and hovels before they are a month old.

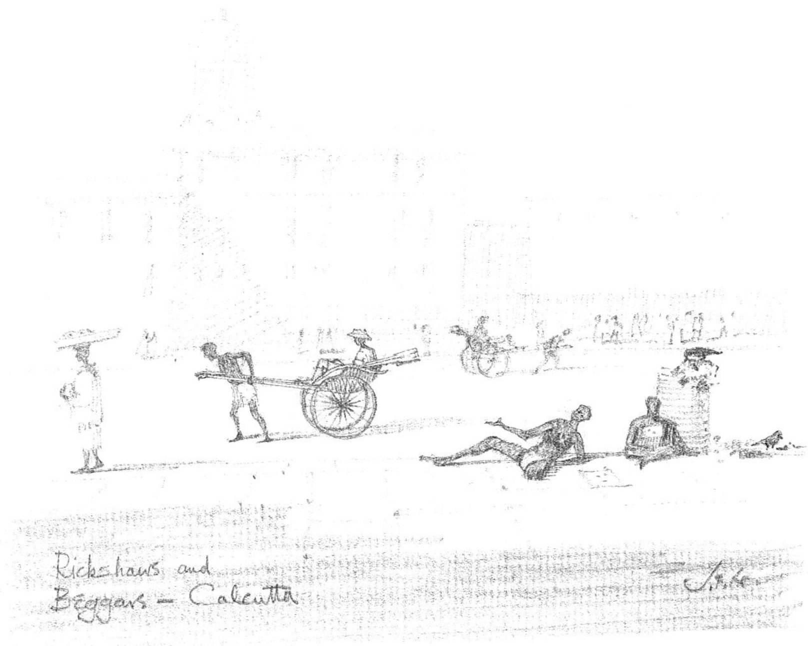

I have already trespassed into the outskirts of politics and will not go further by suggesting who it is that might be responsible for all this gross mismanagement and neglect. I leave that to the imagination of the reader. Suffice it to say that Englishmen have lived and moved and had their being in this city for over 250 years.

In the autumn of 1943 I had received a mysterious and most un-military posting instruction from GHQ ordering me to report to a civilian address in Calcutta and also promoting me to the rank of Major. On arrival, I duly reported to a large office building and was shown into the board room. A middle aged gentleman rose to meet me*. He was a man of medium height, slightly stooping with a round face and a twinkle in the eye, and a large cigar in his mouth; in fact, at that moment, he looked extremely like Mr Churchill.

Charlie, as I was soon to call him, was a man with a frank and friendly manner which won your confidence. He was a pleasure to work for and with, and if his political outbursts were somewhat menacing and of a Communist nature at times – he was of Russian parentage – they were most entertaining and not always incorrect.

I found myself working largely with civilians rather than military colleagues: chemists, factory managers, and company directors were men with whom we made daily contact. Our days were arduous and long and in the evening Charlie and I would sit over our coffee, he smoking the inevitable cigar, and discussing this point and that. How could this opposition be broken down or that mechanical problem be solved. Could I not persuade the army to do so-and-so – well, it was against regulations but we would make it work somehow. I frankly

* EDITORIAL NOTE: He was an American scientist who had been lent to the War Office to advise on the construction of advance airfields for fighter aircraft. This information was Top Secret at the time of my writing this book but at the present time, many years later and not at war, I am free to disclose information on such subjects as this.

By late 1943 it became essential to open up further air/land supply routes for the Burma campaign and to improve the speed of constructing new airfields and roads. A particular need was for fighter aircraft bases to be situated nearer to the enemy positions in Burma so that attacks could be effectively made, and runways constructed into the jungle to bring supplies to our forces. Charles Baskin required immediate introductions to the jute factories of Calcutta in order to instruct them in making a new and secret runway fabric, and also he had to be allowed to visit and inspect forward airfield sites on the Burma Front. He and I were to work together and I was to give him the entrée to any place he needed to visit. Arrangements had been made for American road-making engineers to construct runways on the Burma Front and they had all the latest soil shifting equipment etc.

I visited factories with Baskin on some occasions and there was talk on the factory floor about such things as bitumen viscosity of a suitable type, namely bitumen that would not melt too quickly when exposed to the hot Burma sun, and many other technical construction matters.

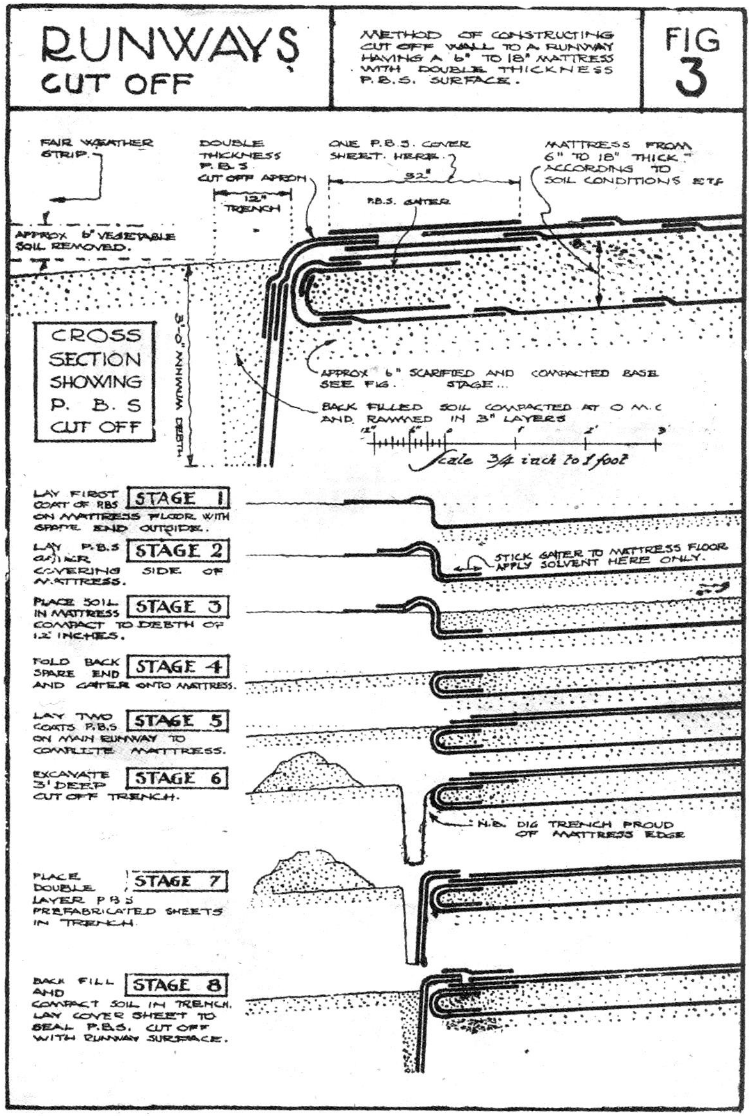

admit I broke more regulations and routine orders during my five months' service as Charlie's A.D.C. than I should care to mention. But it was a rush job and he got the job done which is the main thing. His profound knowledge of his subject and his active brain and forceful opinions on many other subjects, including golf, dogs, music and, to a certain extent, pictures, made him a stimulating and interesting companion.

Our first and foremost challenge was to obtain a staff car. We were continually wanting to go from office to office and from factory to field, so a car was a prime necessity. But could we get one? Not a hope. Charlie, as E-in-C's Adviser, had been allotted a beautiful car all to himself by G.H.Q. Unfortunately this car was only a theoretical car 'on paper' where it remained for three months, passing through diverse official channels. There were rumours of cars from time to time which on investigation proved to be false and I had my work cut out to uphold the prestige of the British Army. This was not easy in the face of a perfect mass of American transport, always scouting in front of our noses. Jeeps, empty except for the American

Left: A construction diagram drawn by Major Fletcher-Watson for the Royal Engineers official pamphlet for Construction of Runways and Roads

officer driving them, would go past us as we walked or taxied to our various appointments. 'Why can't you get one of them,' Charlie would say. At last, I found a temporary solution. Out of the many W.V.S. part-time drivers who offered themselves and their private cars to the services, I discovered a lady who was willing to work six days a week all day, and even the seventh day if necessary. The S.T.O. (Station Transport Officer) did not like letting her do this, for no better reason as far as I could make out than because it was not quite in accordance with regulations. But he was persuaded to think otherwise and so for a time this arrangement worked. Every morning the good lady reported to our office and we went as and when and where we pleased. So far so good. But snags began to crop up. We got a taste of the trouble ahead on the first day, in fact, when we discovered that our woman driver could talk fast, endlessly and untiringly whether the car was stationary or in motion. We might have borne the talk which was the 'He says to her and she says to me' sort of stuff and had its amusing passages, but the erratic consequences this had on her driving was unbearable. We would sit in breathless suspense while the woman recounted events in her past life, apparently completely oblivious to the approach of an eight-wheeler American lorry coming at full tilt in our direction down a single traffic lane where the road was up for repairs. At the last minute she would catch a glimpse of the monster almost upon us and by a dexterous swerve and firm application of the brakes would land us on the green grass at the side of the road, just in time. We breathed again while she commented, 'Oh, these American drivers are awful, don't care about anybody, it shouldn't be allowed. But as I was saying …'

The significant part about all this was the fact that the road to Barrackpore, along which we had to travel almost every day, was rapidly becoming nothing more or less than a death trap to motorists and pedestrians alike. Barrackpore is about eighteen miles out of Calcutta and owing to the large number of military interests which were situated in or beyond this place, the traffic was extremely heavy and increasing daily. The road was narrow, just wide enough for two lorries to pass each other, the camber was great which made small cars bounce when overtaking at speed (ours was a very small car) and the road was up at various points causing one-way traffic and consequent traffic blocks. The most experienced and accomplished of drivers could just hold his own on this 'race track' where everyone tried to overtake everyone else. Imagine our plight, being in the hands of a middle aged woman driving a middle aged small Vauxhall with brakes she admitted were not too reliable. A head strong woman, too, who disputed the right to the centre of the road with powerful military trucks four times our weight and speed! I will admit that the drivers of the larger lorries were apt to hold on to a central course and not give over much to a small car, but it simply did not pay to argue with them. Added to this was our driver's mania for pointing out buildings and landmarks at the roadside, and so our cup of agony was full to overflowing.

Eventually Charlie and I felt something had to be done before we were both sent into the madhouse. Fortunately another type of vehicle became available to us so we gave reasons why we must change our mode of transport. We were prepared to make a lot of sacrifices for country and cause but when it began to affect one's sanity then one was justified in calling a halt, I think. An experimental job of ours was going forward on an airfield where several lorries were employed. These lorries were suddenly made to make an unusual number of trips to Calcutta at unusual hours of the day and in order to replace the tired drivers I did the driving while Charlie sat in the cab beside me. We were both happy now: he could smoke his cigars in peace, and after all a lorry was the safest vehicle to be in when travelling the Barrackpore death run. There was a death of some sort almost every time we went along that road, either a cow or a dog, or an overturned vehicle with a dead occupant or two.

But I must not leave Calcutta in this gloomy vein. Bad as it is, there are lighter aspects. Barrackpore has a very pleasant architectural character. The numerous bungalows are all of that 'delayed-action' Regency style which I have already mentioned as being so well exemplified at Dinapore near Patna. I say 'delayed action' meaning that while England was changing her architecture to the Victorian Copy Gothic style, builders and, I suppose, some British architects in India were still in the throes of full-blooded Regency planning and fenestrating.

I did a sketch of one showing the typical refined Regency character.

I also found a moment to do a rough sketch of bullock carts at Barrackpore (see picture No. 34).

These were literally the only sketches I did over the nine months due to the high pressure of work. All I wanted to do at the end of a long, hard day was relax and Charlie helped me to do this by taking me off to the Royal Calcutta Golf Club on certain evenings , where he had been made an honorary member. Here was an oasis in the midst of the squalor: there were closely cut fairways of wonderfully green grass and groups of dark trees with heavy foliage, a pleasant cool club house which

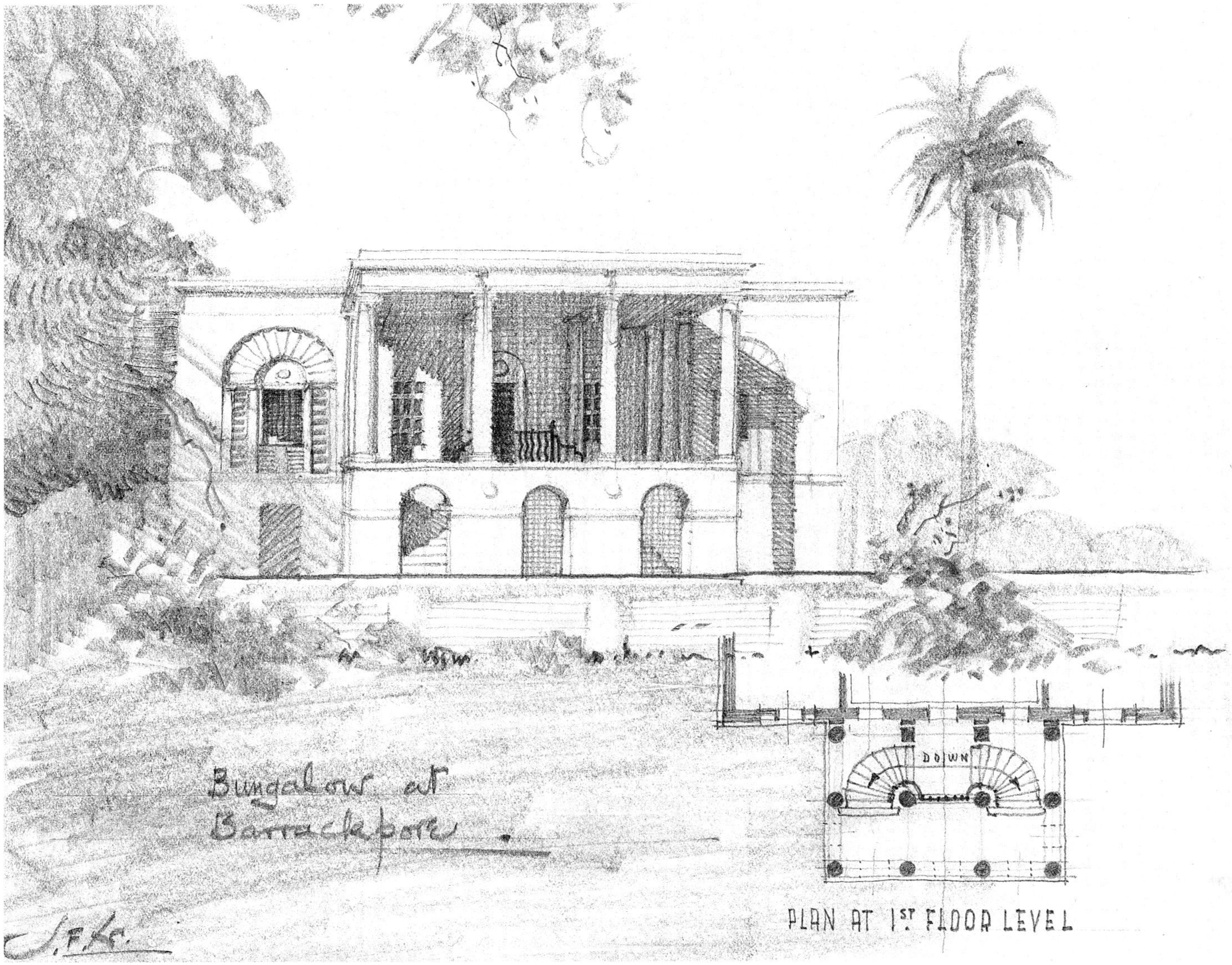
DOWN
Bungalow at Barrackpore.
PLAN AT 1ST FLOOR LEVEL
J.F.Kr.

Left: 33 Bungalow at Barrackpore

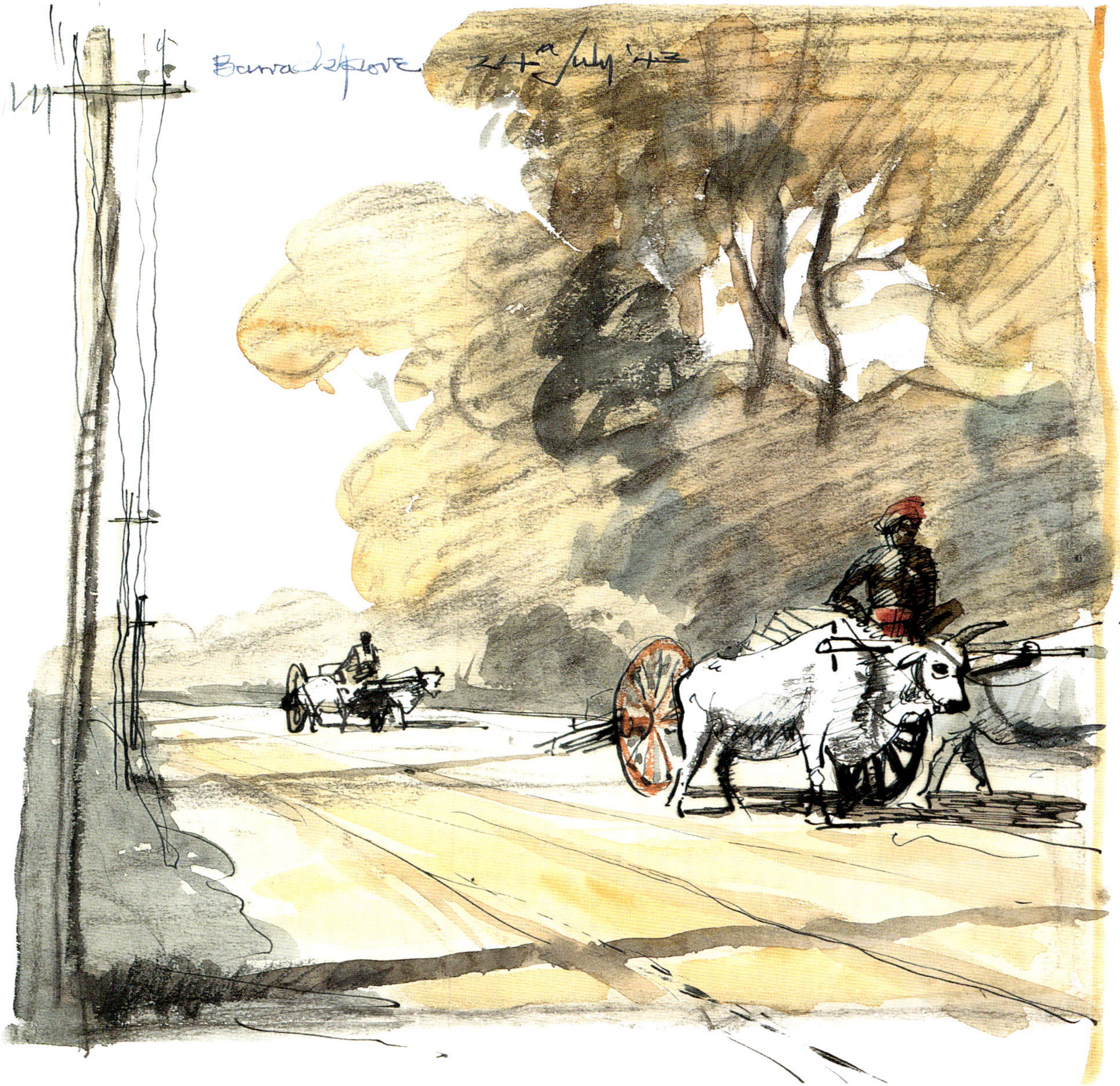

Right: 34 Bullock carts at Barrackpore, a common form of Indian transport

provided a very passable meal and better drink than in most of Calcutta's hotels.

We had some keen contests. I was able to out-drive Charlie but he was steady and that always wins the day against an erratic player like me. There was one decidedly frightful feature to this links. The whole course was littered with most menacing water tanks. Every hole had at least two, secreted away in unexpected places, or sometimes blatantly situated plumb in the middle of the fairway. These proved to be unsurmountable hazards at first and we always lost two or three balls a round. Golf balls, as everyone knows, are as rare as diamonds now-a-days and these losses became a serious problem threatening our very existence as active golfers. We fortunately discovered a place in the Calcutta market where re-paints were sold at a very high price. At once, our golfing improved and we got canny to the methods necessary to avoid 'ponding' our balls. Local boys were employed by the Club to dive for balls; each tank had its diver and very efficient they were at retrieving a ball from the muddy depths.

While I am on the subject of golf, it is interesting to note the difference between Calcutta and Karachi golf courses. At Karachi, the course was flat like the surrounding desert with a yellow sandy soil and not a blade of grass to be seen – the greens were, in fact, called 'browns'. A well-hit drive would go as far as 300 yards without hindrance on the hard smooth surface of the fairway. Approach shots were the devil as can be imagined with the ball on a hard billiard table surface instead of sitting up on a close cropped turf.

Another aspect of the more pleasant side of Calcutta was its night life. This was substantially curtailed by the imposition of a curfew. All ranks had to be indoors by 1 a.m. This law was introduced while I was away from Calcutta but I was told on good authority that quite a large party of brass hats was arrested by that redoubtable body of men, the M.P.s, on the first night together with various junior officers. I am all in favour of early nights, especially when you are working hard, but it does rather cramp the style of a nightclub if it has to pack up at 12.30. The Three Hundred Club was the only worthwhile nightclub in Calcutta where there was a certain lively atmosphere and sense of good living and expensive amusement. The interior colour scheme was cream and red: cream walls and curtains, red bar counters and leather topped stools. The band was quite good, the drinks were no worse than anywhere else, but the food they served definitely let you down. Very expensive but very poor. However, the real amusement, as in all nightclubs, was the people one saw there. There was always one or two of the more well-known celebrities of Calcutta's younger set. Celebrities purely of the frivolous variety, I mean.

I made various journeys and tours of inspection from Calcutta and one of these, a day trip only, consisted of a flight to Imphal. We went in one of the larger American transport planes, ten of which were engaged on a five day special job taking over material for aerodrome construction. This construction was the direct outcome of our recent research work and the first large scale attempt to put it to the test. I was therefore taking a special interest in the whole procedure. These transport aircraft of the U.S.A.A.F. were working themselves to their utmost capacity on this particular job and very considerable credit is due to them. They were making two trips every twenty-four hours which did not leave very much time for maintenance, loading and rest for the pilots. They only lost one plane during the whole episode: it was shot down by a Jap Zero somewhere over the Manipur Hills. The pilot of my plane told me that on the day before he had had a near brush with a Zero himself, the Jap had chased them just as they were approaching the high range of mountains which have to be crossed in order to enter the Imphal Plain. He had power-dived and shaken off his pursuer by dodging low along the steep-sided valleys of the mountainous country. The Zero had eventually run out of ammunition, but not before scoring a hit in the right wing which was unpleasantly near the petrol tank. This was pointed out to me to add weight to his story and perhaps to shake my confidence as well.

We covered the round trip of 800 miles there and back in six hours, spending two hours at the airfield, and no enemies were encountered either way.

The R.E.s were doing a grand job here and showing their customary aptitude for adapting themselves to a new task. They were a special corps of Indian airfield engineers. Nobody had ever seen this process before but they were getting along building this emergency runway at a goodly speed. Things were not made easier for them by the constant daily raids they were receiving from Japanese aircraft, dropping bombs and scattering machine gun fire. The Japs had, in fact, been showing a lively interest in this strange looking work which was going on at such speed. This was at the time when we were beginning to push them back along the road to Tamu in April 1944 and they evidently did not like the look of these feverish airfield activities of ours near Imphal. In ten days the whole show was finished and in active operational use. This was sure proof then that we, in our experimental and pioneer capacity, were succeeding and gave grounds for renewed efforts in improving and perfecting. I am sorry to say, however, that there was still a certain lack of zeal and encouragement on the part of some of my colleagues and superiors. They were not convinced, seeing was not believing with these men. 'There must be something wrong with it somewhere' they said to themselves. And so we struggled on with our experiments. [Soon P.B.S. airstrips were proved to be a huge success. It was also found to be a useful material for new roads. See section on P.B.S. at the end of the chapter.*]

It was a steep climb out of the valley again on our homeward journey. The altimeter read 11,000 feet by the time we were passing over the great Manipur range, stretching from Kohima and the Naga hills to the north, down to the Chin

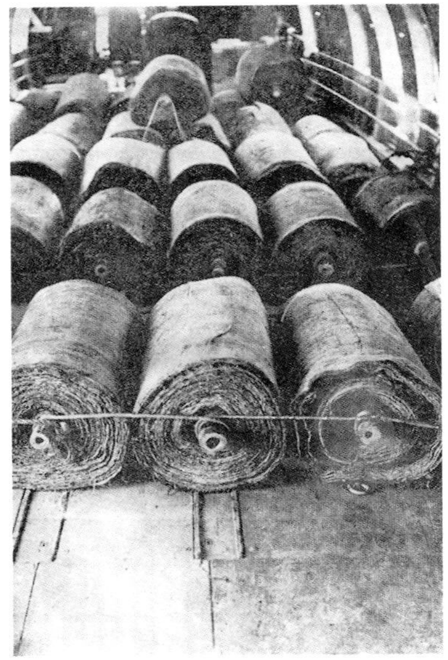

Left: Rolls of Prefabricated Bituminous Surfacing loaded in a transport plane, to be used in runway construction

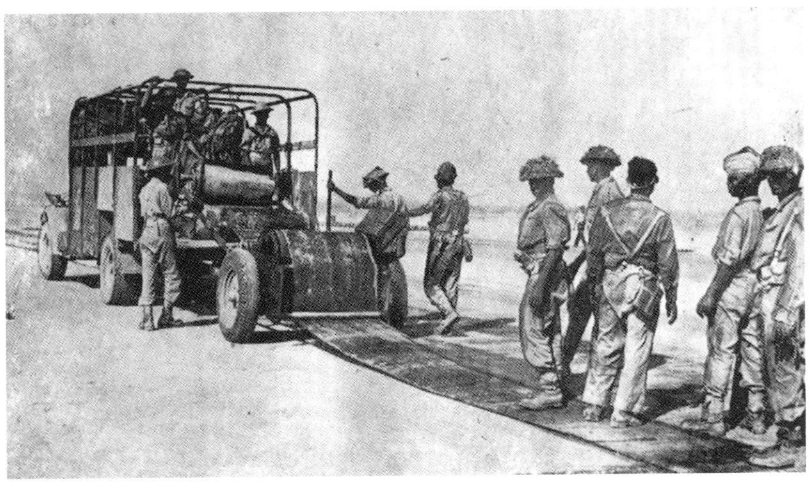

Below left: Laying P.B.S. with the 'Stamplicker'

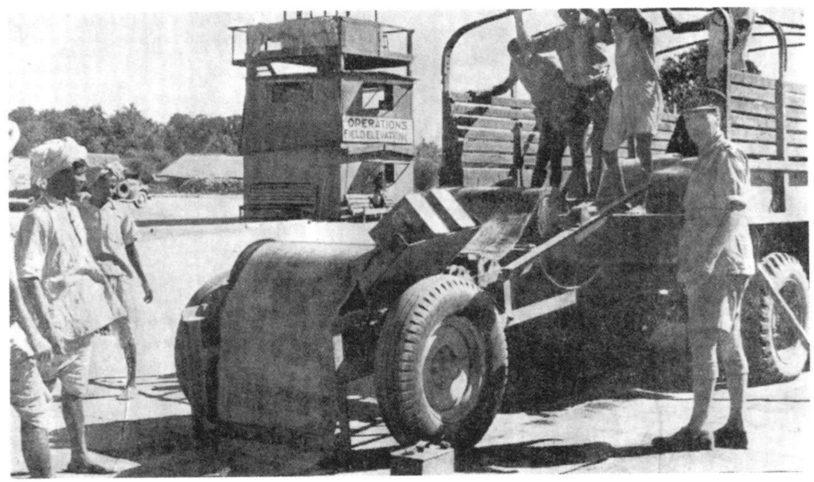

Below: The 'Stamplicker' ready to start laying P.B.S.

hills in the south. Thick jungle territory occupied by the Japs was pointed out to me but we could not see any visible signs of them. The Jap is a master at natural camouflage.

The sky was clear with small yellow tinted clouds in the far distance and the view was superb as we approached the enormous fertile plain of the Ganges Delta. This vast green patchwork quilt of cultivated fields spotted with minute farmsteads, each with its clump of trees and its water tanks, was divided and sub-divided by rivers and tributaries winding across the surface like bunches of silver ribbons strung out in haphazard array.

I had met an old architect friend on the airfield whom I had last seen two and a half years before in England when we were Acting Unpaid Lance Corporals together in a Sapper Training Battalion. He was making an excellent job of this pioneer construction work with his Indian engineer soldier's job which was never dreamt of in our far off training days. It is strange how one meets people one least expects to see, in circumstances quite unpredictable.

If I may indulge a little wishful thinking, I hope that our next meeting may be in England where we shall both be practising architects, planning and building for peaceful ends.

---

*EDITORIAL NOTE: At this point in time, at the beginning of the new century, the year 2000, I am now able to describe the results of Charles Baskin's work with the factories. He invented a material called P.B.S. which stands for Prefabricated Bituminous Surfacing. This consisted of about a three-foot-wide strip of a material which looked like roofing felt and was about 50 yards in length. It was then made into rolls like a large Swiss-roll with a thick bamboo pole in the centre of the roll. The laying operation on an earth-based runway was quite simple. The P.B.S. roll was placed on what Baskin called 'a Stamplicker'. This consisted of a large metal tank filled with petrol and provided with two wheels. The vehicle was towed behind an army truck unwinding the P.B.S. as it progressed. A second layer was unrolled beside the first one, overlapping it by six inches. The roll had passed through the petrol which softened the bitumen surface and made it stick to the adjoining strip of P.B.S. This process was carried on strip after strip, eventually completely covering a runway. A light roller was finally run over the whole runway to ensure the P.B.S. strips would become a homogeneous runway surface.

Experiments were carried out initially by dragging the 'Stamplicker' by hand to decide on what overlap was necessary.

The soil preparation was, of course, very important and Baskin instructed the American soil moving engineers with regard to levelling off the runway area and compacting the soil by means of rolling it with a very heavy machine. We prepared an illustrated pamphlet with instructions for using P.B.S. in the construction of runways, taxi tracks and roads (see photographs from the pamphlet opposite).

CHAPTER TWELVE

LEAVE

I arrived at Darjeeling to spend fourteen days, leave with the conviction that I was going to enjoy every hour and every minute. I was quite prepared to do nothing all day and see nobody, and if the weather was cloudy, misty and wet, as I had been assured it would be by people who knew Darjeeling in June, I would still like it. Such is the mood of someone who has spent recent months in rushing, talking, telephoning, writing and more rushing; in pushing people who did not want to be pushed and interesting people in something which they were determined not to be interested in. Futhermore, I was someone who had not had leave for three long years and was suffering from acute sketching starvation. All this is perhaps putting it on rather thick, so I will add that during those three years I had at least been one of those fortunate metaphors, a square peg in a square hole, doing jobs for the most part about which I had previous knowledge and experience and which I could pursue with willingness and interest.

Sketching above all things was what I was determined to do on this long awaited leave, even if it meant sketching mists and clouds only. The other distractions, or should I say attractions, which usually crowd in upon soldiers on leave, such as tennis, swimming, dancing, propping up the bar and the usual humdrum social activities with wine, women and song, would have to take second place. But did they? Well, I weakened up to a point, but I did achieve about fifteen watercolours and pencil drawings in all.

My friends had been right when they said I was choosing the wrong month for sketching. Low clouds and mist hung over the hills and valleys all day, and blue skies were a rarity. But the early morning and late evenings were usually sunny and it was at an early hour one morning that I caught my first glimpse of that magnificent mountain, Kanchinchanga. The

Right: 35 Kanchinchanga through vapour

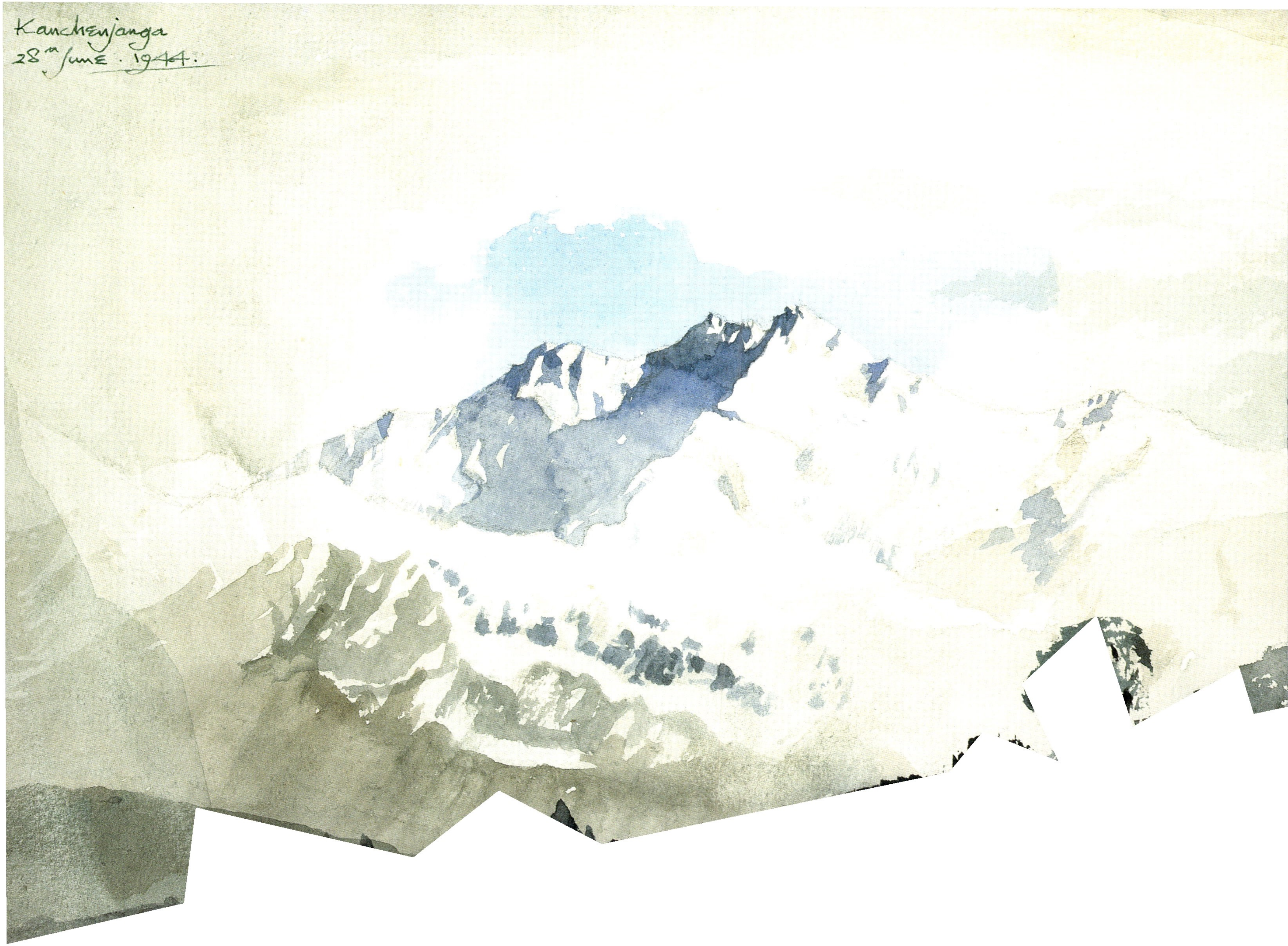
Kanchenjunga
28th June . 1944.

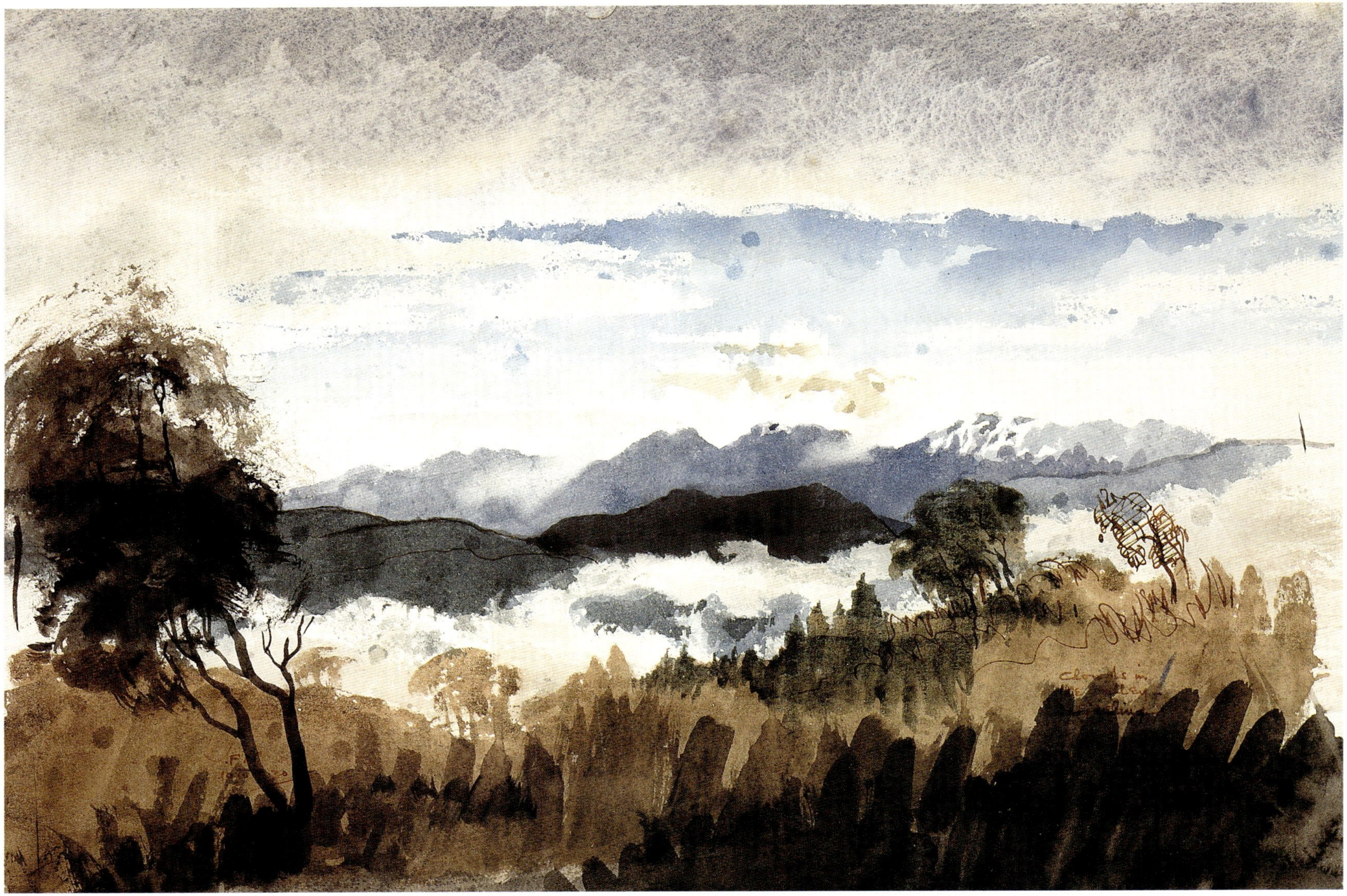

solid line of distant clouds, which always completely masked the whole snow clad range, parted on this occasion in one small sector, revealing as luck would have it, the very peak of Kanchinchanga itself, glistening in all its white brilliance, a phantom spectacle suspended in vapour. Next morning the vision passed as a curtain of cloud drifted across.

My sketch of 'Kanchinchanga through vapour' was an attempt to capture this dramatic view of the third highest mountain in the world. I was not given many opportunities of painting it as I only saw it about six times, at not longer than five minutes a time, during my entire leave. These glimpses were consequently most precious and I had to take the fullest advantage of them in order to build up the complete sketch. Numerous pencil sketches and notes eventually led to a finished drawing on which colour washes could be added as opportunities occurred. I had insisted on getting a room with a window facing the mountain so the task of waiting for 'the moment' when the snow-covered peak chose to expose itself was not so difficult.

Left: 36 Clouds in valley, Darjeeling

Overleaf left: 37 Kanchinchanga, on canvas paper

Overleaf right: 38 Kanchinchanga Range

I must admit I adopted more guile and less honesty in making the other painting of 'Kanchinchanga Range'. I suppose I did actually see every peak in the range at one time or another but certainly never all at once as shown here (see picture No. 38). Everyone was always telling me how marvellous the mountains look in the cloudless fine weather, so I thought I would try and reconstruct this much vaunted view. I resorted to photographs to aid me and all of them showed a little white puff of cloud on Kanchinchanga itself which is rather a pleasing feature and emphasises the amazing sense of height which this mountain possesses. Personally I like the misty view best as there is more movement and drama about it, but that is purely a matter of opinion.

So much for mountains. I did not spend my whole leave, however, watching and waiting for glimpses of mountains but a very deep impression was made on me by this superb range, surely one of the finest mountain scenes in the world and undoubtedly far more impressive than the view of Mount Everest not far away.

I eventually did most of the things that most soldiers do on leave at an Indian hill station, namely drinking in the club,

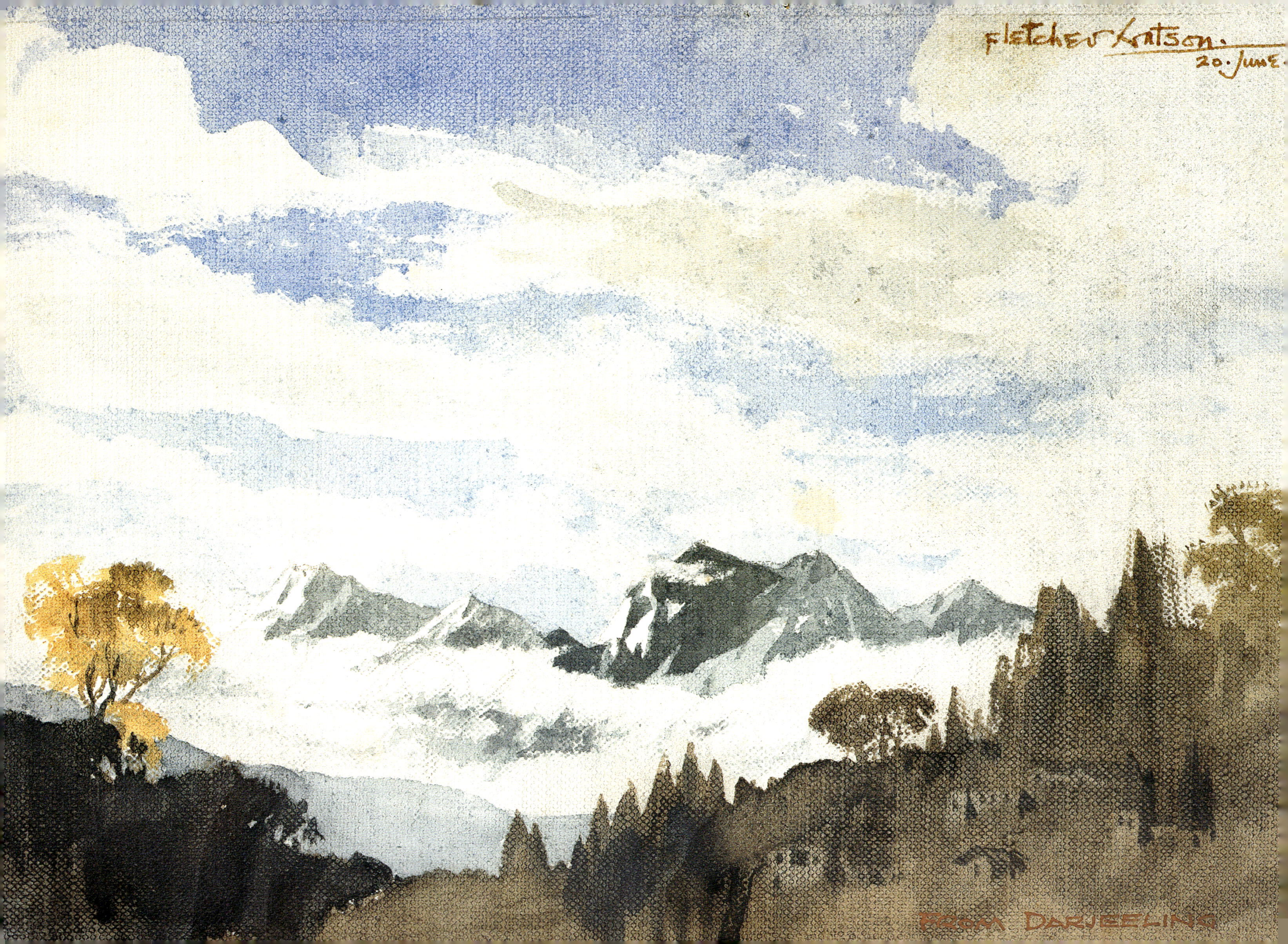
Fletcher Watson.
20. June.
FROM DARJEELING

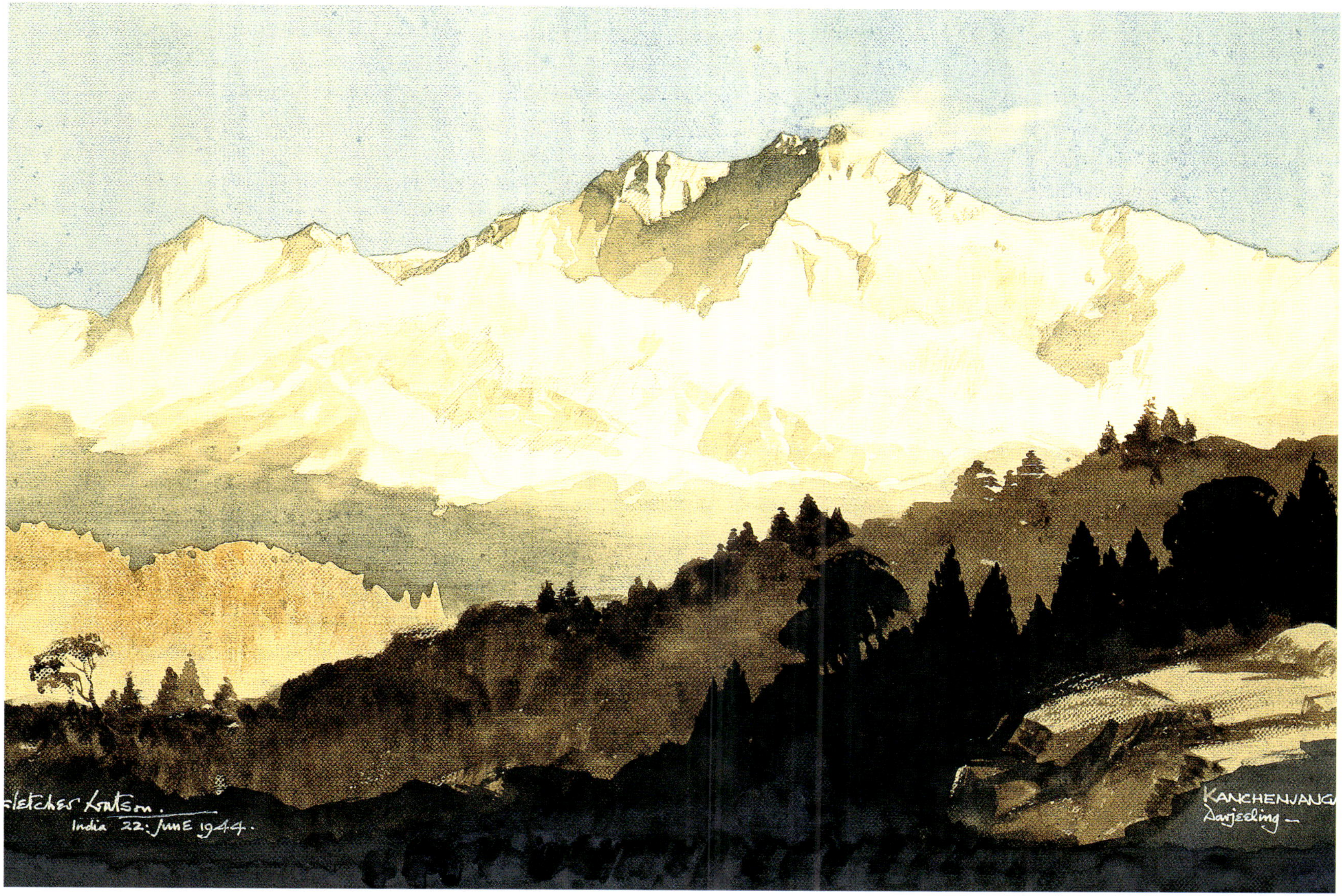
Fletcher Watson.
India 22: JUNE 1944.
KANCHENJANGA
Darjeeling –

dancing and dining at the club, playing tennis and having tea at the club. In fact, the majority of the time the club was the only form of amusement. One went in to the crowded bar and on nearly every occasion saw a fresh face one knew: 'there is old so-and-so, did not know he was having leave' was the phrase constantly on one's lips.

I came to know a very charming young woman whose train of thoughts seemed to run somewhat on the same lines as my own as regards appreciation of scenery and so on. She introduced me to the finest piece of river landscape I have seen in India, the Tista valley. The river Tista runs 5,000 feet below Darjeeling, and to it we repaired in a car one day with picnic baskets, bathing costumes, dogs and most important of all, sketching material.

I do not know how well known the Tista valley is, but if its full beauty were realised by many people it would surely be visited more often. As it was, we had it to ourselves, except for two old local fishermen. This was a type of scenery which reminded me of rivers in South Wales and I do not hesitate to say was quite as beautiful.

After a bathe in icy water, very welcome in the great heat compared with Darjeeling's low temperature, I settled down to the painting 'The Little Ranjit river'. My friend, with her black dog and incidentally her knitting, gave a pleasant form of interest to the flat sandy foreground, while the angle of the tree outlines and hillside in the background made a happy composition with practically no alteration from nature necessary in forming a well balanced picture. In addition, I did the usual two or three pencil sketches annotating the colours of water, rocks and trees, all of which were very attractive. We stopped the car half way on our return journey up the narrow twisting mountain road to let out the boiling water from the radiator and take in a fresh lot of cold. This gave us time for a long last look at the beautiful Tista valley bathed in warm evening sunshine, while we finished off the remains of the picnic. Then back to the heights of Darjeeling shrouded in cloud and mist where they had not seen the sun all day.

There was an appropriately timed land slide on the Darjeeling mountain railway the day before I was due to leave. It succeeded in holding me back for two extra days, a dreadful calamity but one against which I made absolutely no complaint. Both road and rail were affected and the blockage was very nearly of a much more serious and permanent nature: if some of the larger portions of rock had followed the mass of

Right: 39 The Little Ranjit river

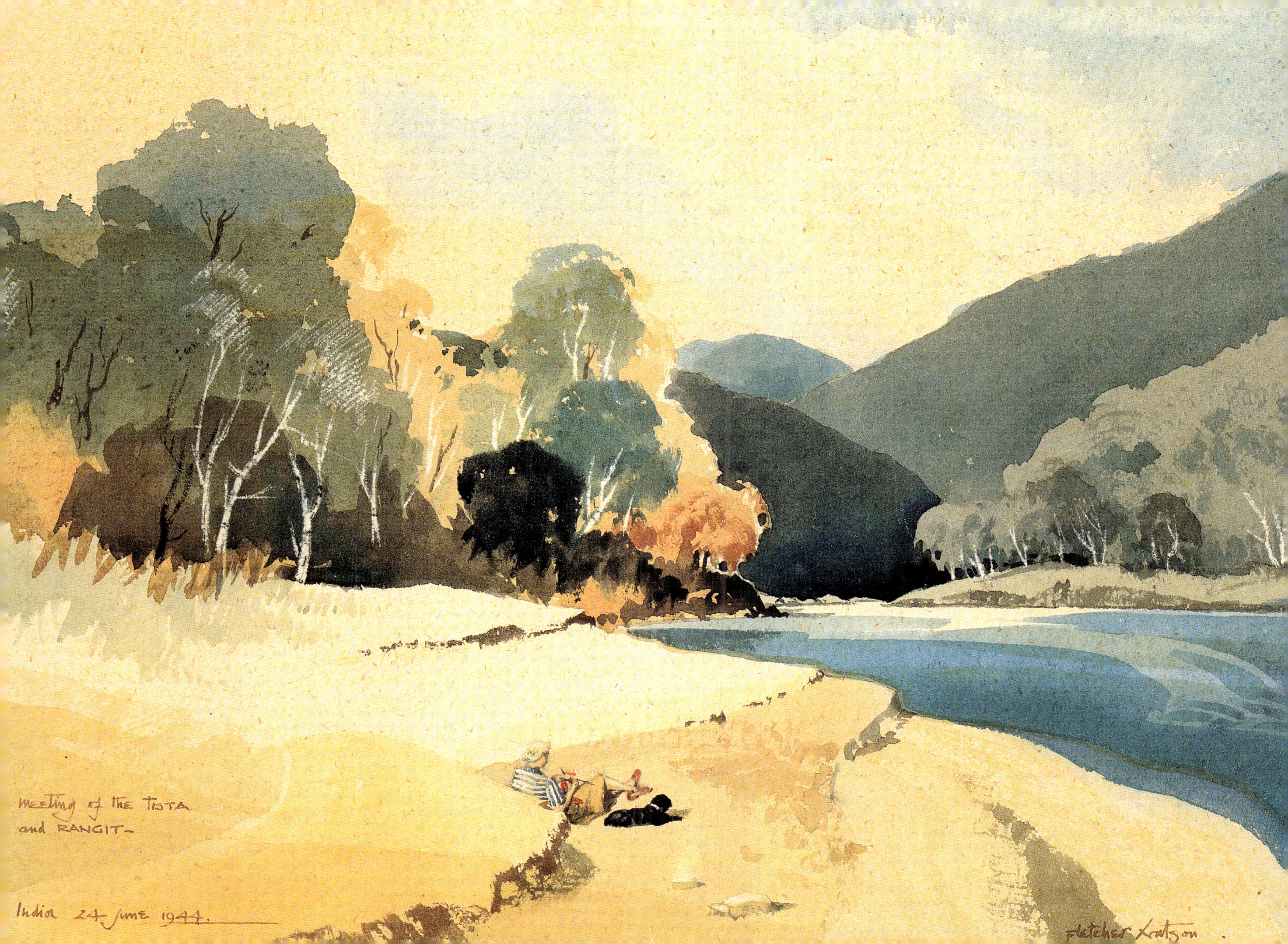
meeting of the Tista
and RANGIT-
India 24 June 1944.
Fletcher Watson

loose stones and earth, we might have been 'stranded' in Darjeeling for two or three weeks. But providence decided not to be as generous as that and the line was cleared sufficiently to allow a train to squeeze slowly past the critical point so as not to make a disturbance and cause further slides.

At Siliguri, where the little mountain railway terminates and the broad gauge begins, I experienced one of those maddening incidents which are rather apt to happen on Indian railways. They are amusing to look back on but simply infuriating at the time. It was late at night and I had been lulled into complacency by the R.T.O (Railways Transport Officer) who said I had plenty of time to have dinner on the station before the train went. I therefore took my time over the meal but as I strolled out of the dining room, I received a horrible shock: the train had actually started to move off. I was immediately galvanised into tremendous activity. No time to ask questions or abuse station masters if one did not want to spend the next twenty-four hours on the station. I tore along the platform, collering my bearer en route and told him to get coolies and throw the luggage into any available carriage door. Seizing a bag myself I leapt into a seemingly empty carriage – there were not lights – and from the step I endeavoured to direct the loading operations of my bags and bearer. I can think of no more hopeless state of affairs, the more I shouted and gesticulated, the more incapable they seemed to become. In the meantime the train gathered speed and I was fighting a losing battle. As I hung out of the train holding onto the hand rail I bumped into a wooden post and knocked it flat on the platform. We then sailed past the R.T.O. gentleman who had so grossly misled me and I gave him a pretty fair sample of bad language in a loud and furious voice. By this time the coolies had given up the chase, they had got in a panic and just ran aimlessly along the platform balancing the bags precariously on their heads and making no effort to push them into the train. My last words were shouted into the darkness as we glided past the end of the platform: 'Bring them on tomorrow.'

After a good many muttered swearings I eventually withdrew into the carriage and shut the door. I discovered that I had an Indian civilian as a companion and murmuring something to him about disgusting inefficiency of Indian railways in general, I curled up on the spare seat and went to sleep. I was slightly put out, therefore, next morning, when daylight revealed the presence of the Indian's wife and child of about two lying on the upper bunk. I made apologies for my indiscreet language of the night before and she was generous enough to say that she quite understood.

I think I must have sufficiently frightened the R.T.O. into taking some action in the matter as my bearer duly turned up complete with all the luggage next day and not a thing missing. He had been put on the first available train by the R.T.O. with no ticket for himself or the luggage. The only box I was really anxious about was the one containing my sketches and paint brushes etc. But all was well that ended well.

In all my four years in India I was only able to take leave twice, and for my second two weeks' leave I was able to visit that very beautiful place, Kashmir.

I took the train from Calcutta and my bearer booked me an air-conditioned carriage – that meant a large block of ice in the centre of the floor! The train journey, heading northwest ended at Rawlpindi, some 1,200 miles distant. From there, going north east about 100 miles by bus, I arrived at Srinagar in the depth of mountains and lakes. We passed through the Gulmara district, the most stunningly beautiful countryside, as seen in my picture 'Gulmara, Kashmir'.

We arrived late on the evening of 11 December 1944 and put up at Nedins Hotel, Srinagar. After supper I sat down in my bedroom at about 10.00 p.m. feeling dog tired and painted the scene of Gulmara from memory by artificial light. The cluster of old houses were probably built of clay lump with thatch roofs. The snow clad mountains made a marvellous back drop.

Not far away on a lake there were house boats moored and my bearer hired one of these sumptuous craft, complete with crew and a cook on board. The boat had two quite big rooms, a bedroom and sitting room with arm chairs and tables, big windows and a cosy stove. The weather was sunny but quite cold for sitting on deck sketching. I indulged in glasses of gin with hot water as I sat outside painting which kept me marvellously warm! Nagin Lake, with a cluster of old houses and trees, is one of my favourites, and my painting of this scene is a lovely composition.

Our boatman was most obliging and ferried our house boat all over the various lakes, anchoring wherever I found a view I wanted to paint.

On 14th December my bearer produced a tailor from a local village who measured me for a new coat and trousers. I

Overleaf left: : 40 Gulmara, Kashmir

Overleaf right: 41 Nagin Lake, Kashmir, painted from a house boat

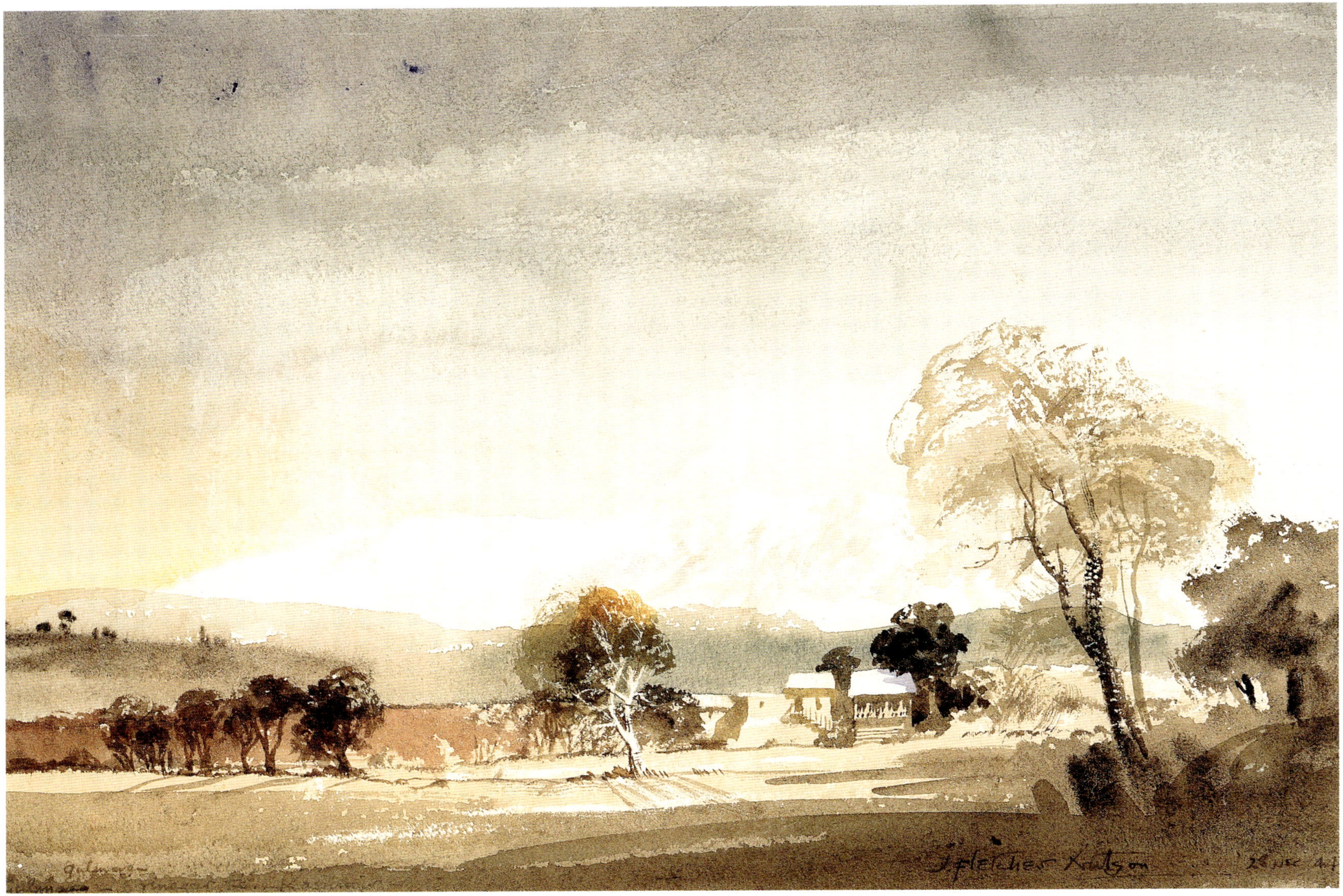

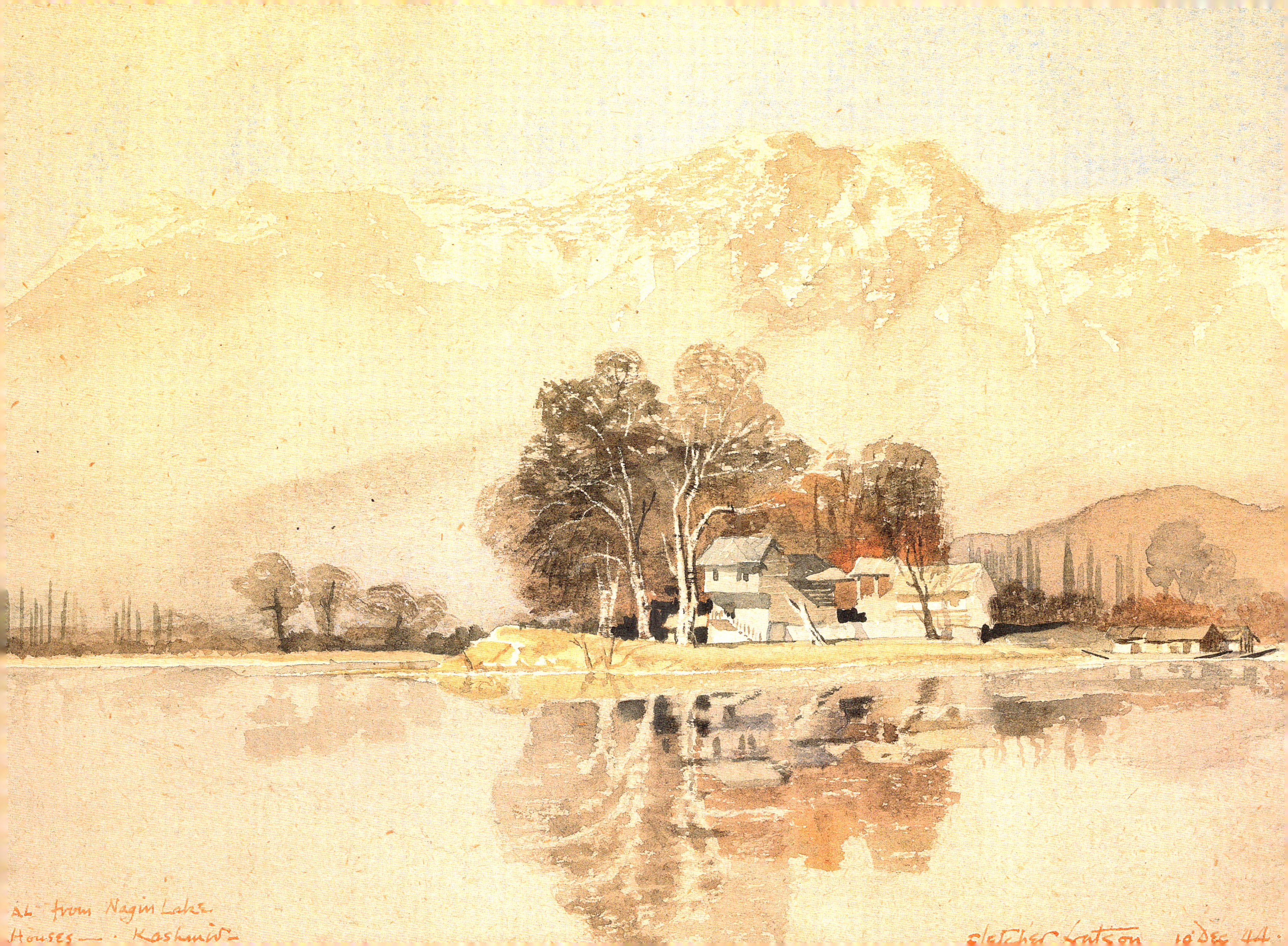
from Nagin Lake
Houses — Kashmir
Fletcher Watson 10 Dec 44

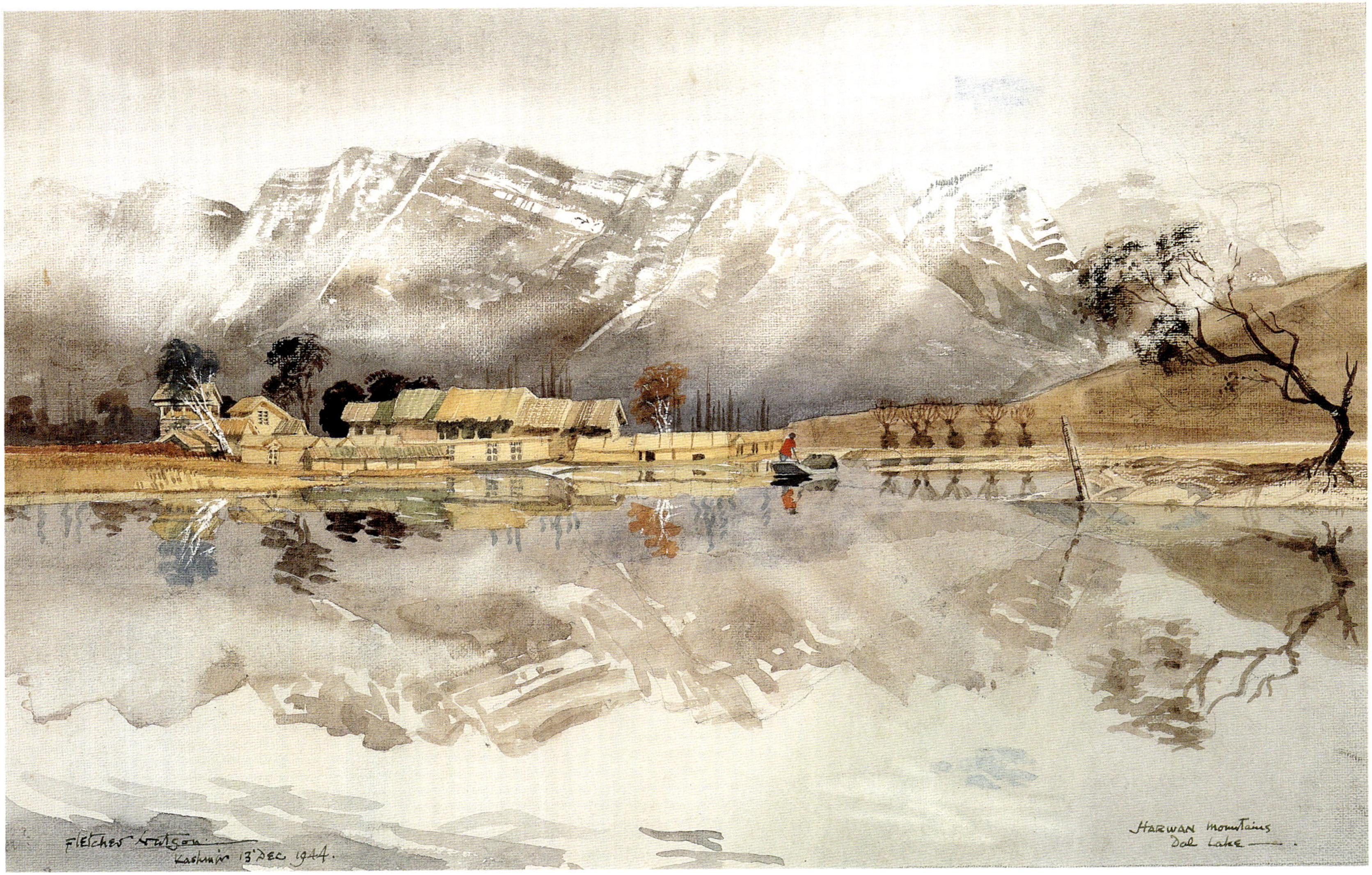

Above: 42 Dal Lake

Right: 43 Harmack mountains

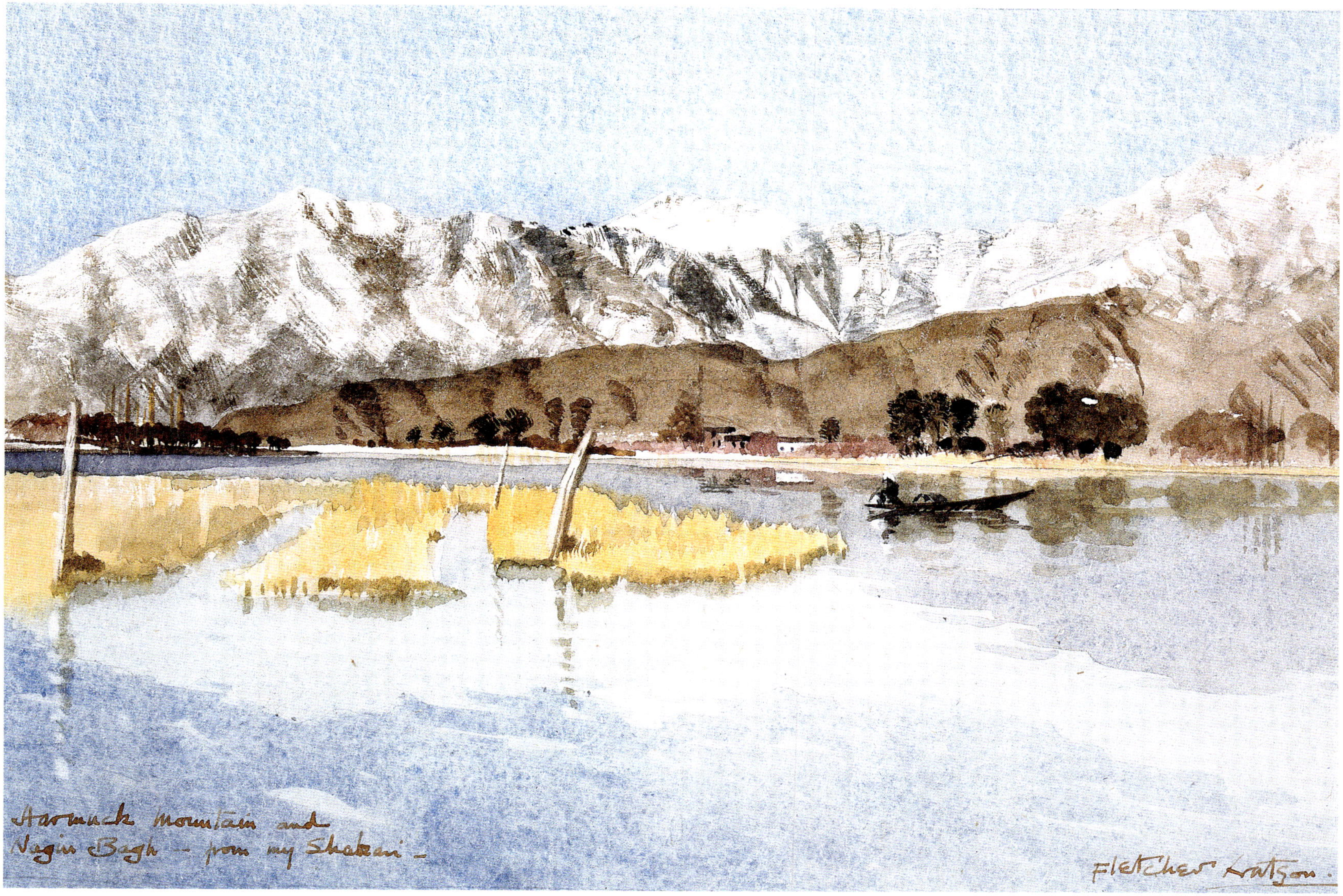
Harmuch mountain and
Nagin Bagh – from my Shikari –
Fletcher Watson.

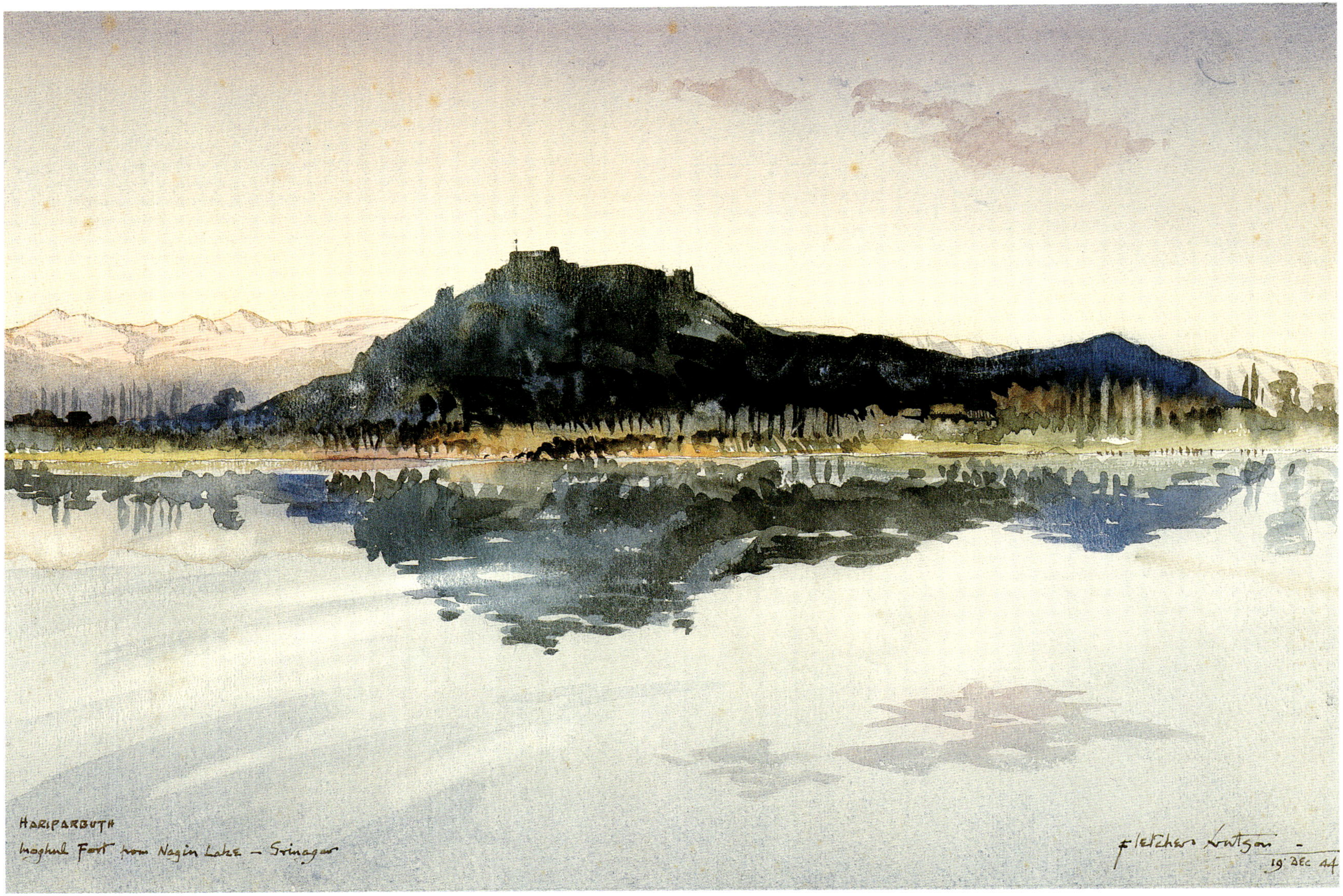
HARIPARBUTH
Moghul Fort from Nagin Lake – Srinagar
Fletcher Watson –
19 DEC 44

Left: 44 Hariparbuth mountain

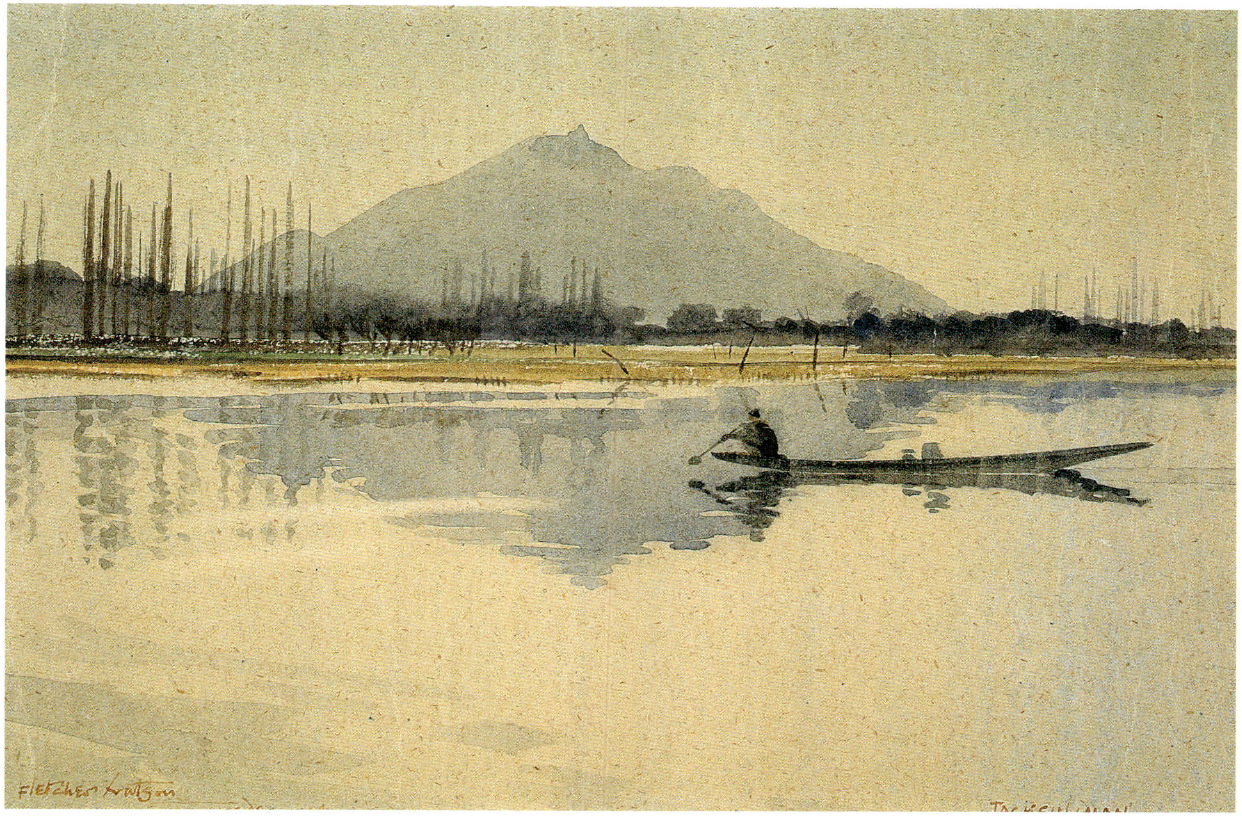

Right: 45 Tacksuliman mountain

only had my uniform and did not want to paint in that. The very next morning the tailor appeared with a lovely new tweed coat and trousers! He must have worked all night – what a marvellous service. I paid him well.

Altogether I painted five more lake and mountain pictures of various sizes, including Dal Lake, Harmack mountains (later exhibited at the Royal Society of British Artists in London, in 1945), and Hariparbuth mountain.

CHAPTER THIRTEEN

BICYCLES, BRASS HATS AND OLD TOMBS

G.H.Q. (General Head Quarters), that enormous arsenal of Staff Officers, completely dominated war time Delhi. Large bungalows, once occupied by Government civil servants living in solitary state, are now crowded with officers of the Army, Navy and Air Force.

The vast monumental secretariat blocks formerly in full use by the Government of India Staff, have been very largely taken over by the military, who have pushed all but the most important civil servants out into small hutments or to the hill station at Simla. Not content with commandeering all this, G.H.Q. have taken over several Maharajas' palaces to make officers' messes. They have also built a number of large blocks of temporary buildings on the ground surrounding the secretariat and in other parts of Delhi. Incidentally, it will surprise me very much if these so called 'temporary' buildings are ever pulled down; they will probably still be there in fifty years time to mar the landscape. 'Temporary' buildings still continue to be erected, and G.H.Q. keeps on expanding like some incurable disease that goes on spreading and which no man can stop.

It can be readily imagined from this, what a terrific number of officers and clerks are employed. I believe the figure is something like twenty five thousand in all. Picture my amazement, then, at being informed by the officer in charge of billeting at the Engineer-in-Chief's branch H.Q. that, as he had not been notified in advance about my arrival, he could not accommodate me for more than one night, after which time he was afraid I would have to return to where I had come from. I literally laughed in his face, whereupon he became rather irate and said that he was not joking, that Delhi was extremely full and that he meant what he said. Thankfully, the Brigadier who had originally sent for me to do a specific job circumnavigated this obstacle by squashing me into his own bungalow for a few days.

Bicycles are the most popular means of transport in Delhi,

RIGHT: Bicycles and brass hats

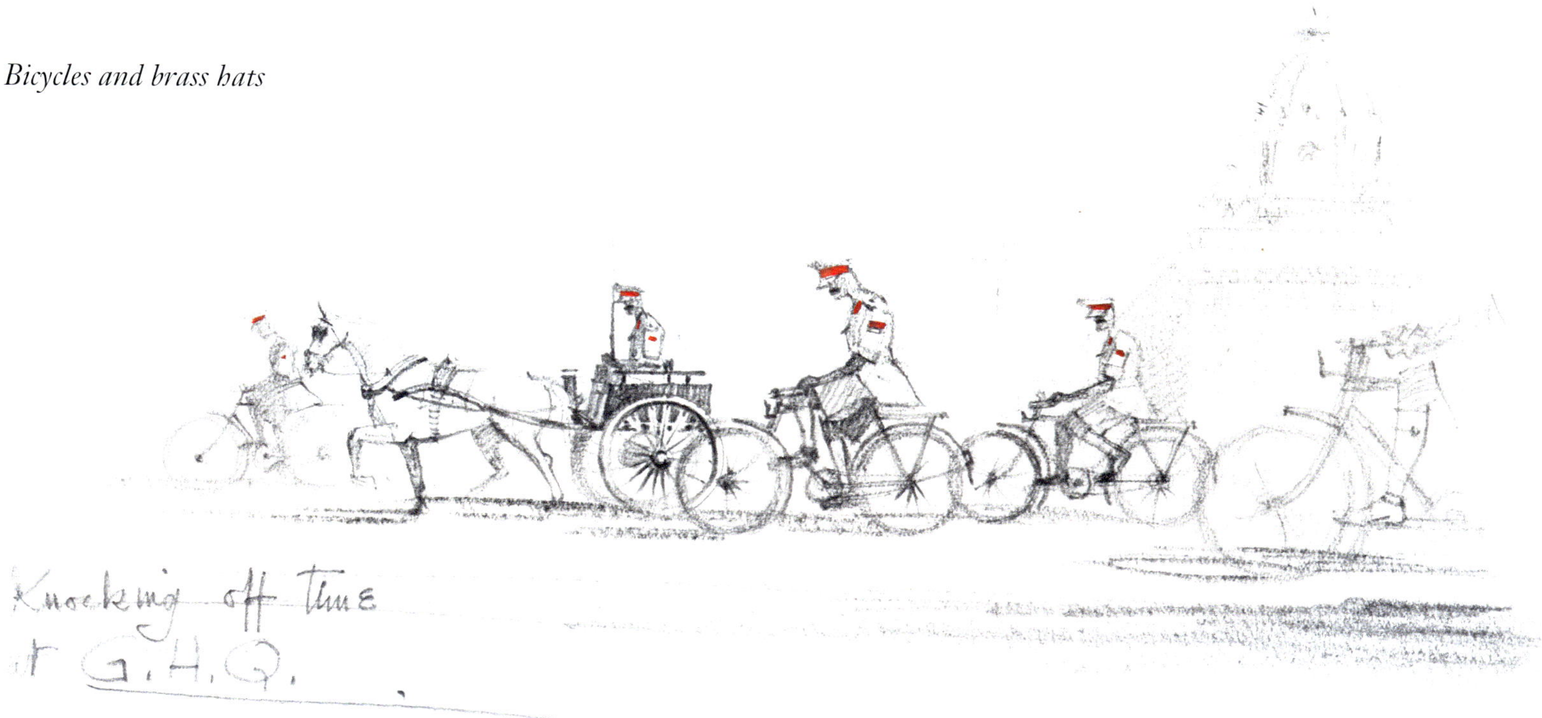

in fact they are a necessity and everybody owns one. If one happens to be outside G.H.Q. at about 6.00 p.m. when the majority are knocking off work, the place is a seething mass of bicycles. Senior officers of all the services together with the W.A.C.I.s and W.R.N.S. and, of course, hundreds of babu clerks, swarm down the roads leading from G.H.Q. in an unquenchable flood. I never actually saw an Admiral or a Field Marshal on a bicycle but I lived in hope.

I will try to describe a typical vision of a staff officer at work in G.H.Q. The scene is roughly this:

Picture a red-faced Englishman sitting at a large flat-topped desk holding a pencil in his right hand, a telephone in his left and a cigarette in his mouth. He has a worried expression on his face as his eyes anxiously scan a thick file of papers in front of him with a letter by its side marked with a blue label which says 'IMMEDIATE'. The thermometer on the wall registers 102°F and the sweat is trickling down his cheeks; a punka is slowly revolving over his head, which causes innumerable

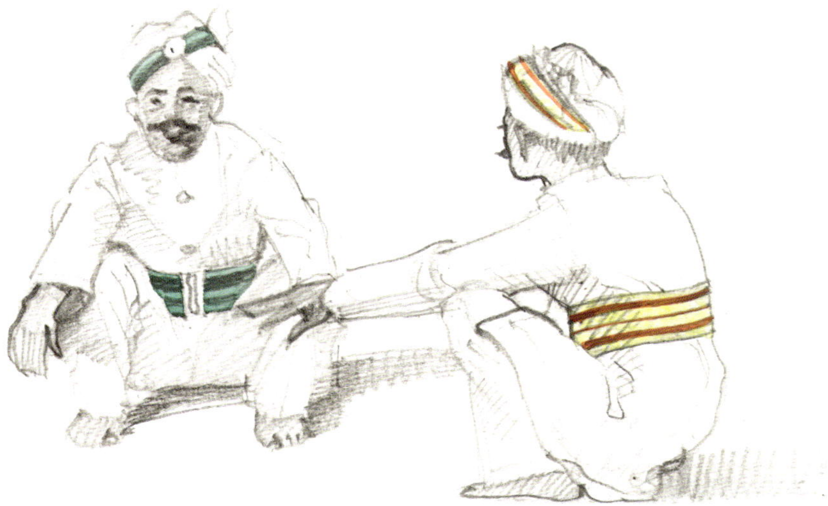

Above: Gossiping bearers

papers to flutter slightly on his desk. They are held down with little brass paperweights. There are two massive ink stands in the centre of the desk, one containing red and the other blue ink and various pens and coloured pencils rest in the wooden tray below. A chaprassi shuffles in carrying a heap of files, which he deposits in the 'IN' tray and shuffles out again. Next a bearer enters with red banded turban carrying a small tray of tea which is deposited on top of some books on the corner of the desk. The telephone conversation ends and the officer wipes the sweat off his brow; muttering something uncomplimentary about somebody, he presses a bell. Nothing happens. He scribbles something on the 'IMMEDIATE' file and presses the bell again. Next he shouts in a loud voice 'chaprassi'. This time something happens: the chaprassi shuffles in again, gets soundly berated and told to take a file 'jaldy, jaldy' to X, Y, Z's office. The face of the chaprassi remains expressionless; he is used to being told to do things quickly and not doing them with any speed. The officer next has a drink of tea, but this is interrupted by the telephone ringing again. It is the General speaking: 'If it is not too inconvenient I would like to have a chat with you.' It is never inconvenient with a General, and the invitation to chat is not always so cordial. And so it goes on.

I may state that the hot weather period in Delhi is not conducive to active brain work, especially during the hours of 2.00 and 4.00 p.m. Speaking for myself, I always feel extremely ineffective at that time of the day.

I was fortunate in having a rather unique job which involved a certain amount of drawing-board work as well as letter writing. But any office job is tedious in India and I welcomed a rather unusual form of diversion caused by a young dove who chose to build her nest precisely three feet from our dining room window. Every lunch time I could switch my mind right off the generals and files, and concentrate on natural history.

RIGHT: 46 The dove on the chick

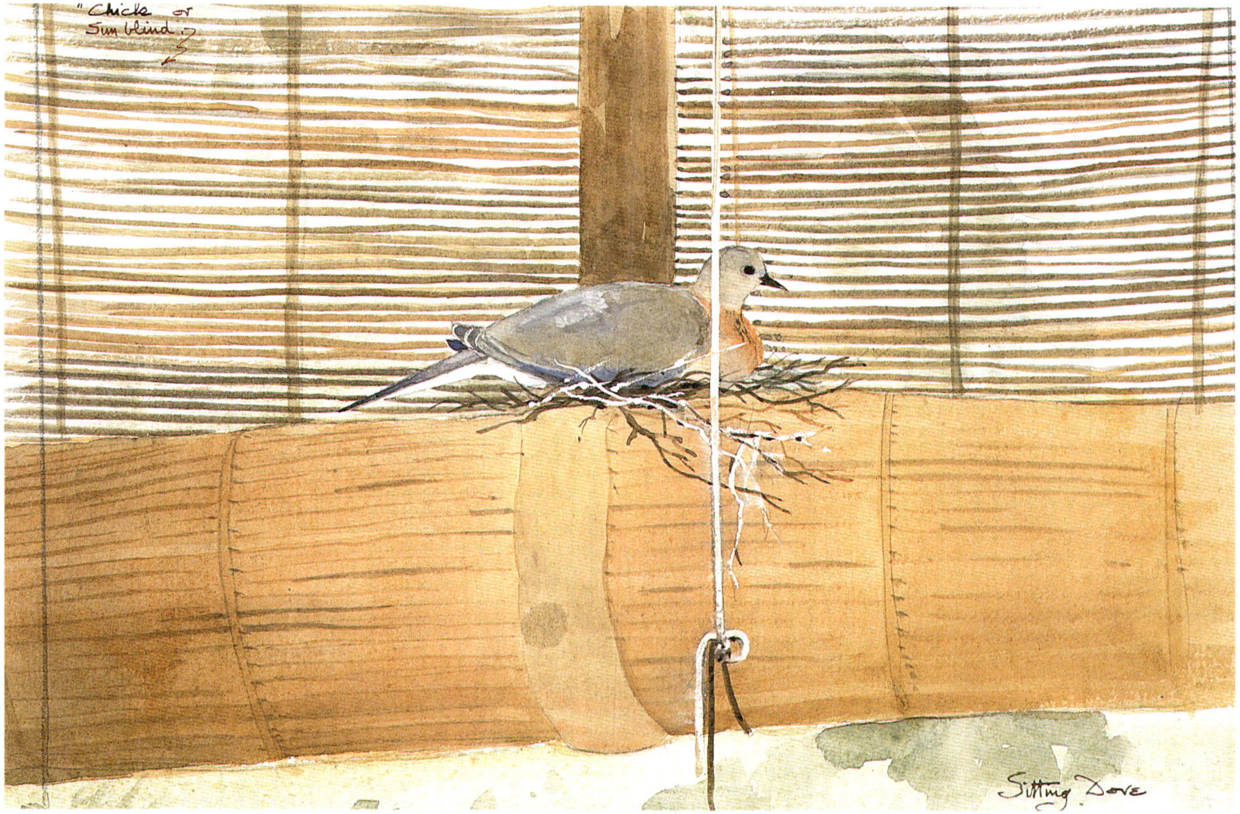

She built her nest, which was only about twenty sticks in all, on the rolled up portion of a chick, or sunblind. This was most awfully convenient for me to make observations but most awfully rash from her point of view as anyone who chose to pull the string holding the chick in position could send the nest rattling to the floor in no time. Strict instructions were therefore given to the staff that no one was to touch the fatal string. Nobody did, fortunately, and I was able to follow all stages of a birth and upbringing in the dove family very closely. Only one baby was produced and just as well as more than that

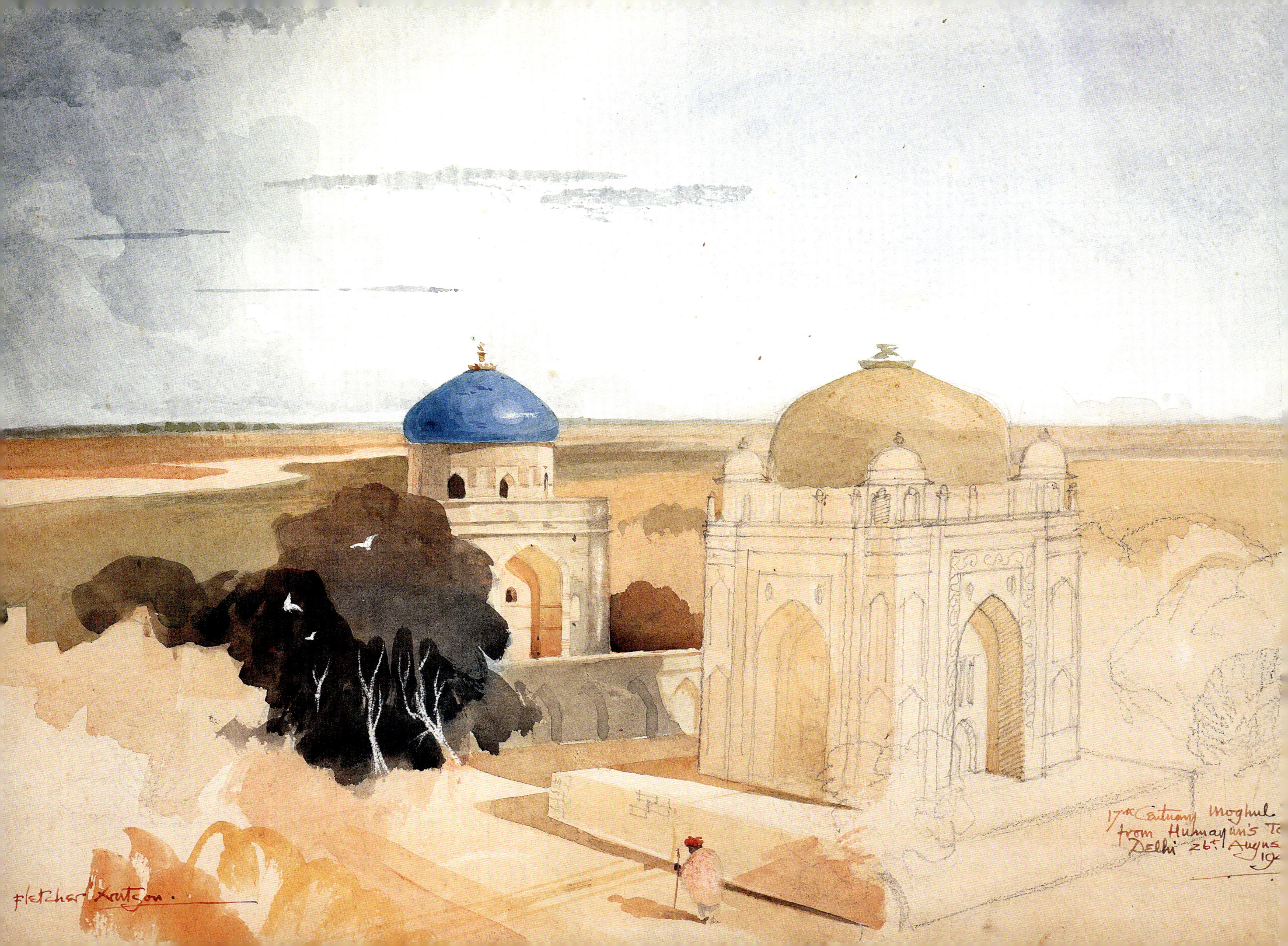
17th Century Moghul
from Humayun's
Delhi 26th

LEFT: 47 Moghul tomb with blue glazed tile dome, built in memory of Humayun's personal barber

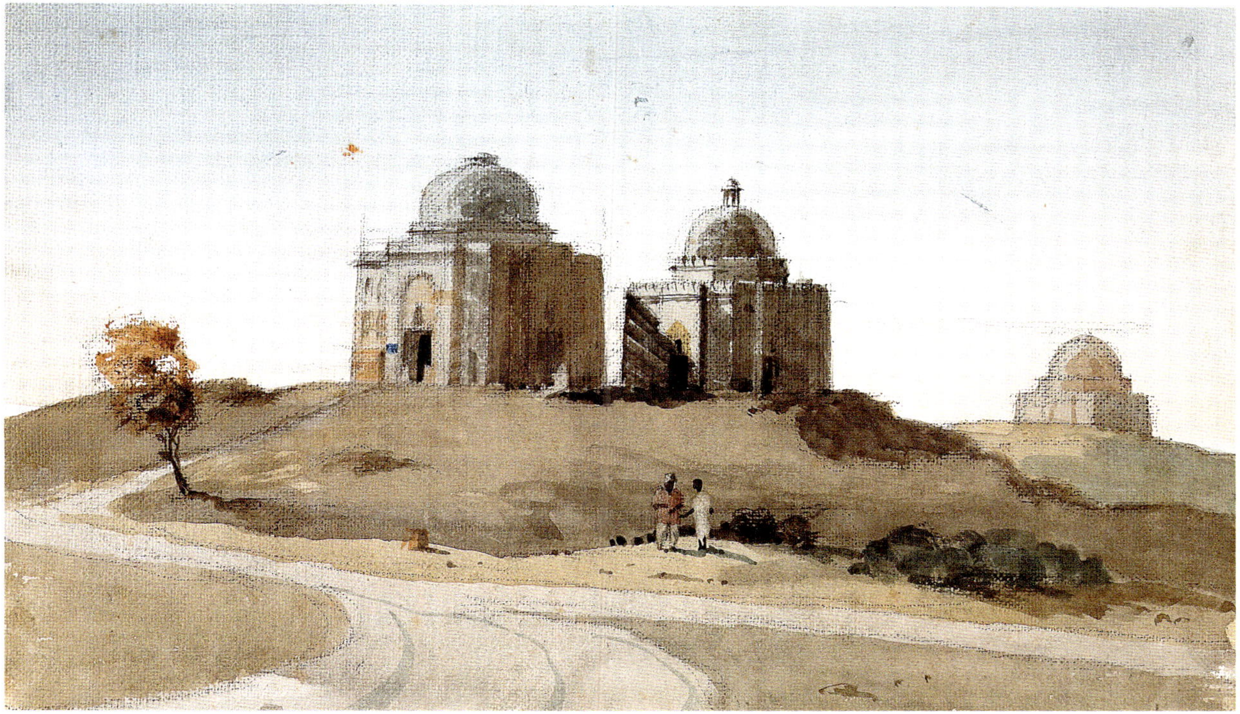

RIGHT: 48 Seventeenth-century Moghul tombs

would have been hard to keep from falling off this narrow cylindrical foundation. With this exceptional private view I was afforded by looking through the glass doors at really close quarters, I could not resist a sketch on a Sunday morning of Mrs Dove sitting on her one white egg.

Delhi is seething with old tombs and mosques of antiquity and great architectural interest, if only one could get away to explore them. Usually explorations got no further than Connought Circus, the main shopping centre of New Delhi, to buy a few of the necessities of life. But one evening a fellow engineer and I did make the effort to visit some tombs. We had a mutual interest in architecture, he being an engineer and town planner in civilian life, and I an architect. As we clambered all over the vast tomb of Humayun, peering into the dark undercroft up winding stone staircases and through archways on higher levels, we suddenly came upon the delightful view of two small tombs which I have tried to sketch, seen through an arched opening leading onto one of the outside balconies (picture No.48). The tomb with the blue glazed tile dome, which was built in memory of Humayun's personal barber, gives a jewel-like sparkle and focal point to the whole scene which would otherwise be sombre. The fading light did not allow me to complete this painting on the spot, and so it remains unfinished.

In the background twists the Jumna river making its way slowly eastwards where it eventually joins the Gangees at a point 400 miles distant, near Allahabad. The scale of the figures on the far bank in my painting 'River Jumna' (picture No.50) shows the amazing width of the river.

We climbed up onto the highest point of Humayun's great tomb into a little domed turret to watch the sunset. From there we could survey the whole prospect of new and old Delhi. The monumental Viceroy's House designed by Lutyens and the Secretariat Buildings by Baker looked very impressive in the middle distance while a little further away rose the many domed buildings and minarets of old Delhi. On the extreme right, Delhi Old Fort stood out on high ground with its massive defensive walls, making grey silhouettes against the fast reddening sky. Here was a spot where perfect peace could be found, away from the madding crowd, from the responsibilities, the petty intrigues and inter-departmental quarrels of G.H.Q. This surely is where all harassed and overworked staff officers should make a visit at least once a week. They would, I feel sure, return as I did, refreshed and elevated above the dust of military officialdom and pen pushing mania.

At the end of March 1945 I was instructed by G.H.Q. Delhi to visit South East Asia Command at Kandy, Colombo (now called Sri Lanka) where Admiral Lord Mountbatten was Supreme Allied Commander of the South East Asia war campaign, Navy, Army and Air Force. Mountbatten wanted to have full details about the top secret work I had been developing with American scientist Charles Baskin to construct Forward Fighter Aircraft runways very rapidly (see explanatory notes in Chapter Eleven, p.00). I spent some hours with Mountbatten's engineer staff explaining methods and procedures and materials to be used.

I found one happy opportunity on Easter Sunday, 1st April

Right: 49 Another Moghul tomb near Nazam-ud-Din, Delhi

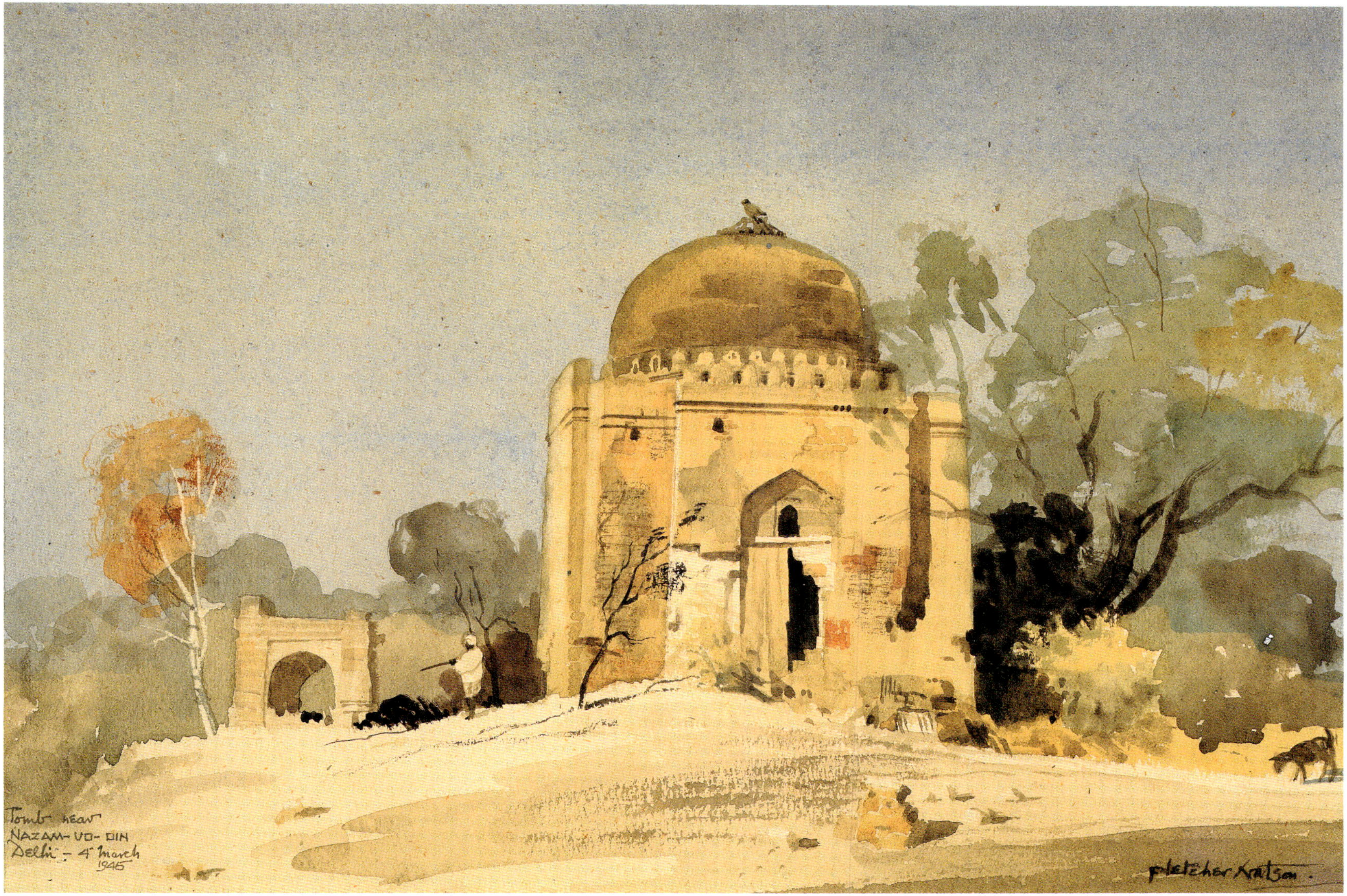
Tomb near
NAZAM-UD-DIN
Delhi - 4 March
1945
Fletcher Watson.

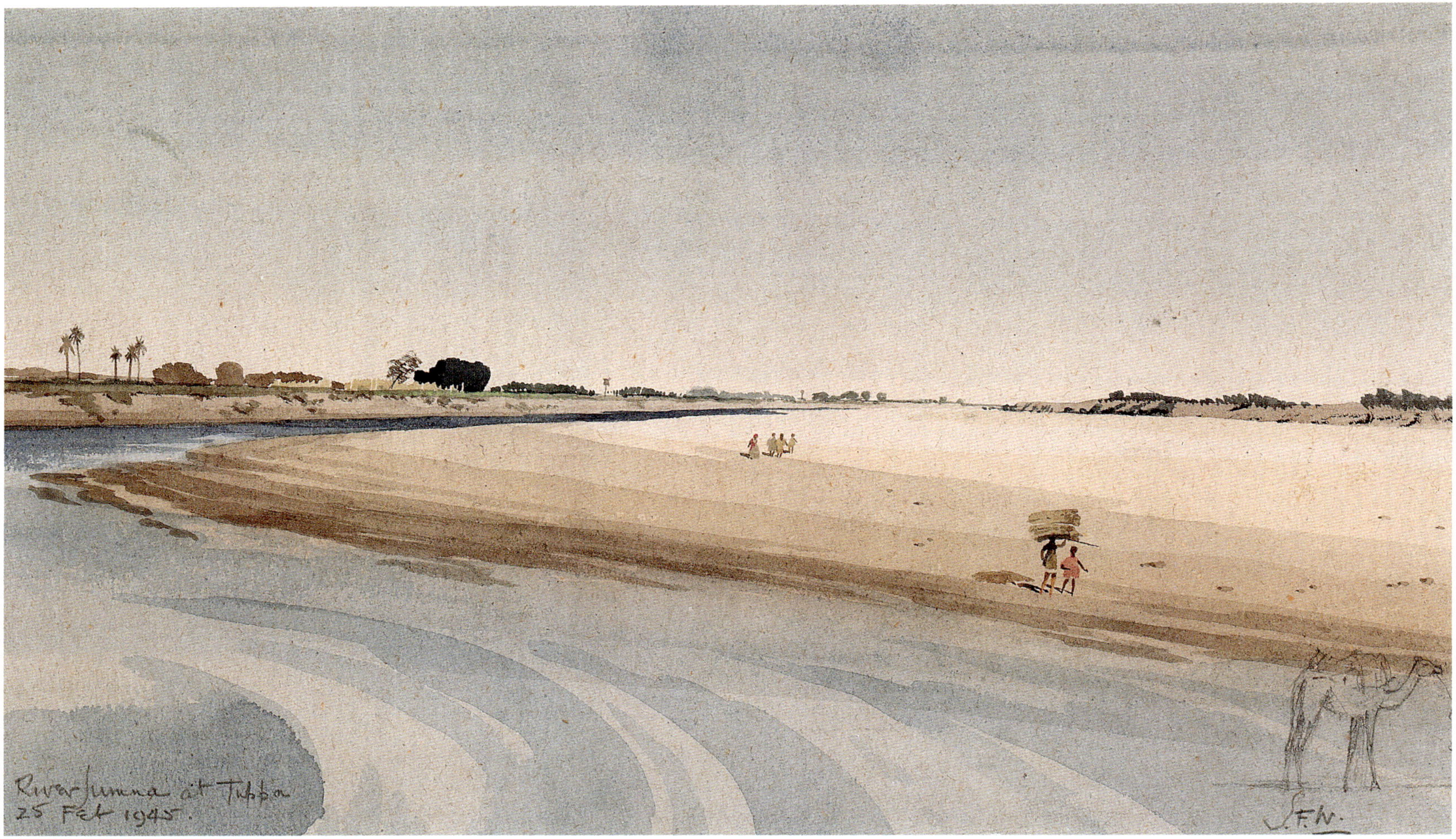

Above: 50 The River Jumna

RIGHT: 51 Octagon-shaped Temple of the Holy Tooth, Kandy

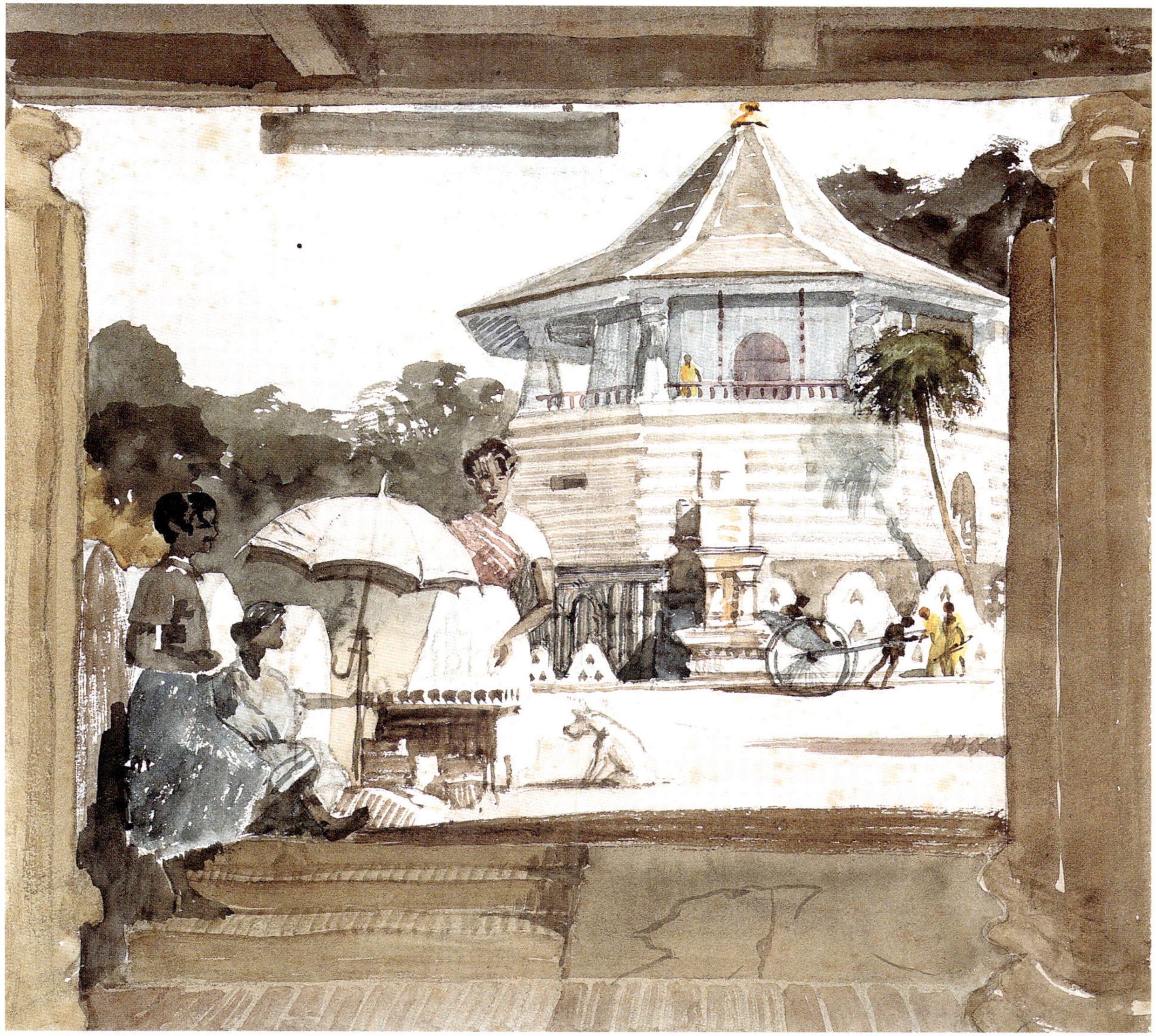

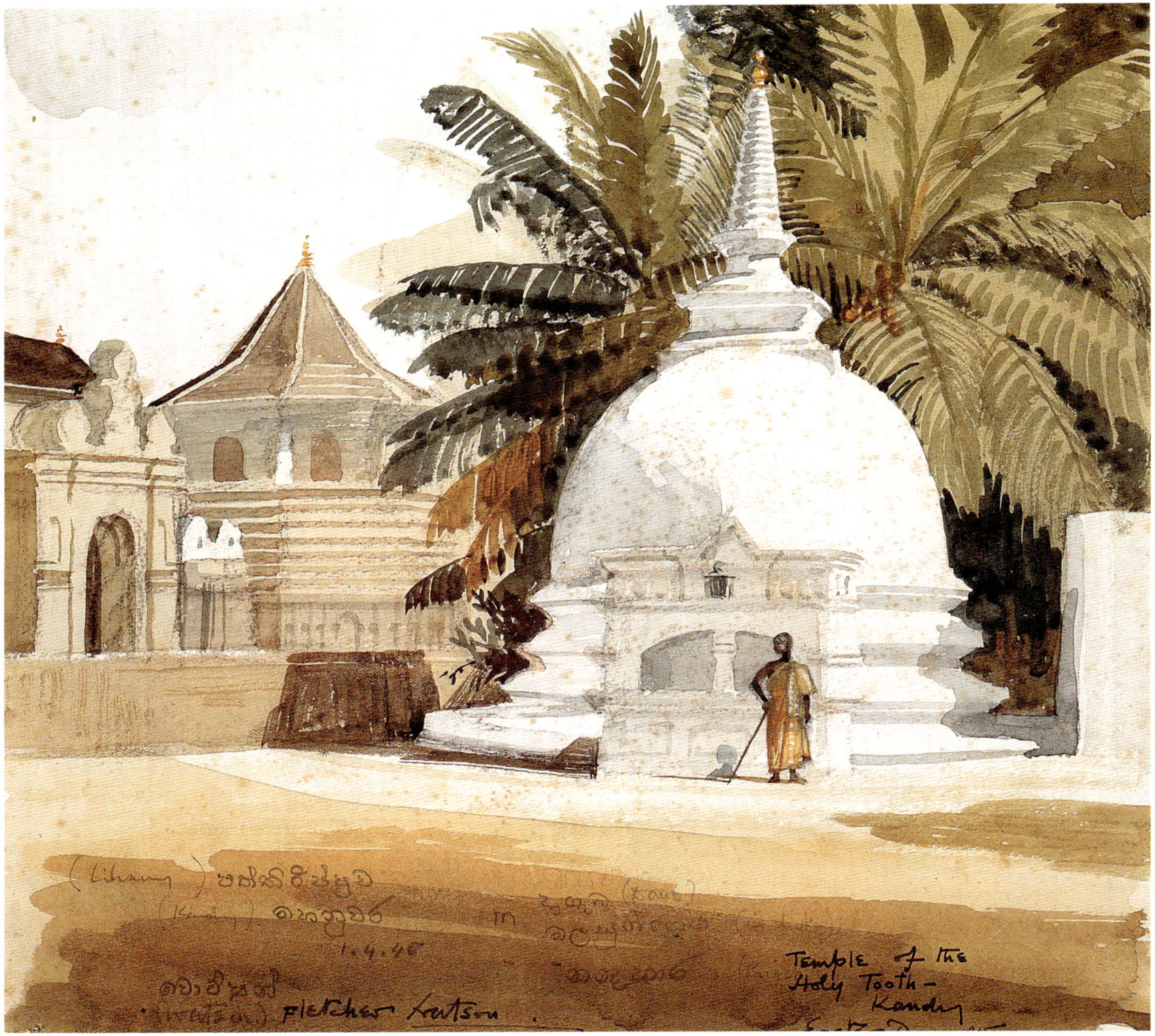

LEFT: 52 Domed tomb, with Temple of the Holy Tooth in the background

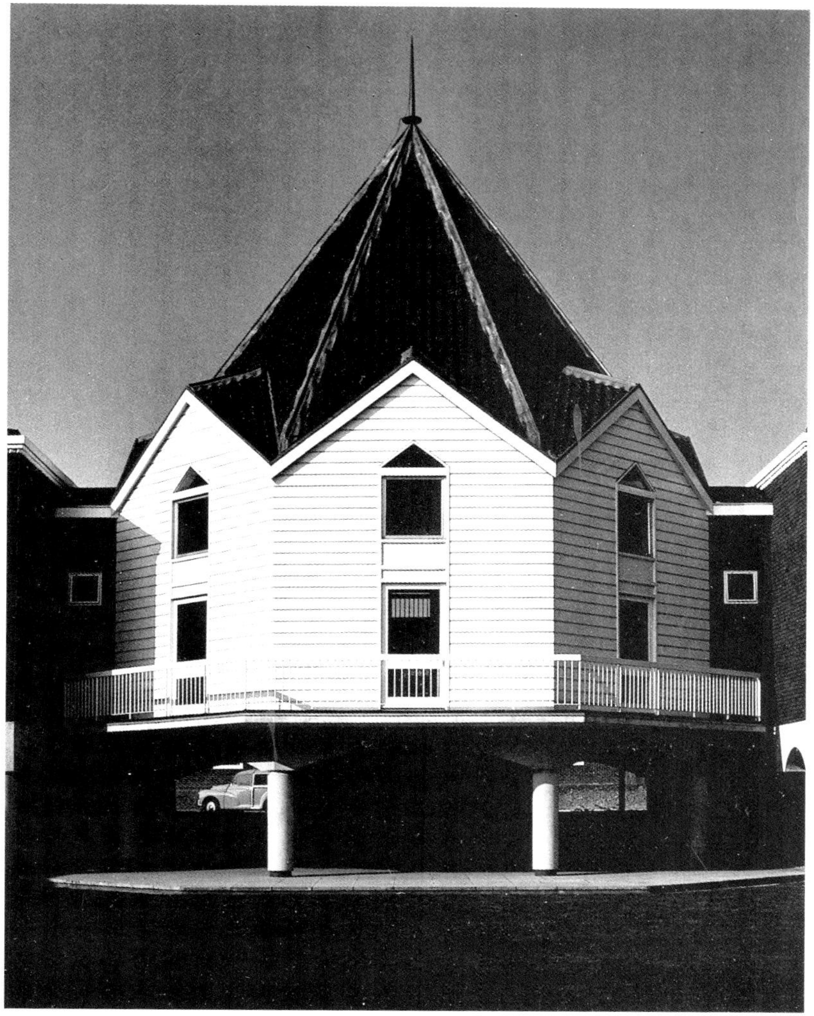

Above: Halls of Residence, Nottingham University

1945 to make a couple of paintings of the simply gorgeous Temple of the Holy Tooth*, Kandy. My picture (No.51) shows the very lovely octagon-shaped temple with its pointed tile roof. Observe the left foreground showing a stall selling models of animals. This was painted in the morning. Picture No.52 was painted in the afternoon of the same day, showing a very fine domed tomb with one of the priests in his yellow robe standing in front. He admired my picture very much and I persuaded him to write a few words in the left bottom corner in his fascinating Singelese writing – the first word was 'Librarian' and he told me this was his official job at the temple. He spoke good broken English.

---

* EDITORIAL NOTE: Long after the war, in 1964, when I was practising as an architect in my London office, I was commissioned by Nottingham University to build two new Halls of Resicence. For ore of these, Rutland Hall, I designed an octagon Library with pointed roof and arcading on the ground floor. This was designed with direct inspiration from the Temple of the Tooth and was a very successful feature of the quadrangle in which it was built!

CHAPTER FOURTEEN

WITH THE 14TH ARMY

My first few days at 14th Army H.Q. were spent sharing a basher hut consisting of a single room, with a sapper Lieutenant Colonel who had just returned from a forward position on the Burma Front where he and his troops had been constructing and defending an airfield.

He had managed to keep with him through all adversities his pet monkey and black mongrel dog, and this menagerie was established in our cramped quarter. We were really quite a matey party, the only snag being the monkey who became a little too presumptuous at times. He was very fond of climbing

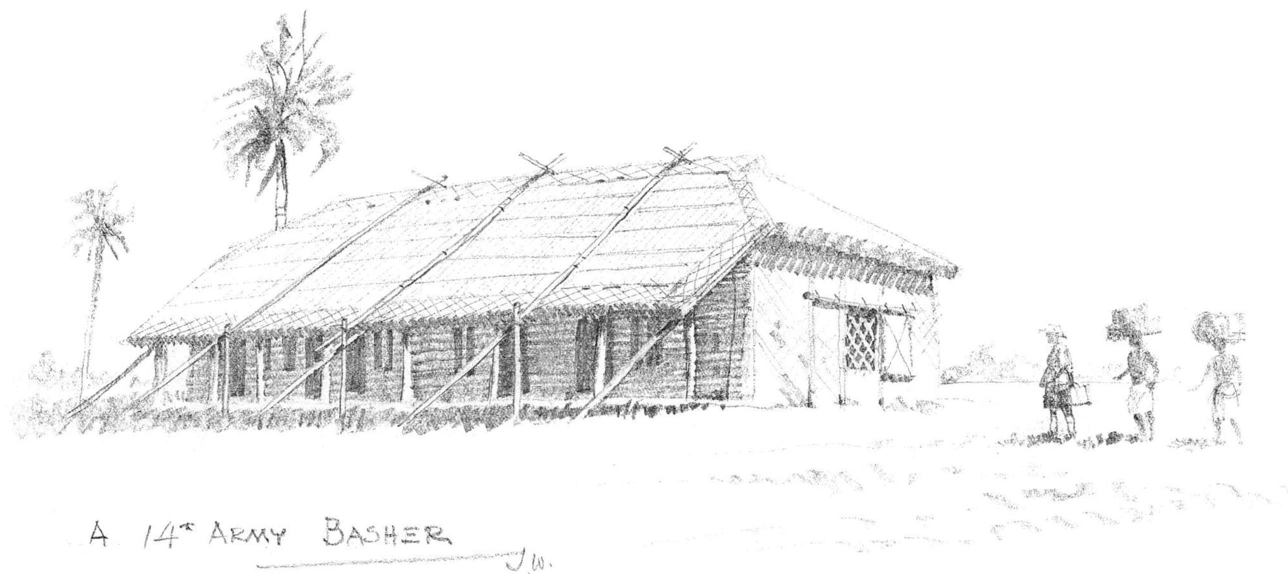

Left: Basher hut

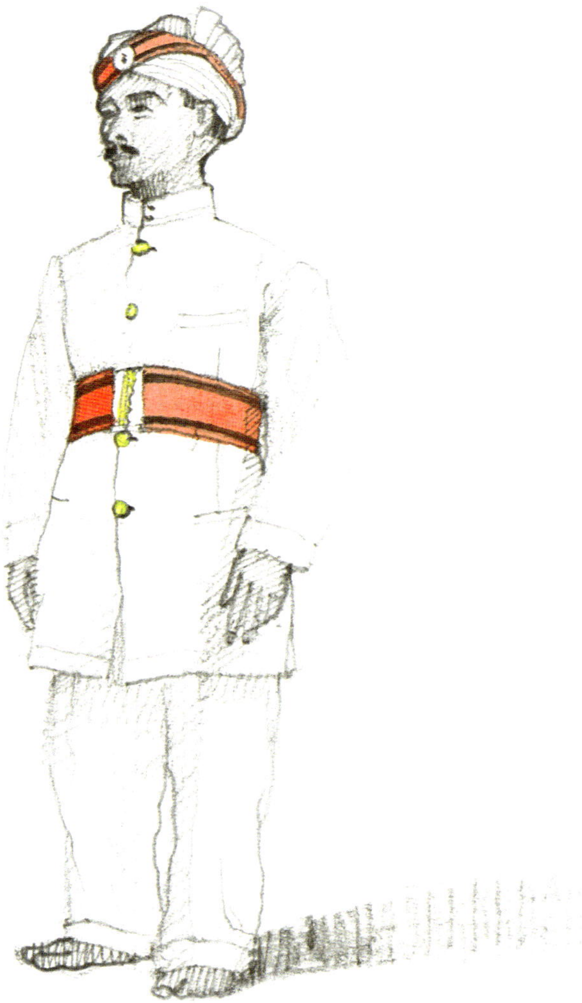

ABOVE: Ramzan

up on to my canvas basin before I came out to wash, and sitting in the water, thereby washing himself, or dabbling with my hot shaving water. I was averse to both these practices but a monkey gets away with an awful lot on account of the amusing way in which he does things. Nothing would ever induce me, however, to keep one of these inquisitive creatures; I have too many small and valuable possessions, such as paints, brushes and other sketching accoutrements that the destructive monkey would love to get his teeth into.

On active service one has to travel light and here I was not able to have with me more than the minimum of drawing equipment. One sketch book, in fact, was the sum total, and of course a few pencils of different grades – not easy to come by in these times when luxury articles were not being manufactured.

The watercolour 'Servicing Hurricanes on the Burma Front' (picture No.53) was painted afterwards from the information contained in pencil sketches made on the spot, as were all my coloured pictures of scenes in this part of India and Burma. This picture is typical of a great many forward airfields from which fighters were operating with the 14th Army, and shows ground staff at work on a Hurricane which is parked on its blast pen at the side of the taxi track. I have endeavoured to impart a feeling of intense heat which always pervaded these airfields. Repairs often have to be made out in the open where there is no shade from trees or hangars: the exposed metal parts of an aircraft become almost too hot to touch from the scorching rays of the sun and the task of the maintenance mechanic is an arduous one.

The construction engineer who builds the aerodromes also has an arduous task. Mechanical plant for cutting and levelling the ground is not always available and thousands of coolies have to be employed instead of machines, to remove large volumes of earth. The sketch already referred to, indicates the sort of work that has to be done. The embankment on the far side had to be cut away by hand in this case with shovels or 'cadalies' and carried away in small baskets. Excavations were made in a similar manner round where the aircraft are standing, giving them bomb blast protection. Sometimes earth banks had to be thrown up when no natural embankments existed. Engineers in charge of such work have to spend a great deal of time on the spot checking widths of taxiways to allow clearance for aircraft wing tips, watching the levels of the finished roadway surface and organising and distributing the native labour to the best possible advantage. Problems arise in the handling of local labour that never occur when working with British labour at home. When fields are wanted in a hurry for some tactical reason, these problems are increased. To make 600 coolies work faster than their customary sluggish pace is no small achievement and in fact any rush work with local labour takes a great deal of energy and urging on the part of the man in charge. A line from Kipling comes to mind, written over the grave of a European in India: 'Here lies the man who tried to hurry the East'!

I did many hours of flying in small aircraft while I was with the 14th Army. The monsoon was approaching and every day now was an anxious one. Would the rain come and stop our urgent work, or would it hold off yet another twenty-four hours? The skies were dramatic seen from the open cockpit of a reconnaissance plane. Great banks of nimbus storm cloud hanging ominously over the land threatening to make their watery descent.

I have a great desire to create a picture which really gives the feeling of being in an open aircraft 2,000 feet up, looking out over the flat paddy land of Bengal with one of these cloudy skies through which pass thin shafts of light, picking out fields in brilliant emerald spots, vivid as if lit by a search light, whilst the remainder of the country is in grey shadow. But this must wait to be worked out in more leisurely times.

Right: 53 Servicing Hurricanes on the Burma Front

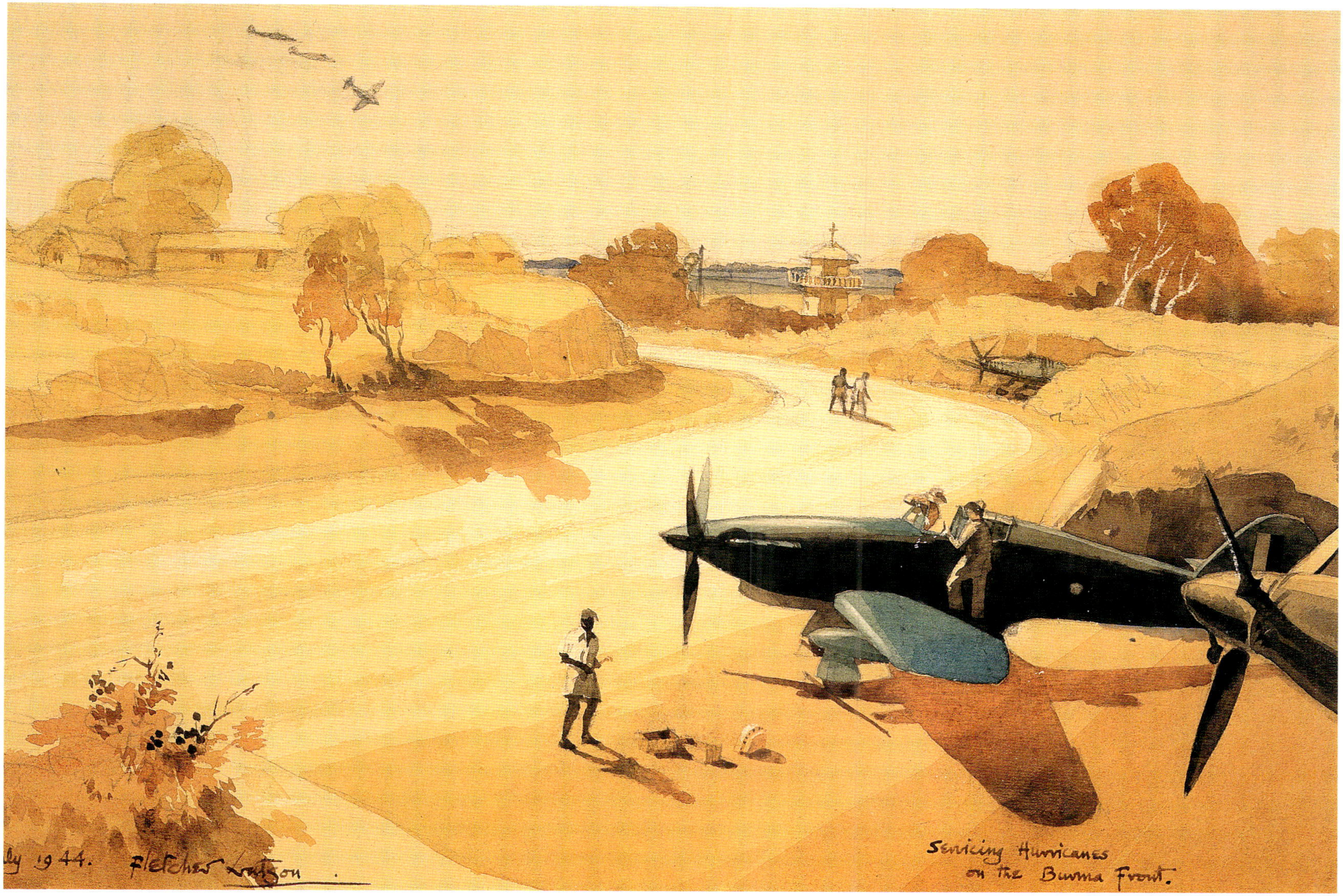
Servicing Hurricanes
on the Burma Front.

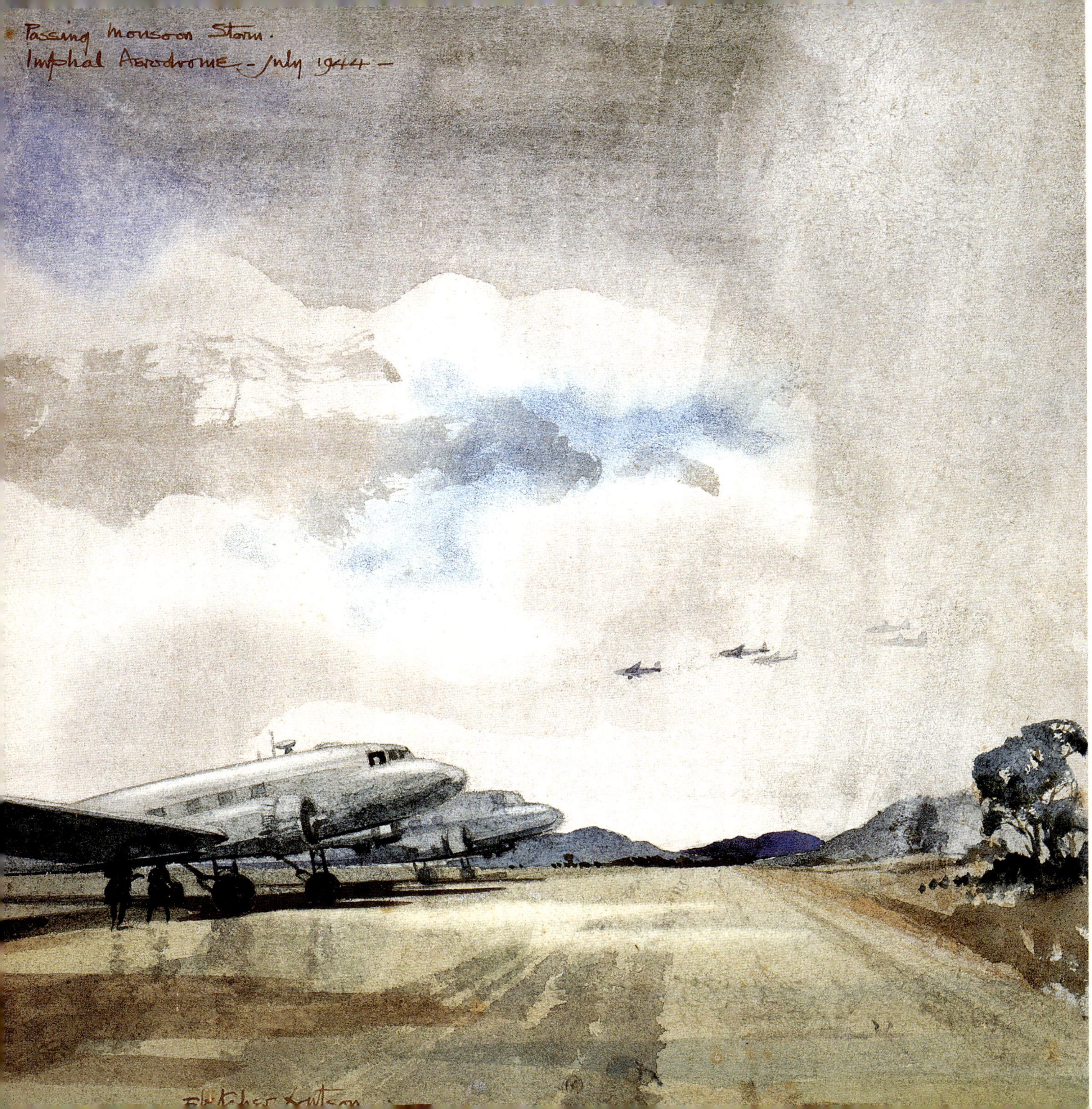
Passing Monsoon Storm.
Imphal Aerodrome - July 1944 -

Left: 54 Imphal Aerodrome with Dakotas on the runway

Right: 55 Fighter airfield with the 14th Army

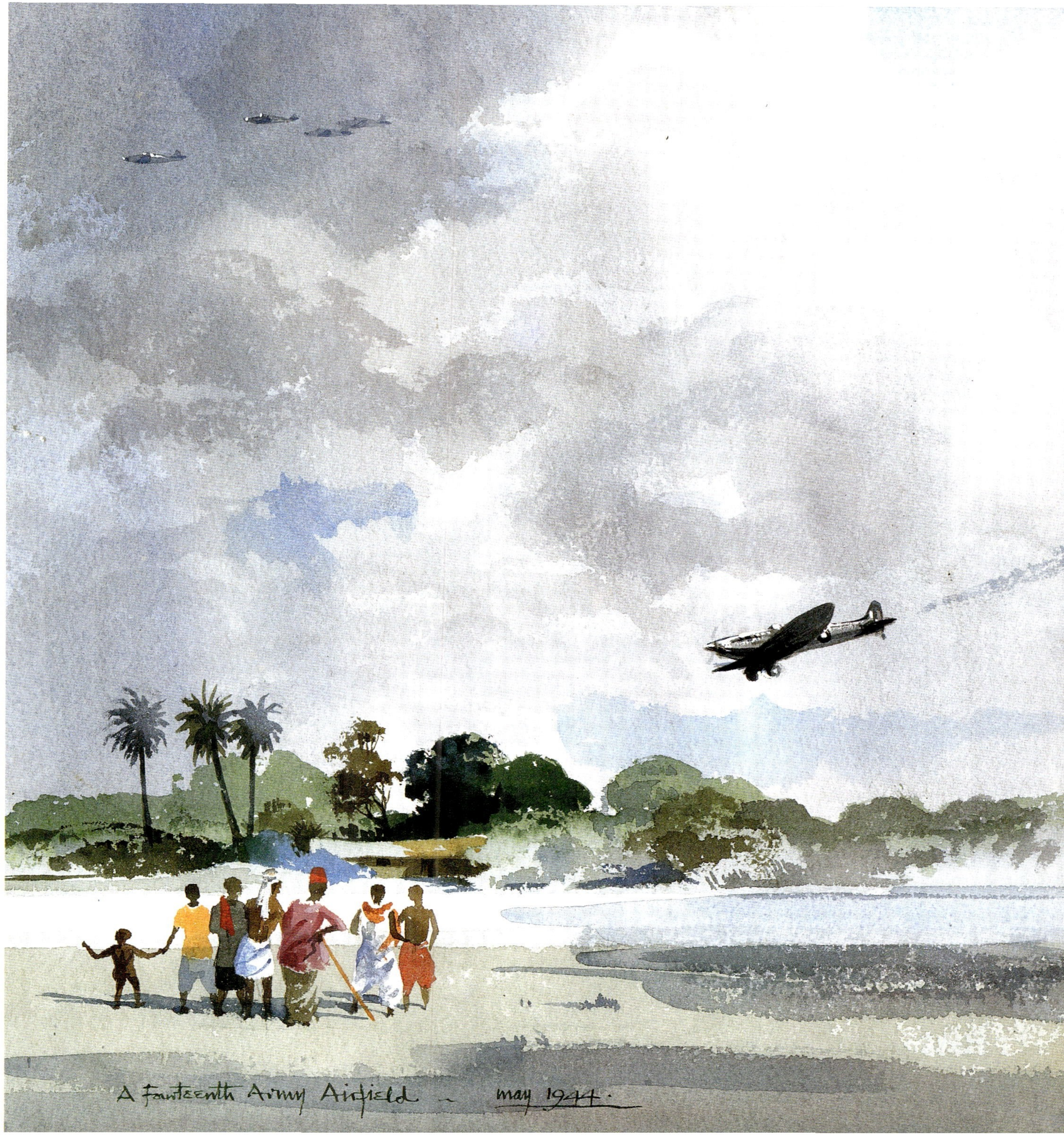

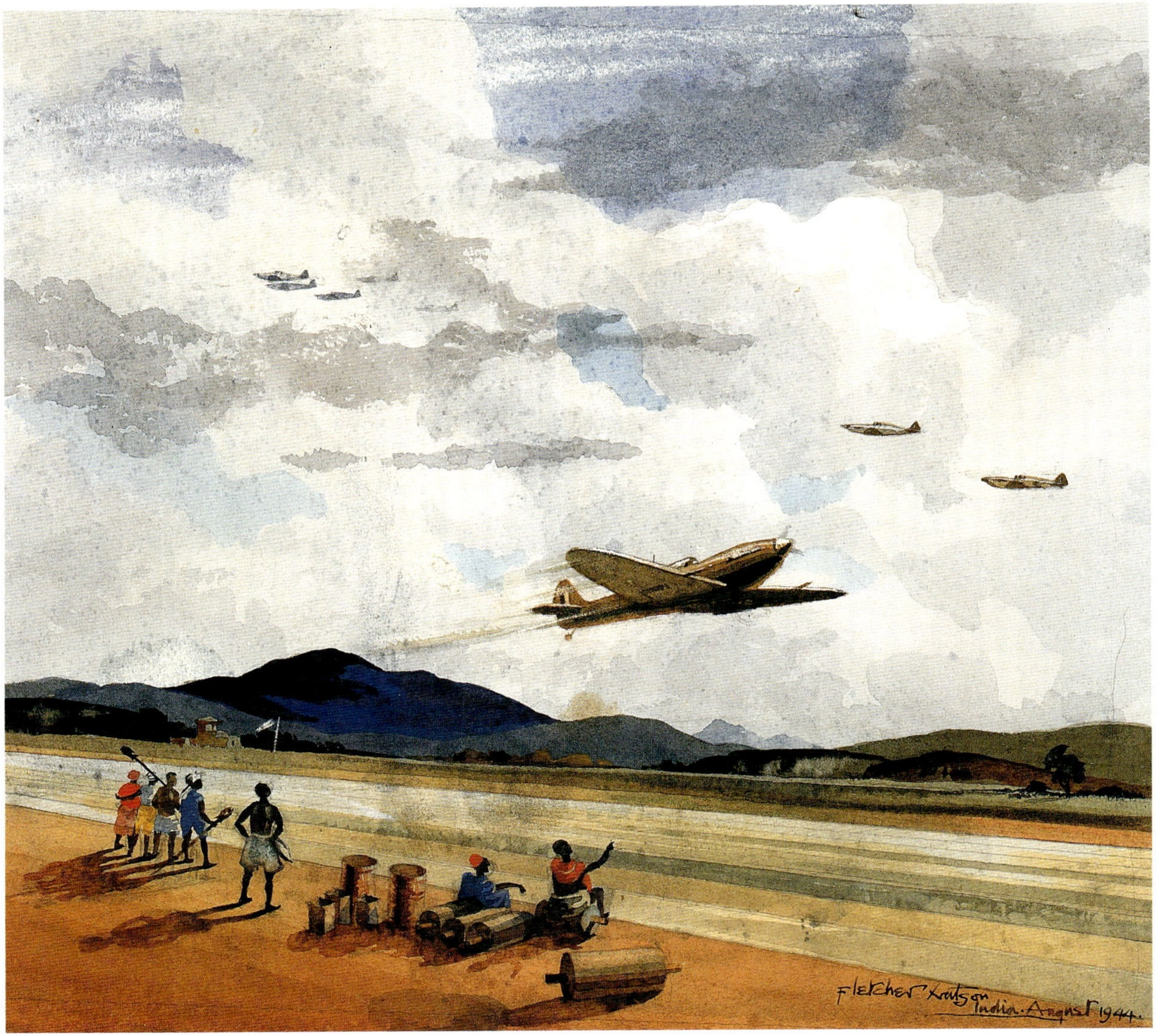

Left: 56 Fighter taking off

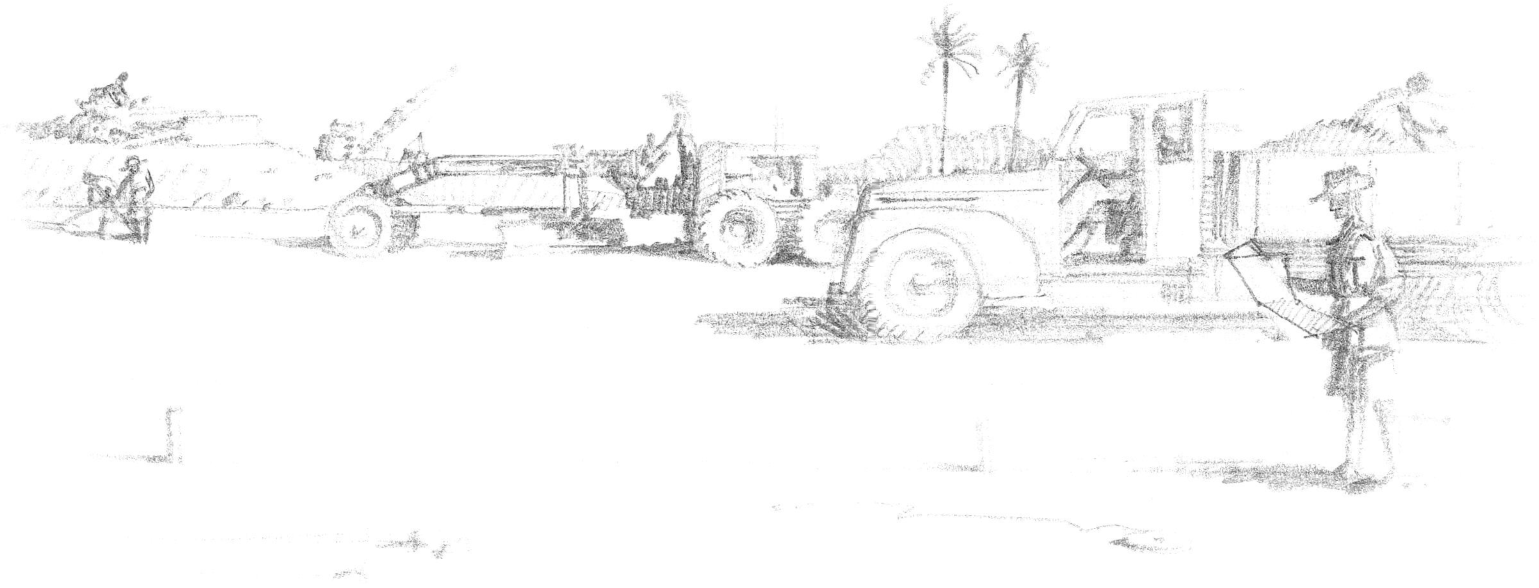

Above: Excavating machinery

The picture of Imphal Aerodrome (No.54) was painted from a pencil sketch made on one of these typical cloudy days. A rain storm had just passed over the runway, leaving it wet and slippery, and the distant blue mountains stand out sharply in the fresh clear atmosphere. There is some very beautiful scenery in the Imphal valley which I think rivals the mountain scenery of Quetta. In other circumstances I should like to spend several days sketching this part of the world.

The war conditions under which one saw these places offered no inducement to sketch. Everything was dash and rush and one had to be content with making hasty pencil scribbles only. I stayed for three weeks on one airfield project where we were doing a special fast job trying to complete work before the monsoon broke. We were working flat out from dawn till dusk, but somehow or other I did manage to do four pencil sketches during that time. The pink 'Airfield taxi track' picture is typical of a scene constantly surrounding us at this job. I made the drawing from which this sketch was done from the front seat of a lorry, seizing the opportunity by stopping on the way back to lunch in the R.E. mess one day.

I did this on two or three occasions; it was the only hope of ever getting a moment for drawing. The drill was simple: stop lorry, draw view for ten minutes, drive on again. No fussing around to obtain the most perfect viewpoint before starting, as in peace time. It was certainly an entirely new approach to sketching from the artist's point of view. I was used to walking round and round looking at a subject from all angles before settling on the most advantageous composition. The angle of the road, the position of a tree in relation to the distance, shadows, all were fully weighed up before taking the final step of starting to draw. One useful dodge is to look at a view upside down: this is achieved by turning one's back on the subject then bending down like playing leap-frog and peering between one's legs. It enables one to asses tone values of different parts of the landscape without being influenced by actual shapes of objects which subconsciously suggest dark or light tones when viewed the correct way up. This method is not to be recommended in towns or crowded places because the ungainly attitude causes a lot of undesirable attention to the sketcher and subsequent embarrassment!

In this part of the Indian-Burma frontier, the landscape is full of unusual colour in the foliage of trees and shrubs. Note the bright blue and vivid pink trees in picture No.58 and the strong green and light blue ground crops in No.59. In both pictures there are palm trees which denote the hot climate. How I wished that I had had more time to paint this unusual and colourful landscape.

I was stopping with the Assistant Garrison Engineer who ran the R.E. mess at this airfield, and one night a vicious pre-monsoon hurricane passed over our basher camp. It completely lifted off the corrugated iron cook-house roof, and the cook was left in the pouring rain to cope with our half-cooked dinner. He did cope most magnificently and if the soup was a trifle watery it was certainly hot, which to my mind was a miraculous achievement. The Indian has a great gift of keeping fires going under almost any conditions and our cook lived up to form on this occasion. These basher huts that we lived in are thatch roofed buildings with a framework of thick bamboo poles (see pencil drawing on page 146). The walls are chattai matting, like basket work in appearance, and windows are made with big open work matting or split bamboo. Bamboo shutters hang on horizontal poles just above the window

Right: 57 Airfield taxi track

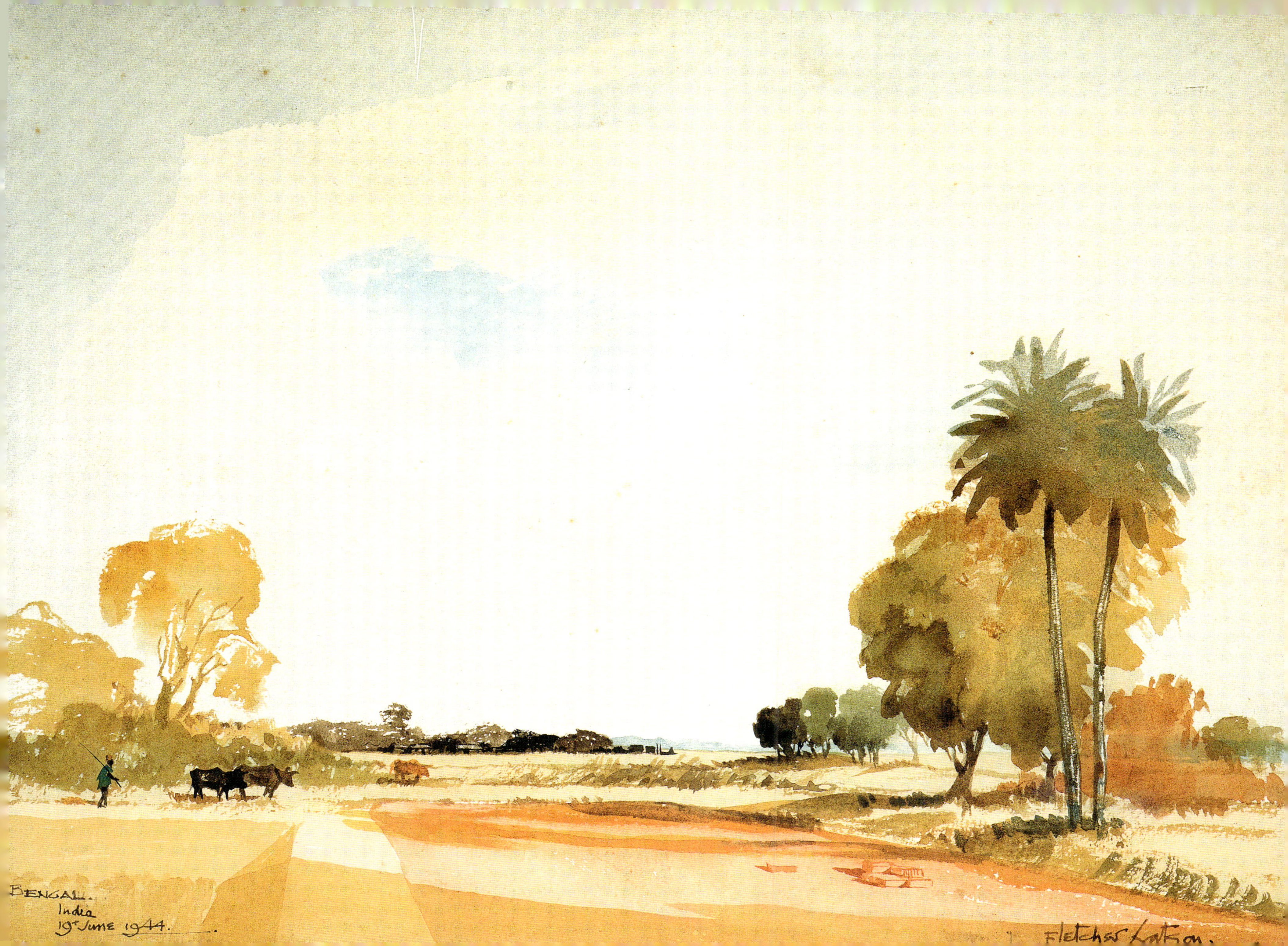
BENGAL.
India
19th June 1944.
Fletcher Watson.

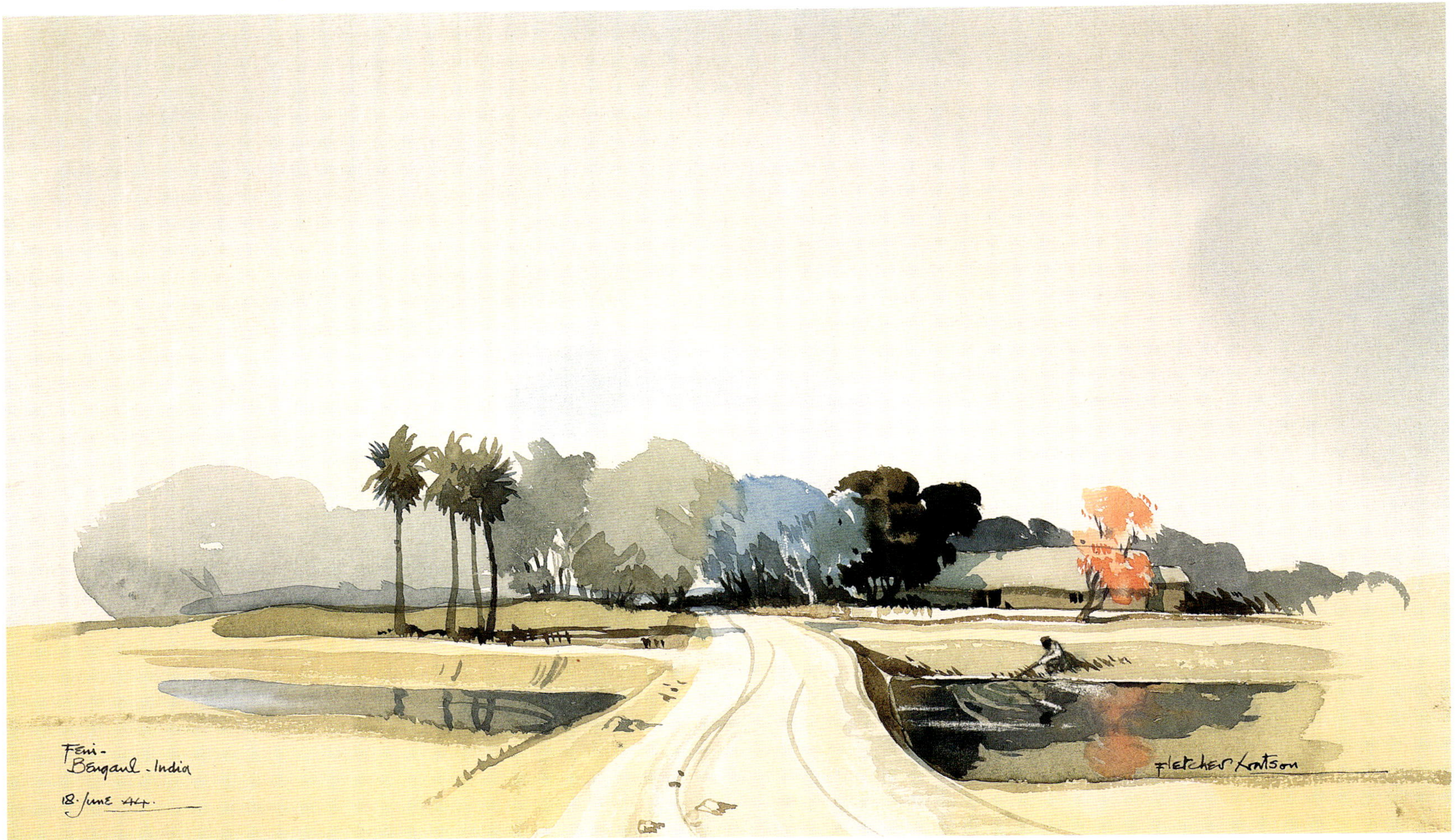

ABOVE: 58 Road to an airfield, Feni

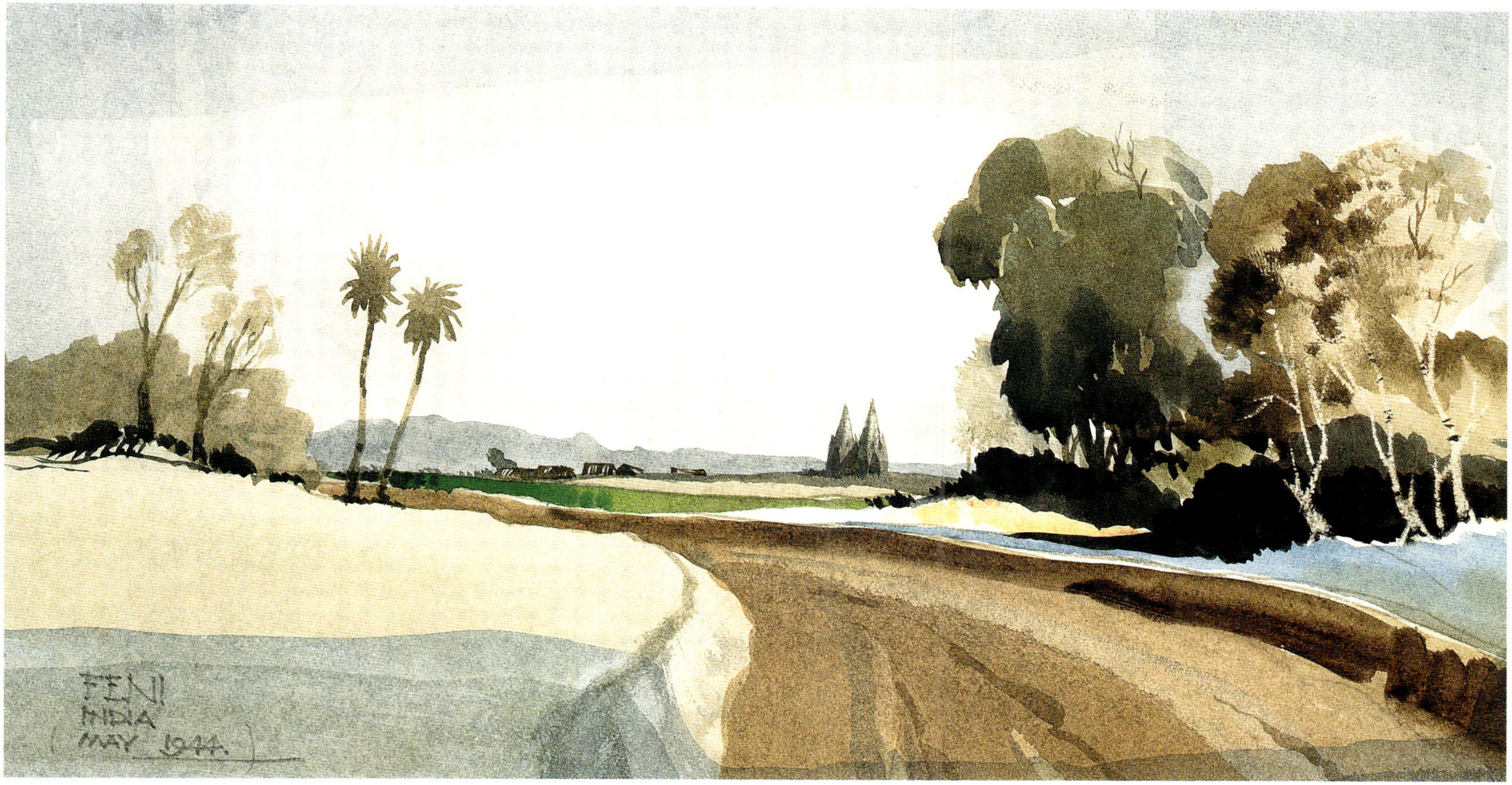

Above: 59 Another view of the road to the airfield, Feni

outside and can be drawn across for protection against the rain. They were very much drawn across when the hurricane hit us that night. While it lasted it felt as if the whole hut was going to collapse, swaying and groaning under the strain. But they are well designed huts and are surprisingly rigid and strong. The whippy nature of the bamboo allows the whole structure to give without breaking.

A few days after the hurricane episode, I flew back to Army H.Q. in Delhi, and as I walked into the mess ante-room the 1.30 news was just coming over the wireless. 'Invasion of the Continent.' It had come at last, the beginning of the end. There was tremendous excitement and speculation by the would-be tactical experts as to how well it would all go. We were beginning to push the Japs back at our end of the war too by this time, so altogether the outlook was very promising.

In due course, orders came through for my own posting back to the U.K. The prospect of seeing one's home and loved ones again was great after four years of service abroad.

My army career during this time in India had been extremely varied and I had to act as a freelance engineer almost all the time, receiving orders from Army G.H.Q. Delhi and reporting back at intervals as required. Looking back, I realise how lucky I was to be so independent and virtually out of danger most of the time, except for a fairly short period with the 14th Army in Burma. I was priviledged to meet a great many Indian soldiers and civilians connected with the defences of India and in due time I came to realise what a very fine body of people they all were.

My camouflage work included Army training camps, airfields, anti aircraft gun emplacements, roads, bridges, and various forms of defence. Indian women joined the services in large numbers and were highly trained for various military duties like our own W.A.F. people in the U.K.

I met a lot of Indian civilians from many walks of life who were immensely kind and helpful. One was left with the impression of what a truly wonderful nation they are from every part of the vast Indian peninsula. [Since this book was written, India has had partition and Pakistan now exists as a separate country in the north west, but my comments include both countries, of course.]

My final word has to be about the terrain of the country itself. It is romantic and colourful and truly magical, with superb ancient architecture and wonderful mountain regions and rivers that are all very attractive to the landscape painter.

Right: 60 The Straits of Gibraltar, going home

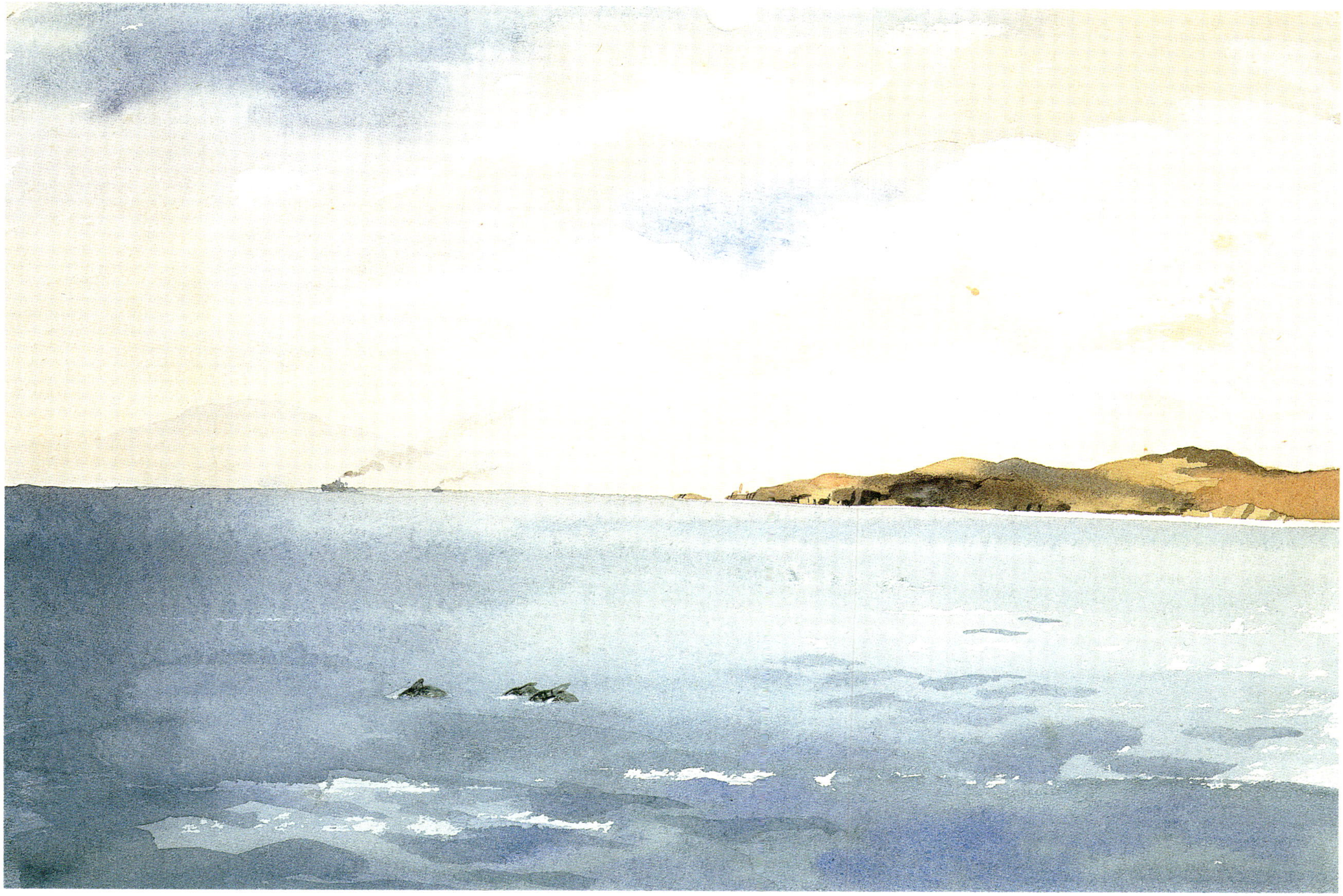

OTHER BOOKS BY JAMES FLETCHER-WATSON, R.I., R.B.A.

The Magic of Watercolour
Outdoor Painting
The Secret of Watercolour

These books are priced at £20.00 including postage, available from Country Heritage.

WATERCOLOUR PAINTING VIDEOS

Three sixty-minute videos, *The Magic of Watercolour*, *Outdoor Painting* and *The Secret of Watercolour*, in which James Fletcher-Watson can be seen painting a range of landscape scenes, are available. Produced by APV films, the videos are priced at £26.00 each including postage from Country Heritage.

Country Heritage
Windrush House
Windrush
Nr. Burford
Oxon OX18 4TU

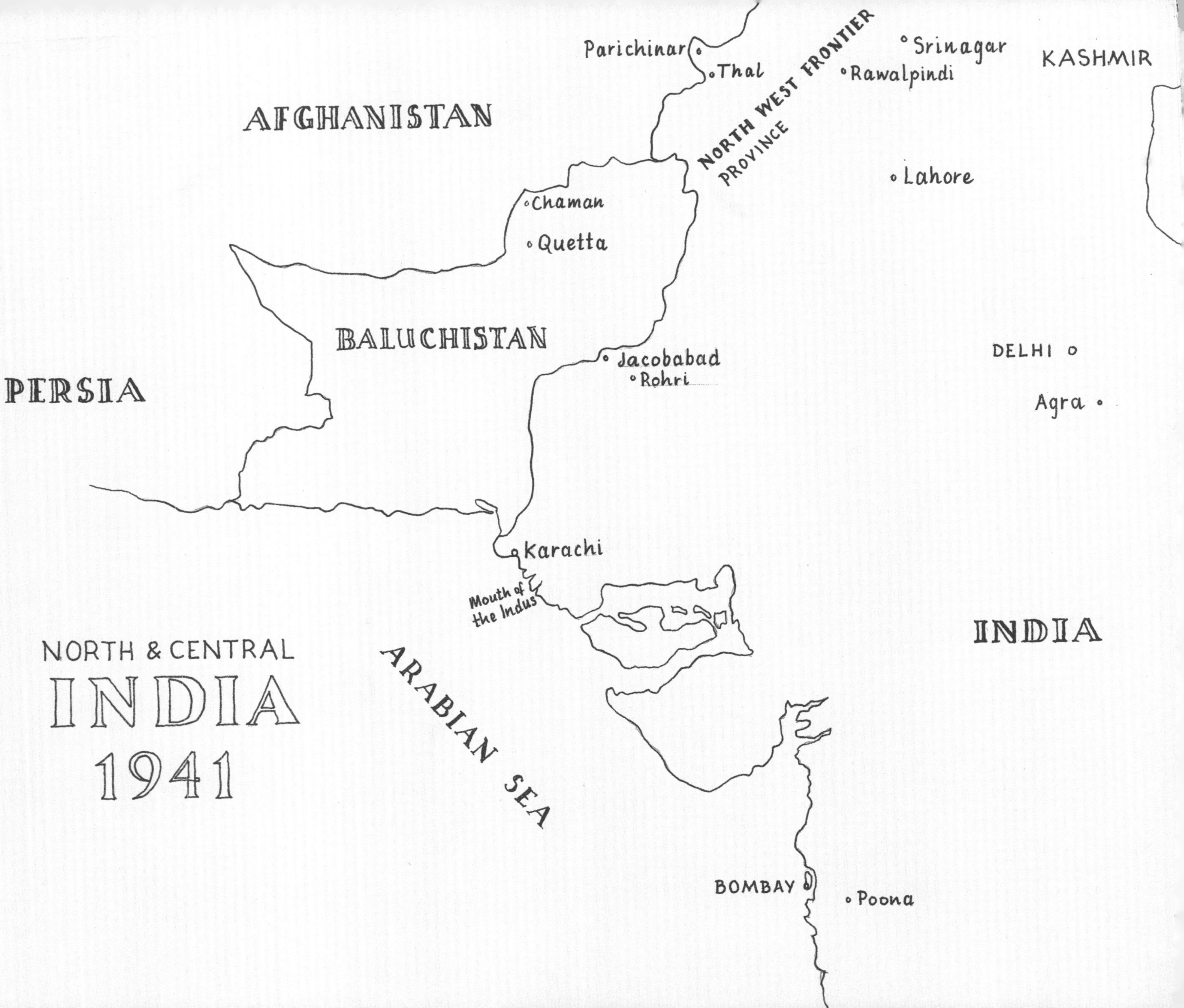

Parichinar
Thal
NORTH WEST FRONTIER
PROVINCE
Srinagar
Rawalpindi
KASHMIR
AFGHANISTAN
Lahore
Chaman
Quetta
BALUCHISTAN
Jacobabad
Rohri
DELHI
PERSIA
Agra
Karachi
Mouth of the Indus
INDIA
NORTH & CENTRAL
INDIA
1941
ARABIAN SEA
BOMBAY
Poona